CONTEMPORARY LAW SERIES

ALSO BY LEONARD W. LEVY

The Law of the Commonwealth and Chief Justice Shaw *(1957)*

Legacy of Suppression: Freedom of Speech and Press in Early American History *(1960)*

The American Political Process *(1963)*, ed.

Jefferson and Civil Liberties: The Darker Side *(1963)*

Major Crises in American History: Documentary Problems *(1963)*, ed.

Congress *(1964)*, ed.

The Judiciary *(1964)*, ed.

Political Parties and Pressure Groups *(1964)*, ed.

The Presidency *(1964)*, ed.

American Constitutional Law: Historical Essays *(1966)*

Freedom of the Press from Zenger to Jefferson: Early American Libertarian Theories *(1966)*, ed.

Freedom and Reform *(1967)*, ed.

Origins of the Fifth Amendment: The Right Against Self-Incrimination *(1968)*

Essays on the Making of the Constitution *(1969)*, ed.

The Fourteenth Amendment and the Bill of Rights *(1971)*, ed.

Judgments: Essays on Constitutional History *(1972)*

The Supreme Court Under Warren *(1972)*, ed.

Blasphemy in Massachusetts *(1973)*, ed.

Against the Law: The Nixon Court and Criminal Justice *(1974)*

Jim Crow Education *(1974)*, ed.

Treason Against God—A History of the Offense of Blasphemy *(1981)*

Emergence of a Free Press *(1985)*

Constitutional Opinions: Aspects of the Bill of Rights *(1986)*

The Establishment Clause: Religion and the First Amendment *(1986)*

Encyclopedia of the American Constitution *(1986)*, ed.

The Framing and Ratification of the Constitution *(1987)*, ed.

The American Founding *(1988)*, ed.

Original Intent and the Framers' Constitution *(1988)*

Supplement One: Encyclopedia of the American Constitution *(1992)*, ed.

Blasphemy: Verbal Offense Against the Sacred from Moses to Salman Rushdie *(1993)*

Encyclopedia of the American Presidency *(1993)*, ed.

Seasoned Judgments: Constitutional Rights and American History *(1994)*

Supplement Two: Encyclopedia of the American Constitution *(1998)*, ed.

Origins

of the

Bill of Rights

Leonard W. Levy

Yale Nota Bene

Yale University Press   *New Haven and London*

First published as a Yale Nota Bene book in 2001. Published in 1999 by Yale University Press. Copyright © 1999 by Yale University.

For information about this and other Yale University Press publications, please contact:

    U.S. office   sales.press@yale.edu
    Europe office   sales@yaleup.co.uk

Printed in the United States of America by R. R. Donnelley and Sons, Harrisonburg, Va.

The Library of Congress has cataloged the hardcover edition as follows:
Levy, Leonard Williams, 1923–
    Origins of the Bill of Rights / Leonard W. Levy.
       p.   cm.—(Contemporary law series)
    Includes bibliographical references and index.
    ISBN 0-300-07802-1 (cloth : alk. paper)
    1. United States. Constitution. 1st–10th Amendments.—History.
2. Civil Rights—United States—History. I. Title. II. Series.
KF4749.L488   1999
342.73'085—dc21
                                   98-44965

ISBN 0-300-08901-5 (pbk.)

A catalog record for this book is available from the British Library.

10 9 8 7 6 5 4 3 2 1

Dedicated to

Elyse

My wonderful wife of fifty-four years

Contents

Preface

This is my thirty-sixth book, and at the age of seventy-five I am beginning to think of retiring as an author, although I have at least one more book to do—on the origins of trial by jury. And, if I know myself, when that one is done, another will come to mind. In the past forty-plus years, I have written on a considerable variety of subjects, including Chief Justice Lemuel Shaw, Jim Crow, Thomas Jefferson, blasphemy, the right against self-incrimination, the forfeiture of property, and criminal justice. I may now be getting to the point where repeating myself becomes inevitable, especially on the subject of the beginnings of the history of our rights. Parts of this book draw heavily on previous ones. The subject of the origins of the Bill of Rights has long absorbed me. I have written several volumes on aspects of the Bill of Rights, as the list opposite the title page of this book indicates. In addition to my books on the First Amendment, I devoted several chapters on provisions of the Bill of Rights in *Original Intent and the Framers' Constitution,* but this is my first attempt to be systematic and comprehensive concerning the origins of the Bill of Rights. I have included coverage of the provisions of the unamended Constitution that also protect rights (writ of habeas corpus, ex post facto laws, and bills of attainder).

I wrote this book alone, contracting no debts to anyone, especially not to my grandchildren: Natalie, Elon, and Avishai Glucklich and Aaron, Adam, Jacob, and Nathan Harris. But I do want them to see their names in print. I should also acknowledge that several useful suggestions for improving the manuscript derived from an unknown reader employed by Yale University Press and from my editors John Covell and Laura Jones Dooley.

Chronology

1690 John Locke's *Treatise of Civil Government*

1691 New York Declaration of Rights

1692 Massachusetts Habeas Corpus Act

1693 Case of Sir Thomas Lawrence

1698 Henry Care's *English Liberties, or, The Free-Born Subject's Inheritance*

1701 Pennsylvania Charter of Privileges

1734–1735 Case of John Peter Zenger

1763 Case of John Wilkes

1765–1769 Sir William Blackstone's *Commentaries on the Laws of England*

1765 Declaration of Rights and Grievances of Stamp Act Congress

1770 Case of Alexander McDougall

1772 Sommersett's case

1772 Boston's Rights of the Colonies and A List of Infringements and Violations of Rights

1774 Address to Inhabitants of Quebec

1774 Declaration and Resolves of First Continental Congress

1775 Declaration of Continental Congress

1776 Declaration of Independence

1776 Virginia Declaration of Rights

1776 Bills of Rights in Pennsylvania, Delaware, Maryland, and Vermont

1780 Massachusetts Declaration of Rights

1787 Northwest Ordinance

1787 United States Constitution

1787 George Mason's Objections to proposed Constitution

1787 Reasons of Dissent by Minority of Pennsylvania Convention

1788 Alexander Hamilton's *The Federalist*, Nos. 84, 85

1787–1789 Thomas Jefferson–James Madison correspondence on bills of rights

1788 Amendments proposed by state ratifying conventions

1789 Madison proposes amendments to Constitution

1789 Congress proposes amendments to Constitution

1791 Bill of Rights ratified by states

1798 Alien and Sedition Acts

1798 Virginia and Kentucky Resolutions

CHAPTER ONE

Why We Have the Bill of Rights

THE BILL OF RIGHTS consists of the first ten amendments to the Constitution. The traditions that gave shape and substance to the Bill of Rights had English roots, but a unique American experience colored that shape and substance. "We began with freedom," as Ralph Waldo Emerson wrote in "The Fortune of the Republic." The first charter of Virginia (1606) contained a provision that the colonists and their descendants "shall have and enjoy all Liberties, Franchises, and Immunities . . . as if they had been abiding and born, within this our Realm of England." Later charters of Virginia contained similar clauses, which extended to legal rights of land tenure and inheritance, trial by jury, and little else. But the vague language was repeated in numerous other charters for colonies from New England to the South, and Americans construed it handsomely. As the Continental Congress declared, Americans believed that they were entitled to all the rights of Englishmen, their constitutional system, and their common law. American experience with and interpretations of charters eased the way to written constitutions of fundamental law that contained bills of rights.

Freedom was mainly the product of New World conditions, the English legal inheritance, and skipping a feudal stage. Because of American's postfeudal beginnings, it was unencumbered by oppressions associated with an ancien régime—a rigid class system dominated by a reactionary and hereditary aristocracy, arbitrary government by despotic kings, and a single established church extirpating dissent. "America was opened," Emerson wrote, "after the feudal mischief was spent, and so the people made a good start. We began well. No inquisitions here, no kings, no nobles, no dominant church. Here heresy has lost its terrors." Americans were the freest people, therefore the first colonials to rebel. A free people, as Edmund Burke said, can sniff tyranny in a far-off breeze—even if nonexistent. American "radicals" actually believed that the Stamp Act reduced Americans to slavery. They resorted to arms in 1775, the Continental Congress believed, not to establish new liberties but to defend old ones. In fact, they did establish many new liberties but convinced themselves that those liberties were old. That was an English custom: marching forward into the future facing backward to the past, while adapting old law to changing values. Thus, Magna Carta had come to mean indictment by grand jury, trial by jury, and a cluster of related rights of the criminally accused, and Englishmen believed, or made believe, that it was ever so. The habit crossed the Atlantic.

So did the hyperbolic style of expression by a free people outraged by injustice. Thus, James Madison exclaimed that the "diabolical Hell conceived principle of persecution rages" because some Baptist ministers were jailed briefly for unlicensed preaching. By European standards, however, persecution hardly existed in America, not even in the seventeenth century, except on a local and sporadic basis. America never experienced anything like the Inquisition, the fires of Smithfield, the Saint Bartholomew's Day Massacre, or the deaths of more than five thousand nonconformist ministers in the jails of Restoration England. Draconian colonial statutes existed but were rarely enforced. Broad libertarian practices were the rule, not the exception.

On any comparative basis, civil liberty flourished in America, a fact that intensified the notoriety of exceptional abridgments, such as the hanging of four Quakers in Massachusetts in 1659 or the 1735 prosecution of John Peter Zenger for seditious libel. Although a stunted concept of the meaning and scope of freedom of the press existed in America until the Jeffersonian reaction to the Sedition Act of 1798, an extraordinary degree of freedom of the press existed in America, as it did in England. And nowhere did freedom of religion prosper as in America.

The predominance of the social compact theory in American thought reflected a condition of freedom and, like the experience with charters, contributed to the belief in written bills of rights. The social compact theory hypothesized a prepolitical state of nature in which people were governed only by laws of nature, free of human restraints. From the premise that man was born free, the deduction followed that he came into the world with God-given or natural rights. Born without the restraint of human laws, he had a right to possess liberty and to work for his own property. Born naked and stationless, he had a right to equality. Born with certain instincts and needs, he had a right to satisfy them—a right to the pursuit of happiness. These natural rights, as John Dickinson declared in 1766, "are created in us by the decrees of Providence, which establish the laws of our nature. They are born with us; exist with us; and cannot be taken from us by any human power without taking our lives." When people left the state of nature and compacted for government, the need to secure their rights motivated them. A half-century before John Locke's *Second Treatise on Government*, Thomas Hooker of Connecticut expounded the social compact theory. Over a period of a century and a half, America became accustomed to the idea that government existed by consent of the governed, that the people created the government, that they did so by a written compact, that the compact reserved their natural rights, and that it constituted a fundamental law to which the government was subordinate. Constitutionalism, or the theory of limited government, was in part an outgrowth of the social compact.

In America, political theory and law, as well as religion, taught that government was limited. But Americans took their views on such matters from a highly selective and romanticized image of seventeenth-century England, and they perpetuated it in America even as that England changed. Seventeenth-century England was the England of the great struggle for constitutional liberty by the common law courts and Puritan parliaments against Stuart kings. Seventeenth-century England was the England of Edward Coke, John Lilburne, and John Locke. It was an England in which religion, law, and politics converged to produce limited monarchy and, ironically, parliamentary supremacy. To Americans, however, Parliament had irrevocably limited itself by reaffirmations of the Magna Carta and passage of the Petition of Right of 1628, the Habeas Corpus Act of 1679, the Bill of Rights of 1689, and the Toleration Act of 1689. Americans learned that a free people are those who live under a government so constitutionally checked and controlled that its powers must be reasonably exercised without abridging individual rights.

In fact, Americans had progressed far beyond the English in securing their rights. The English constitutional documents limited only the crown and protected few rights. The Petition of Right reconfirmed Magna Carta's provision that no freeman could be imprisoned but by lawful judgment of his peers or "by the law of the land"; it also reconfirmed a 1354 version of the great charter that first used the phrase "by due process of law" instead of "by the law of the land." The Petition of Right invigorated the liberty of the subject by condemning the military trial of civilians as well as imprisonment without cause or on mere executive authority.

Other sections provided that no one could be taxed without Parliament's consent or be imprisoned or forced to incriminate himself by having to answer for refusing an exaction not authorized by Parliament. The Habeas Corpus Act safeguarded personal liberty, without which other liberties cannot be exercised. The act secured an old right for the first time by making the writ of habeas corpus an effective remedy for illegal imprisonment. The only loophole in the act, the possibility of excessive bail, was plugged by the Bill of Rights ten years later. That enactment, its exalted name notwithstanding, had a narrow range of protections, including the freedom of petition, free speech for members of Parliament, and, in language closely followed by the American Eighth Amendment, bans on excessive bail, excessive fines, and cruel and unusual punishments. As an antecedent of the American Bill of Rights, the English one was a skimpy affair, though important as a symbol of the rule of law and of fundamental law. The Toleration Act was actually "A Bill of Indulgence," exempting most nonconformists from the penalties of persecutory laws of the Restoration, leaving those laws in force but inapplicable to persons qualifying for indulgence. England maintained an establishment of the Anglican Church, merely tolerating the existence of non-Anglican trinitarians, who were still obligated to pay tithes and endure many civil disabilities.

In America, England promoted Anglicanism in New York and in the southern colonies but wisely prevented its establishments in America from obstructing religious peace because immigrants were an economic asset, regardless of religion. England granted charters to colonial proprietors on a nondiscriminatory basis—to Cecil Calvert, a Catholic, for Maryland; to Roger Williams, a Baptist, for Rhode Island; and to William Penn, a Quaker, for Pennsylvania and Delaware. The promise of life in America drew people from all of Western Christendom and exposed them to a greater degree of liberty and religious differences than previously known.

James Madison, whose practical achievements in the cause of freedom of religion were unsurpassed, said that it arose from "that multiplicity of sects which pervades America."

But a principled commitment to religious liberty came first in some colonies. Maryland's Toleration Act of 1649 was far more liberal than England's Toleration Act of forty years later. Until 1776 only Rhode Island, Pennsylvania, Delaware, and New Jersey guaranteed fuller freedom than Maryland by its act of 1649, which was the first to use the phrase "the free exercise of religion," later embodied in the First Amendment. The act also symbolized the extraordinary fact that for most of the seventeenth century in Maryland, Catholics and Protestants openly worshiped as they chose and lived in peace, if not amity. The act applied to all trinitarian Christians but punished others; it also penalized the reproachful use of such divisive terms as heretic, puritan, papist, anabaptist, or antinomian. The Maryland act was a statute, but the Charter of Rhode Island, which remained its constitution until 1842, made the guarantee of religious liberty a part of the fundamental law. It secured for all inhabitants "the free exercise and enjoyment of their civil and religious rights" by providing that every peaceable person might "freely and fullye hav and enjoye his and theire owne judgements and consciences, in matters of religious concernments." Thus, the principle that the state has no legitimate authority over religion was institutionalized in some American colonies, including those under Quaker influence.

Massachusetts, the colony that least respected private judgment in religious matters, was the first to safeguard many other rights. Its Body of Liberties, adopted in 1641, was meant to limit the magistrates in whom all power had been concentrated. As John Winthrop observed, the objective was to frame limitations "in remarkable resemblance to Magna Charta, which . . . should be received for fundamental laws." The Body of Liberties was, in effect, a comprehensive bill of rights. In comparison, the later

English Bill of Rights was rudimentary and the liberties of Englishmen few in number. Among the guarantees first protected in writing by Massachusetts were freedom of assembly and of speech (at least in public meetings), the equal protection of the laws, just compensation for private property taken for public use, the freedom to emigrate, the right to bail, the right to employ counsel, trial by jury in civil cases, the right to challenge jurors, restrictions on imprisonment for debt, speedy trial, no double jeopardy, and no cruel or excessive punishments. In addition to traditional liberties, such as trial by jury in criminal cases, and Magna Carta's principle of the rule of law, the Body of Liberties also protected some rights of women: widows received a portion of the estate of husbands, even if cut off by will; physical punishment of women by their husbands was prohibited; and daughters received a right to inherit if parents died intestate and without male heirs. Servants, slaves, foreigners, and even animals received humane consideration.

The Body of Liberties was a statute, but the Charter of Fundamental Laws of West New Jersey (1677), which was probably the work of William Penn, functioned as a written constitution because it began with the provision that the "common law or fundamental rights" of the colony should be "the foundation of government, which is not to be altered by the Legislative authority." The liberty documents of England limited only the crown, not the legislature. The principle of limiting all governmental authority was written into Penn's Frame of Government for Pennsylvania in 1682, a document that extensively enumerated rights that were to last "for ever," including for the first time a ban on excessive fines, a guarantee of indictment by grand jury in capital cases, delivery to the accused of a copy of the charges against him, and assurance that a jury's verdict of not guilty was final. Penn's charter carefully particularized the rights of the criminally accused. Americans were learning that charters of liberty must assure fair and regularized procedures, without which there could be no liberty.

Vicious and ad hoc procedures had been used to victimize religious and political minorities. One's home could not be his castle or his property be his own, nor could his right to express his opinion or to worship his God be secure, if he could be searched, arrested, tried, and imprisoned in some arbitrary way.

The case of Sir Thomas Lawrence in 1693 illustrates. Secretary of Maryland, a judge, and a member of the governor's council, Lawrence broke politically with the government and denounced it. Summoned by the council for examination, he was accused of having a treasonable letter. On his refusal to produce it, the council had him searched against his protests, found the letter, convicted him of unspecified crimes, deprived him of his offices, and jailed him without bail. Lawrence appealed his conviction to the assembly on the grounds of having been forced to incriminate himself by an illegal search, of having been convicted without trial by jury and without knowing the charges against him or the names of his accusers, and of having been denied bail and habeas corpus, "which is the great security of the lives & Libertyes of every English Subject." The assembly vindicated English liberties by supporting Lawrence on every point, found all proceedings against him illegal, and freed and restored him.

The American colonial experience, climaxed by the controversy with England leading to the Revolution, honed American sensitivity to the need for written constitutions that protected rights grounded in the "immutable laws of nature" as well as in the British constitution and colonial charters. To the English, the Americans had the wrong ideas about the British constitution. English and American ideas did differ radically, because the Americans had a novel concept of *constitution*. The word signified to them a supreme law creating government, limiting it, unalterable by it, and paramount to it. A town orator of Boston announced that independence offered the people a chance of reclaiming rights "attendant upon the original state of nature, with the opportunity of establishing a government for ourselves." "To secure these rights," Thomas Jefferson declared, "governments are instituted among men."

The Virginia constitution of 1776, the first permanent state constitution, began with a Declaration of Rights that restrained all branches of government (see Appendix: Key Documents). As the first such document it contained many constitutional "firsts," such as the statements that "all men" are equally free and have inherent rights that cannot be divested even by compact; that among these rights are the enjoyment of life, liberty, and property and the pursuit of happiness; and that all power derives from the people, who retain a right to change the government if it fails to secure its objectives. The declaration recognized "the free exercise of religion" and freedom of the press, and included clauses that were precursors, sometimes in rudimentary form, of the Fourth through the Eighth Amendments of the Constitution of the United States. Inexplicably, the convention voted down a ban on bills of attainder and on ex post facto laws and omitted the freedoms of speech, assembly, and petition, the right to the writ of habeas corpus, grand jury proceedings, the right to compulsory process to secure evidence in one's own behalf, the right to counsel, and freedom from double jeopardy. Although religious liberty was guaranteed, the ban on an establishment of religion awaited enactment of the Virginia Statute for Religious Freedom in 1786.

Pennsylvania's bill of rights was more comprehensive than Virginia's. Pennsylvania omitted the right to bail and bans on excessive fines and cruel punishments but added freedom of speech, assembly, and petition; separated church and state; recognized the right of conscientious objection; protected the right to counsel in all criminal cases; secured the right to keep arms; and guaranteed the right to travel or emigrate—all constitutional "firsts." Pennsylvania also recognized that "the people have a right to hold themselves, their houses, papers, and possessions free from search and seizure," in contrast to Virginia's mere prohibition of general warrants. Delaware's bill of rights was the first to ban ex post facto laws and the quartering of troops in homes during peacetime; Maryland added a prohibition on bills of attainder. Vermont's contribution was the first to outlaw slavery and the first constitutional provision for just compensation in cases of eminent domain. Connecticut and Rhode Island retained their charters as their constitutions, while New Jersey, Georgia, New York, and South Carolina protected some rights in their constitutional texts but had no separate bills of rights and no noteworthy innovations.

Massachusetts, the last of the original states to adopt a constitution (1780), contributed the most to the concept of a bill of rights. It had the most comprehensive bill of rights and was the first to secure citizens against "all unreasonable searches and seizures," the formulation closest to that of the later Fourth Amendment. Massachusetts was also the first state to replace the weak "ought not" found in all previous bills of rights (for example, "the liberty of the press ought not be restrained") with the injunction "shall not," which Madison later followed. Most important, Massachusetts was the first state that framed its fundamental law by a specially elected constitutional convention, which exercised no legislative authority (and submitted the document to the towns for popular ratification). In every other state before 1780, legislatures, sometimes calling themselves conventions, wrote the fundamental law and promulgated it. Theoretically, a bill of rights framed by a legislature could be changed by ordinary legislation, a fact deplored by Jefferson as a capital defect in Virginia's model. The procedure first adopted by Massachusetts was copied by New Hampshire when it revised its constitution in 1784, with the first guarantee against double jeopardy; thereafter the Massachusetts procedure prevailed.

The framing of the first constitutions with bills of rights ranks among America's foremost achievements, the more remarkable because they were unprecedented and they were realized during wartime. Nevertheless, the phrasing of various rights and the inclusion or omission of particular ones in any given state constitution seems careless. Why so few states protected the rights against double jeopardy and bills of attainder, and why so many omitted habeas corpus and freedom of speech, among others, is inexplicable except in terms of shoddy craftsmanship. Even so, the existence of eight state bills of rights with constitutional status invigorated Anti-Federalist arguments that a bill of rights should be appended to the Constitution of 1787. The state ratifying conventions produced about seventy-five recommendations, providing Madison with an invaluable list from which to create the proposals that he submitted to Congress.

Congress itself supplied a final precedent, the Northwest Ordinance of 1787, which planned the evolution of territories to statehood. The ordinance was the first federal document to contain a bill of rights. To extend "the fundamental principles of civil and religious liberty," Congress included articles that were to remain "forever . . . unalterable," guaranteeing to territorial inhabitants habeas corpus, trial by jury, representative government, judicial proceedings "according to the course of the common law," and, as an additional assurance of due process, an encapsulated provision from Magna Carta protecting liberty and property from being deprived except "by the judgment of . . . peers, or the law of the land." The ordinance also included articles protecting the right to bail except in capital cases, enjoined that all fines should be "moderate," and prohibited "cruel or unusual punishment." Another article provided a federal precedent for still another provision of the Bill of Rights: just compensation for property taken for public purposes. The ordinance also protected the sanctity of private contracts, outlawed sex discrimination in land ownership, banned slavery, and provided for religious liberty. Thus the federal as well as colonial and state experience with written instruments to safeguard rights enhanced the claim that a bill of rights should bridle the new national government.

The Bill of Rights did just that: it was a bill of restraints on the United States. Congress submitted those restraining amendments to the states for ratification on September 25, 1789, and the requisite number of state legislatures ratified them by December 15, 1791. The triumph of individual liberty against government power is one of history's noblest themes, epitomized by the Bill of Rights. Yet James Madison of Virginia, justly remembered as the "father" of the Bill of Rights, privately referred on August 19, 1789, to the "nauseous project of amendments." In the First Congress, he had proposed the amendments that became the Bill of Rights, in part because "it will kill the opposition everywhere"—a suggestion that party politics saturated the making of the first ten amendments. Thomas Jefferson, who must have been profoundly gratified by the ratification of the amendments, which he had urged, was the secretary of state who officially notified the governors of the states that ratification was an accomplished fact: he had the honor, he listlessly wrote, of enclosing copies of an act "concerning certain fisheries," another establishing the post office, and "the ratifications by three fourths of the . . . States, of certain articles in addition and amendment of the Constitution." The history of the Bill of Rights from its rejection by the Philadelphia Constitutional Convention to its belated ratification is not as passionless, because the omission of a bill of rights in the original Constitution had been the most important obstacle in the way of its adoption by the states.

The omission of a bill of rights was a deliberate act of the Constitutional Convention. The Convention's work was almost done when it received from the Committee of Style copies of the proposed Constitution and the letter by which the Convention would submit it to Congress. The major task that remained was to adopt, engross, and sign the finished document. The weary delegates, after a hot summer's work in Philadelphia, were eager to return home. At that point, on September 12, 1787, George Mason of Virginia remarked that he "wished the plan had been prefaced by a Bill of Rights," because it would "give great quiet" to the people. Mason thought that with the aid of state bills of rights as models, "a bill might be prepared in a few hours." He made no stirring speech for civil liberties in general or any rights in particular. He did not even argue the need for a bill of rights or move the adoption of one, though he offered to second a motion if one were made. Elbridge Gerry of Massachusetts then moved for a committee to prepare a bill of rights, and Mason seconded the motion. Roger Sherman of Connecticut observed that the rights of the people should be secured if necessary, but because the Constitution did not repeal the state bills of rights, the Convention need not do anything. Without further debate, the delegates, voting by states, defeated the motion 10–0. Two days later, on the fourteenth, after the states unanimously defeated a motion by Mason to delete from the Constitution a ban on ex post facto laws by Congress, Charles Pinckney of South Carolina, seconded by Gerry, moved to insert a declaration "that the liberty of the Press should be inviolably observed." Sherman laconically replied, "It is unnecessary. The power of Congress does not extend to the Press," and the motion lost 7–4. Three days later the Convention adjourned. Two months later James Wilson of Pennsylvania would report to his state ratifying convention that "so little account was the idea [of a bill of rights] that it passed off in a short conversation, without introducing a formal debate or assuming the shape of a motion."

In the Congress of the Confederation, Richard Henry Lee of Virginia moved that a bill of rights, which he had adapted from his own state's constitution, be added to the Constitution. Lee was less interested in the adoption of a bill of rights than in defeating the Constitution. Under the Articles of Confederation amendments recommended by Congress required ratification by all the state legislatures, not just nine state ratifying conventions. Lee's motion was defeated, but it showed that, from the start of the ratification controversy, the omission of a bill of rights became an Anti-Federalist mace with which to smash the Constitution. Its opponents sought to prevent ratification and exaggerated the bill of rights issue because it was one with which they could enlist public support. Their prime loyalty belonged to states' rights, not civil rights.

Mason, the author of the celebrated Virginia Declaration of Rights of 1776, soon wrote his influential "Objections to the Constitution," which began, "There is no Declaration of Rights." The sincerity of Mason's desire for a bill of rights is beyond question, but he had many other reasons for opposing the Constitution. Almost two weeks before he raised the issue of a bill of rights on September 12, he had declared "that he would sooner chop off his right hand than put it to the Constitution as it now stands." A bill of rights might protect individuals against the national government, but it would not protect the states. He believed that the new government would diminish state powers and by the exercise of its commerce power could "ruin" the southern states; the control of commerce by a mere majority vote of Congress was, to Mason, "an insuperable objection." But the lack of a bill of rights proved to be the most powerful argument against ratification of the Constitution in the Anti-Federalist armory.

Why did the Constitutional Convention omit a bill of rights? No delegate opposed one in principle. As George Washington informed the Marquis de Lafayette, "there was not a member of the Convention, I believe, who had the least objection to what is contended for by the advocates for a Bill of Rights." All the Framers were civil libertarians as well as experienced politicians who had the confidence of their constituents and the state legislatures that elected them. Even the foremost opponents of ratification praised the makeup of the convention. Mason himself, for example, wrote that "America has certainly upon this occasion drawn forth her first characters . . . of the purest intentions," and Patrick Henry, who led the Anti-Federalists in Virginia, conceded that the states had trusted the "object of revising the Confederation to the greatest, the best, and most enlightened of our citizens." Their liberality of spirit is suggested by the fact that many—Protestants all and including the entire Virginia delegation—made a point of attending divine service at Saint Mary's Chapel in Philadelphia. As Washington recorded in his diary, "Went to the Romish church to high mass." How could such an "assembly of demigods," as Jefferson called them, neglect the liberties of the people?

On July 26 the Convention had adjourned until August 6 to permit a Committee of Detail to frame a "constitution conformable to the Resolutions passed by the Convention." The committee introduced a number of significant changes, such as the explicit enumeration of the powers of Congress, and without recommendations from the Convention decided on a preamble. Edmund Randolph left a fragmentary record of the committee's decision that the preamble did not seem a proper place for a philosophic statement of the ends of government because "we are not working on the natural rights of men not yet gathered into society" but upon rights "modified by society and interwoven with what we call . . . the rights of states." According to American revolutionary theory, the natural rights to which Randolph referred were possessed by individuals in the state of nature, which existed before people voluntarily contracted with each other to establish a government whose purpose was to secure their rights. In the state of nature, when only the law of nature governed, the theory posited that—as the first section of the Virginia Declaration of Rights stated—"all men are by nature equally free and independent, and have certain inherent rights, of which, when they enter into a state of society, they cannot, by any compact, deprive or divest their posterity; namely, the enjoyment of life and liberty, with the means of acquiring and possessing property, and pursuing and obtaining happiness and safety." Because the adoption of the state constitutions ended the state of nature, there was no need to enumerate the rights reserved to the people—or so the Framers of the Constitution reasoned.

And yet, they recognized that the existence of organized society and government required the affirmation of certain rights that did not exist in the state of nature but that served to protect natural rights. Trial by jury, for example, was unknown in the state of nature but was necessary for the protection of one's life, liberty, and property. Accordingly, the Framers recognized a class of rights "modified by society," just as they recognized that the legitimate powers of government that did not belong to the central government of the Union could be called "the rights of the states." The principal task of the Convention was to provide for an effective national government by redistributing the powers of government. The Committee of Detail, when enumerating the powers of Congress, began with the power to tax and the power to regulate commerce among the states and with foreign nations (the two great powers that the Articles of Confederation had withheld from Congress) and ended with an omnibus clause that granted implied powers: "And to make all laws that shall be necessary and proper for carrying into execution the foregoing powers, and all other powers vested, by this Constitution, in the government of the United States, or in any department thereof." That "necessary and proper" clause was the most formidable in the array of national powers, therefore the most controversial, and the one most responsible, later, for the demand for a bill of rights to ensure that the United States did not violate the rights of the people or of the states.

The Committee of Detail, again on its own initiative, recommended some rights ("modified by society"), among them trial by jury in criminal cases, a tight definition of treason to prevent improper convictions, a ban on titles of nobility (a way of guaranteeing against a privileged class), freedom of speech and debate for members of the legislature, and a guarantee that the citizens of each state should have the same privileges and immunities as citizens in other states. In addition, the committee introduced the clause guaranteeing to each state a republican form of government. In the minds of the Framers, many provisions of the Constitution had a libertarian character: the election of public officials, the representative system, the separation of powers among three branches of government, and the requirement that revenue and appropriation measures originate in the House of Representatives—a protection of the natural right to property and a bar against taxation without representation. During the controversy over ratification of the Constitution, when the omission of a bill of rights was the major issue, many Framers argued, as did Alexander Hamilton in *The Federalist*, No. 84, "that the Constitution is itself, in every rational sense, and to every useful purpose, a Bill of Rights."

All the rights recommended by the Committee of Detail eventually found their way into the Constitution, but Charles Pinckney believed that the committee had neglected several others that also deserved constitutional recognition. On August 20 he recommended "sundry propositions," including a guarantee of the writ of habeas corpus, which protected citizens from arbitrary arrest; an injunction that the liberty of the press should be "inviolably preserved"; a ban on maintaining an army in time of peace except with the consent of Congress; an explicit subordination of the military to the civil power; a prohibition on the quartering of troops in private homes during peacetime; and a ban on religious tests as a qualification for any United States office.

None of these provisions secured what theoreticians regarded as natural rights. The freedoms of speech and conscience were natural rights, but the liberty of the press was distinguishable as a right that did not exist in the state of nature. The ban on religious tests, though protecting the right of conscience, was another example of what Edmund Randolph had called a right "modified by society," not preexisting it. Significantly, Pinckney had not recommended a protection of freedom of religion or of speech. Without debate or consideration the Convention referred his proposals to the Committee of Detail, but it made no recommendations on any of them.

On the floor of the Convention, Elbridge Gerry moved that Congress should be denied the power to pass bills of attainder and ex post facto laws. The motion passed with hardly any discussion. Bills of attainder were legislative declarations of the guilt of individuals and legislative impositions of criminal penalties, without the usual judicial proceedings. No instrument of the criminal law was more dreaded or violative of the fair procedures associated with trial by jury than a bill of attainder, the most expeditious way of condemning political opponents. Ex post facto laws in the field of criminal law were nearly as notorious and as unfair, for they were legislative acts that made criminal any conduct that was not a crime at the time committed or acts that retroactively increased the penalty for a crime or changed the rules of evidence in order to obtain a conviction. With little debate the Convention also placed prohibitions on the power of the states to enact bills of attainder and ex post facto laws. Some delegates, including George Mason, opposed the ban on the latter because they did not wish to limit the power of the states to enact retroactive legislation in civil cases, and they insisted, against the supposed authority of Sir William Blackstone's *Commentaries on the Laws of England* (1765–1769) that ex post facto laws included civil legislation as well as criminal. The Supreme Court in 1798 would settle the matter in favor of the Blackstonian interpretation, ruling that ex post facto laws are criminal only.

Bills of attainder and ex post facto laws, being legislative enactments, came into existence after the people had compacted to form a government. Banning such enactments, therefore, constituted a means for the protection of natural rights, but the bans did not protect natural rights as such. The same may be said of protecting the cherished writ of habeas corpus as a device for ensuring the personal liberty of an individual wrongfully imprisoned. After the Convention unanimously adopted the Committee of Detail's recommendation for a clause on trial by jury in criminal cases, Pinckney urged the Convention to secure the benefit of the writ as well, and by a vote of 7–3 a habeas corpus clause was adopted.

Pinckney also moved a prohibition on religious tests, which the Convention summarily adopted by unanimous vote. In so doing the Convention demonstrated a rare liberality of spirit, because all the Framers except those who represented New York and Virginia came from states whose constitutions discriminated against some religious denominations by imposing a religious test as a qualification for public office. In Pennsylvania, for example, a state whose constitution contained the broadest guarantee of religious freedom and a provision that no man acknowledging God should be deprived of any civil right on account of his religion, the oath of office required an acknowledgment of the divine inspiration of the New Testament. A Jew from Philadelphia petitioned the Constitutional Convention not to frame a similar oath of office, which would impose a civil disability upon him. Unitarians, Deists, and Catholics suffered from various religious disabilities in many states. By prohibiting religious tests, the Convention showed a greater regard for religious liberty than most states; yet the Convention did not protect religious liberty itself.

Thus, all the protections written into the Constitution were means of vindicating natural rights, but only one natural right was constitutionally protected. The overwhelming majority of the Convention believed, as Roger Sherman of Connecticut succinctly declared, that a bill of rights "is unnecessary." Why was it unnecessary, given the fact that the Convention recommended a new and powerful national government that could operate directly on individuals? The Framers believed that the national government could exercise only enumerated powers or powers necessary to carry out those enumerated, and no provision for the Constitution authorized the government to act on any natural rights. A bill of rights would restrict national powers, but, Hamilton declared, such a bill would be "dangerous" as well as unnecessary, because it "would contain various exceptions to powers not granted; and, on this very account, would afford a colorable pretext to claim more than were granted. For why declare that things shall not be done which there is no power to do? Why, for instance, should it be said that the liberty of the press shall not be restrained, when no power is given by which restrictions may be imposed?"

Hamilton expressed a standard Federalist position, echoing other Framers and advocates of ratification. Excluding a bill of rights from the Constitution was fundamental to the constitutional theory of the Framers. James Wilson of Pennsylvania, whose influence at the Convention had been second only to that of Madison, led the ratificationist forces in Pennsylvania and several times sought to explain the omission of a bill of rights. The people of the states, he declared, had vested in their governments all powers and rights "which they did not in explicit terms reserve," but the case was different as to a federal government whose authority rested on positive grants of power expressed in the Constitution. For the federal government, "the reverse of the proposition prevails, and everything which is not given, is reserved" to the people or the states. That distinction, Wilson argued, answered those who believed that the omission of a bill of rights was a defect. Its inclusion would have been "absurd," because a bill of rights stipulated the reserved rights of the people, whereas the function for the Constitution was to provide for the existence of the federal government rather than enumerate rights not divested. Like Hamilton and other Federalists, Wilson believed that a formal declaration on freedom of the press or religion, over which Congress had no powers whatsoever, could "imply" that some degree of power had been granted because of the attempt to define its extent. Wilson also insisted on the impossibility of enumerating and reserving all the rights of the people. "A bill of rights annexed to a constitution," he added, "is an enumeration of the powers reserved. If we attempt an enumeration, everything that is not enumerated is presumed to be given. The consequence is, that an imperfect enumeration would throw all implied powers into the scale of the government; and the rights of the people would be rendered incomplete."

Civil liberties, the supporters of the Constitution believed, faced real dangers from the possibility of repressive state action, but that was a matter to be guarded against by state bills of rights. They also argued, inconsistently, that some states had no bills of rights but were as free as those with bills of rights. They were as free because personal liberty, to Federalist theoreticians, did not depend on "parchment provisions," which Hamilton called inadequate in "a struggle with public necessity"; it depended, rather, on public opinion, an extended republic, a pluralistic society of competing interests, and a free and limited government structured to prevent any interest from becoming an overbearing majority.

The fact that six states had no bills of rights and that none had a comprehensive list of guarantees provided the supporters of ratification with the argument, made by Wilson among others, that an imperfect bill of rights was worse than none at all because the omission of some rights might justify their infringement by implying an unintended grant of government power. The record was not reassuring: the states had very imperfect bills of rights, which proved to be ineffective when confronted by "public necessity," and the state governments did in fact abridge rights that had not been explicitly reserved.

Virginia's Declaration of Rights, for example, did not ban bills of attainder. In 1778 the Virginia assembly adopted a bill of attainder and outlawry, drafted by Jefferson at the instigation of Governor Patrick Henry, against a reputed cutthroat Tory, one Josiah Philips, and some fifty unnamed "associates." By legislative enactment they were condemned for treason and murder, and on failure to surrender were subject to being killed by anyone. At the Virginia ratifying convention, Edmund Randolph, irked beyond endurance by Henry's assaults on the Constitution as dangerous to personal liberties, recalled with "horror" the "shocking" attainder. When Henry defended the attainder, John Marshall, who supported ratification without a bill of rights, declared, "Can we pretend to the enjoyment of political freedom or security, when we are told that a man has been, by an act of Assembly, struck out of existence without a trial by jury, without examination, without being confronted with his accusers and witnesses, without the benefits of the law of the land?"

The Framers of the Constitution tended to be skeptical about the value of "parchment barriers" against "overbearing majorities," as Madison said. He had seen repeated violations of bills of rights in every state. Experience proved the "inefficacy of a bill of rights on those occasions when its control is most needed," he said. In Virginia, despite an explicit protection of the rights of conscience, the legislature had favored an establishment of religion, which was averted only because Madison turned the tide of opinion against the bill. As realists, the Framers believed that constitutional protections of rights meant little during times of popular hysteria; any member of the Constitutional Convention could have cited examples of gross abridgments of civil liberties in states that had bills of rights.

Virginia's bill was imperfect not just because it lacked a ban on bills of attainder. The much vaunted Declaration of Rights of Virginia also omitted the freedoms of speech, assembly, and petition; the right to the writ of habeas corpus; the right to grand jury proceedings; the right to counsel; separation of church and state;

and freedom from double jeopardy and from ex post facto laws. The rights omitted were as numerous and important as those included. Twelve states, including Vermont, had framed constitutions, and every one of them secured the right to trial by jury in criminal cases. Although every one also protected religious liberty, five either permitted or provided for establishments of religion. Two states passed over a free press guarantee. Four neglected to ban excessive fines, excessive bail, compulsory self-incrimination, and general search warrants. Five ignored protections for the rights of assembly, petition, counsel, and trial by jury in civil cases. Seven omitted a prohibition of ex post facto laws. Nine failed to provide for grand jury proceedings, and nine failed to condemn bills of attainder. Ten said nothing about freedom of speech, while eleven were silent on double jeopardy. Whether omissions implied a power to violate, they seemed, in Federalist minds, to raise dangers that could be prevented by avoiding an unnecessary problem entirely: omit a bill of rights when forming a federal government of limited powers.

That the Framers of the Constitution actually believed their own arguments to justify the omission of a bill of rights is difficult to credit. Some of the points they made were patently absurd, like the insistence that the inclusion of a bill of rights would be dangerous, and on historical grounds, unsuitable. The last point most commonly turned up in the claim that bills of rights were appropriate in England but not in America. Magna Carta, the Petition of Right of 1628, and the Bill of Rights of 1689 had been grants wrested from kings to secure royal assent to certain liberties and therefore had "no application to constitutions . . . founded upon the power of the people" who surrendered nothing and retained everything. That argument, made in *The Federalist*, No. 84, and by leading ratificationists as sophisticated as James Wilson and Oliver Ellsworth, was so porous that it could persuade no one. Excepting Rhode Island and Connecticut, the two corporate colonies that retained their charters (with all royal references deleted), eleven states had framed written constitutions during the Revolution, and seven drew up bills of rights; even the four without such bills inserted in their constitutions provisions normally found in a bill of rights.

To imply that bills of rights were un-American or unnecessary merely because in America the people were the source of all power was unhistorical. Over a period of a century and a half America had become accustomed to the idea that government existed by a consent of the governed, that people created government, that they did it by written compact, that the compact constituted fundamental law, that the government must be subject to such limitations as are necessary for the security of the rights of the people, and, usually, that the reserved rights of the people were enumerated in bills of rights. Counting Vermont (an independent republic from 1777 until its admission to the Union in 1791), eight states had bills of rights—notwithstanding any opinion that such bills properly belonged only in a compact between a king and his subjects. The dominant theory in the United States from the time of the Revolution was that the fundamental law limited all branches of the government, not just the crown as in England, where the great liberty documents did not limit the legislative power.

When Randolph for the Committee of Detail alluded to the fact that "we are not working on the natural rights of men not yet gathered into society," he referred to the framing of the state constitutions. The constitution of James Wilson's state began with an elaborate preamble whose first words established the proposition that "all government ought to be instituted . . . to enable the individuals who compose [the commonwealth] to enjoy their natural rights" and whose preamble was followed by as comprehensive a "Declaration of the Rights of the Inhabitants" as existed in any state. Yet Wilson repeatedly informed Pennsylvania's ratifying convention that rights and liberties could be claimed only in a contract between king and subjects, not when "the fee simple of freedom and government is declared to be in the people." Governor Randolph merely exaggerated at the Virginia ratifying convention when he claimed that the Virginia Declaration of Rights "has never secured us against any danger; it has been repeatedly disregarded and violated." But Randolph's rhetoric became unpardonable when he declared that although a bill of rights made sense in England to limit the king's prerogative, "Our situation is radically different from that of the people of England. What have we to do with bills of rights? . . . A bill of rights, therefore, accurately speaking, is quite useless, if not dangerous to a republic." At the Constitutional Convention, Randolph had been able to distinguish natural rights from some rights modified by society.

That supporters of the Constitution could ask, "What have we to do with a bill of rights?" suggests that they had made a colossal error of judgment, which they compounded by refusing to admit it. Their single-minded purpose of creating an effective national government had exhausted their energies and good sense, and when they found themselves on the defensive, accused of threatening the liberties of the people, their frayed nerves led them into indefensible positions. Any Anti-Federalist could have answered Randolph's question, Wilson's speeches, or Hamilton's *Federalist*, No. 84, and many capably did so without resorting to Patrick Henry's grating hysteria. "Centinel," who answered Wilson in a Philadelphia newspaper, declared that the explanation for the omission of a bill of rights "is an insult on the understanding of the people."

Abroad, two wise Americans serving their country in diplomatic missions, coolly appraised the proposed Constitution without the obligation of having to support a party line. After receiving a copy of the document in London, John Adams wrote a short letter to Thomas Jefferson in Paris. The Constitution seemed "admirably calculated to preserve the Union," Adams wrote, and he hoped it would be ratified with amendments adopted later. "What think you," he asked, "of a Declaration of Rights? Should not such a Thing have preceded the Model?" Jefferson, in his first letter to Madison on the subject of the Constitution, began with praise but ended with what he did not like: "First the omission of a bill of rights." After listing rights he thought deserved special protection, starting with freedom of religion and of the press, Jefferson dismissed as campaign rhetoric Wilson's justification for the omission of a bill of rights and concluded: "Let me add that a bill of rights is what the people are entitled to against every government on earth, general or particular, and what no just government should refuse, or rest on inference."

Adams and Jefferson in Europe were much closer to popular opinion than the Framers of the Constitution, who had worked secretly for almost four months and, with their supporters, became locked into a position that defied logic and experience. During the ratification controversy, some Federalists argued that the Constitution protected basic rights, exposing them to the reply that they had omitted the liberty of the press, religious freedom, security against general warrants, trial by jury in civil cases, and other basic rights. If the Framers intended to protect only non-natural rights, those arising from the existence of society and government and unknown in a state of nature, they were inconsistent. First, they protected only some of the nonnatural rights; the first ten amendments are crowded with such rights that the Framers neglected. Second, any reader of John Locke would realize that the clause in Article I, section 10, prohibiting the states from impairing the obligation of contracts, protected a natural right. At the close of Chapter 2 of *Second Treatise on Government*, Locke wrote that the "promises and bargains" between two men on a desert island or between a Swiss and an Indian in the woods of America "are binding to them, though they are perfectly in a State of Nature to one another." Oddly, the Convention had failed to adopt the contract clause when it was proposed; the Committee of Style inserted it into the Constitution, and the Convention, without discussion, agreed to the clause in its closing days. The inclusion of one natural right raises the question of why all others were excluded. The contract clause, of course, operates only against state infringement and raises the additional question of why the Convention failed to include a comparable prohibition on the United States.

Natural rights, in accordance with American theory and experience, required protection in any government made by compact. At the Convention, Madison declared that the delegates had assembled to frame "a compact by which an authority was created paramount to the parties, and making laws for the government of them." Some of the states, when formally ratifying the Constitution, considered themselves to be "entering into an explicit and solemn compact," as Massachusetts declared. During the ratification controversy, publicists on both sides referred to the Constitution as a compact. Chief Justice John Jay, who had been one of the authors of *The Federalist,* observed in *Chisholm v. Georgia* (1793) that "the Constitution of the United States is . . . a compact made by the people of the United States in order to govern themselves."

The new compact created a government whose powers seemed intimidating. Article VI established the Constitution, laws made in its pursuance, and treaties of the United States to be the supreme law of the land, anything in the state constitutions to the contrary notwithstanding. That struck many Anti-Federalists as dangerous, because they thought it superseded their state bills of rights and authorized laws repugnant to personal rights. Most Anti-Federalists believed that enumerated powers could be abused at the expense of fundamental liberties. Congress's power to tax, for example, might be aimed at the press and was thus, in the words of Richard Henry Lee, "a power to destroy or restrain the freedom of it." Others feared that taxes might be exacted from the people for the support of a religious denomination. According to Patrick Henry, tax collectors unrestrained by a ban on general warrants might invade homes "and search, ransack, and measure, everything you eat, drink, and wear."

The necessary and proper clause particularly enraged advocates of a bill of rights. They saw that clause as the source of undefined and unlimited powers to aggrandize the national government and victimize the people, unless, as "An Old Whig" declared, "we had a bill of rights to which we might appeal." "A Democratic Federalist" wrote: "I lay it down as a general rule that wherever the powers of government extend to the lives, the persons, and properties of the subject, all their rights ought to be clearly and expressly defined, otherwise they have but a poor security for their liberties." Henry warned that Congress might "extort a confession by the use of torture" in order to convict a violator of federal law. Numerous opponents of ratification contended that Congress could define as crimes the violation of any laws it might legitimately enact, and in the absence of a bill of rights, accused persons might be deprived of the rights to counsel, to indictment, to cross-examine witnesses against them, to produce evidence in their own behalf, to be free from compulsory self-incrimination, to be protected against double jeopardy or excessive bail, to be exempt from excessive fines or cruel and unusual punishments, and to enjoy other rights traditionally belonging to accused persons. Such an argument was, invariably, advanced as one among many refuting the Federalist claim that a bill of rights was unnecessary.

If a bill of rights was unnecessary, Anti-Federalists asked, why did the Constitution protect some rights? The protection of some rights opened the Federalists to devastating rebuttal. They claimed that because no bill of rights could be complete, the omission of any particular right might imply a power to abridge it as unworthy of respect by the government. The argument that to include some rights would exclude all others boomeranged. The protection of trial by jury in criminal cases, the bans on religious tests, ex post facto laws, and bills of attainder, the narrow definition of treason, and the provision for the writ of habeas corpus by the Federalists' own reasoning was turned against them. Robert Whitehall, answering Wilson on the floor of the Pennsylvania ratifying convention, noted that the writ of habeas corpus and trial by jury had been expressly reserved, and in vain he called on Wilson to reconcile the reservation with his "favorite proposition." "For, if there was danger in the attempt to enumerate the liberties of the people," Whitehall explained, "lest it should prove imperfect and defective, how happens it, that in the instances I have mentioned, that danger has been incurred? Have the people no other rights worth their attention, or is it to be inferred, agreeable to the maxim of our opponents, that every other right is abandoned?" Stipulating a right, he concluded, destroyed the "argument of danger." Surely, Anti-Federalists said, their opponents might think of some rights in addition to those protected. The ban on religious tests could have reminded them of freedom of religion. Did not its omission, by their reasoning, necessarily mean that the government could attack freedom of religion?

Patrick Henry cleverly observed that the "fair implication" of the Federalist argument against a bill of rights was that the government could do anything not forbidden by the Constitution. Because the provision on the writ of habeas corpus allowed its suspension when required for public safety, Henry reasoned, "It results clearly that, if it had not said so, they could suspend it in all cases whatsoever. It reverses the position of the friends of this Constitution, that every thing is retained which is not given up; for, instead of this, everything is given up which is not expressly reserved." In his influential *Letters of a Federal Farmer*, Richard Henry Lee observed that a clause of the Constitution prohibited Congress from granting titles of nobility. If the clause had been omitted, he wondered whether Congress would have the power to grant such titles, and he concluded that it would not under any provision of the Constitution. "Why then by a negative clause, restrain congress from doing what it had power to do? This clause, then, must have no meaning, or imply, that were it omitted, congress would have the power in question . . . on the principle that congress possess the powers not expressly reserved." Lee objected to leaving the rights of the people to "logical inferences," because Federalist principles led to the implication that all the rights not mentioned in the Constitution were intended to be relinquished.

Far from being dangerous, a bill of rights, as "A Federal Republican" stated in answer to Wilson, "could do no harm, but might do much good." Lee, discoursing on the good it might do, observed that a bill of rights would assist popular "education," because it taught "truths" upon which freedom depends and that the people must believe as "sacred." James Winthrop of Massachusetts, writing as "Agrippa," explained another positive value of a bill of rights. It "serves to secure the minority against the usurpations and tyranny of the majority." History, he wrote, proved the "prevalence of a disposition to use power wantonly. It [a bill of rights] is therefore as necessary to defend an individual against the majority in a republick as against the king in a monarchy."

In sum, the usually masterful politicians who had dominated the Convention had blundered by botching constitutional theory and making a serious political error. Their arguments justifying the omission of a bill of rights were impolitic and unconvincing. Mason's point that a bill of rights would quiet the fears of the people was unanswerable. Alienating him and the many who agreed with him was bad politics and handed to the opposition a stirring cause around which they could muster sentiment against ratification. The single issue that united Anti-Federalists throughout the country was the lack of a bill of rights. No rational argument—and the lack of a bill of rights created an intensely emotional issue because people believed that their liberties were at stake—could possibly allay the fears generated by demagogues like Henry and principled opponents of ratification like Mason. Washington believed that even Mason's "Objections" were meant "to alarm the people." And, when Anti-Federalists in New York demanded a bill of rights, Hamilton alleged, "It is the plan of men of this stamp to frighten the people with ideal bugbears, in order to mould them to their own purposes. The unceasing cry of these designing croakers is, My friends, your liberty is invaded!" The Anti-Federalists capitalized on the Federalist blunder, hoping to defeat the Constitution or get a second convention that would revise it in order to hamstring the national government.

In Pennsylvania, the second state to ratify, the minority demanded a comprehensive bill of rights similar to that in their state constitution. Massachusetts, the sixth state to ratify, was the first to do so with recommended amendments. Only two of the recommended amendments, dealing with jury trial in civil suits and grand jury indictment, belonged in a bill of rights. Supporters of the Constitution in Massachusetts had withdrawn a proposed bill of rights on the supposition that Anti-Federalists would use it as proof that the Constitution endangered liberty. Maryland would also have recommended a bill of rights, but the Federalist majority jettisoned it when the Anti-Federalists tried to insert curbs on national powers to tax and regulate commerce. Nevertheless, Federalists grudgingly accepted ratification with recommended amendments to ward off conditional ratification or the defeat of the Constitution. New Hampshire, whose approval as the ninth state made ratification an accomplished fact, urged the adoption of a partial bill of rights after the new government went into operation. Virginia and New York, whose ratification was politically indispensable, followed suit with more comprehensive recommendations. North Carolina was the fourth state to ratify with recommendations that included a bill of rights. But the states also recommended crippling restrictions on delegated powers.

Thus, the Constitution was ratified only because crucial states, where ratification had been in doubt, were willing to accept the promise of a bill of rights in the form of subsequent amendments to the Constitution. State recommendations for amendments, including those of the Pennsylvania minority, received nationwide publicity, adding to the clamor for a bill of rights. Every right that became part of the first ten amendments was included in state recommendations except the clause in the Fifth Amendment requiring just compensation for private property taken for public use.

James Madison was one of the Federalists who finally realized that statecraft and political expediency dictated a switch in position. At the Virginia ratifying convention in June 1788, Madison had upheld the usual Federalist arguments for the omission of a bill of rights, but finally voted to recommend such a bill in order to avoid previous amendments. He later conceded that the Constitution would have been defeated without a pledge from its supporters to back subsequent amendments. In Virginia, Madison's own political position deteriorated because he had opposed a bill of rights. The Anti-Federalists, who controlled the state legislature, elected two of their own, Richard Henry Lee and William Grayson, as the state's first United States senators. Madison faced a tough contest for election to the House of Representatives, and he feared that the Anti-Federalists might succeed in their call for a second constitutional convention. He needed to clarify his position on a bill of rights.

Although Madison had periodically apprised Jefferson, in Paris, on ratification developments, he had not answered Jefferson's letter of December 1787 supporting a bill of rights. On October 17, 1788, the eve of his campaign for a House seat, Madison faced the issue. He favored a bill of rights, he wrote, but had "never thought the omission a material defect" and was not "anxious to supply it even by subsequent amendments"; he did not even think the matter important. Still agreeing with Wilson that the delegated powers did not extend to reserved rights, Madison also worried about the difficulty of adequately protecting the most important rights; experience proved, he asserted, that a bill of rights was a mere parchment barrier when most needed. Government, after all, was the instrument of the majority, which could endanger liberty. "What use then . . . can a bill of rights serve in popular Governments?" Its political truths, he conceded by way of an answer, could educate the people, thereby inhibiting majority impulses.

Jefferson's reply of March 15, 1789, had a profound influence on Madison, as Madison's great speech of June 8 would show. An argument for a bill of rights that Madison had omitted, wrote Jefferson, was "the legal check which it puts into the hands of the judiciary." Jefferson believed that an independent court could withstand oppressive majority impulses by holding unconstitutional any acts violating a bill of rights. The point was not new to Madison, for he himself, when defending a ban on ex post facto laws at the Constitutional Convention, had declared that it would "oblige the Judges to declare [retrospective] interferences null and void." As for the point that the delegated powers did not reach the reserved rights of the people, Jefferson answered that because the Constitution protected some rights but ignored others, it raised implications against them, making a bill of rights "necessary by way of supplement." Moreover, he added, the Constitution "forms us into one state as to certain objects," requiring a bill of rights to guard against abuses of power. As for the point that a bill of rights could not be perfect, Jefferson replied with the adage that half a loaf is better than none; even if all rights could not be secured, "let us secure what we can." Madison had also argued that the limited powers of the federal government and the jealousy of the states afforded enough security, to which Jefferson answered that a bill of rights "will be the text whereby to try all the acts of the federal government." That a bill of rights was inconvenient and not always efficacious did not impress Jefferson. Sometimes, he replied, it was effective, and if it inconveniently cramped the government, the effect was short-lived and remediable, while the inconveniences of not having a bill of rights could be "permanent, afflicting, and irreparable." Legislative tyranny, Jefferson explained, would be a formidable dread for a long time, and executive tyranny would likely follow.

Jefferson's arguments, however persuasive, would have been unproductive but for the dangerous political situation, which Madison meant to ameliorate. Four states, including his own and New York, had called for a second convention, whose purpose, Madison feared, would be to "mutilate the system," especially as to the power to tax. Lack of that power "will be fatal" to the new federal government. Madison correctly believed that many Anti-Federalists favored an effective Union on the condition that a bill of rights bridle the new government. His strategy was to win them over by persuading the First Congress to adopt protections of civil liberties, thereby alleviating the public's anxieties, providing popularity and stability for the government, and isolating those Anti-Federalists whose foremost objective was "subverting the fabric . . . if not the Union itself."

In the First Congress, Representative Madison sought to fulfill his pledge of subsequent amendments. His accomplishment in the face of opposition and apathy entitles him to be remembered as father of the Bill of Rights even more than as father of the Constitution. Many Federalists thought that the House had more important tasks, such as the passage of tonnage duties and a judiciary bill. The opposition party, which had previously exploited the lack of a bill of rights in the Constitution, realized that its adoption would sink the movement for a second convention and make unlikely any additional amendments that would cripple the substantive powers of the government. Having used the bill of rights issue as a smokescreen for objections to the Constitution that could not be dramatically popularized, they now sought to scuttle Madison's proposals. They began by stalling, then tried to annex amendments aggrandizing state powers, and finally depreciated the importance of the very protections of individual liberty that they had formerly demanded as a guarantee against impending tyranny. Madison meant to prove that the new government was a friend of liberty; he also understood that his amendments, if adopted, would thwart the passage of proposals aggrandizing state powers and diminishing national ones. He would not be put off; he was insistent, compelling, unyielding, and, finally, triumphant.

On June 8, 1789, he made his long, memorable speech before an apathetic House, introducing amendments culled mainly from state constitutions and state ratifying convention proposals, especially Virginia's. All power, he argued, is subject to abuse and should be guarded against by constitutionally securing "the great rights of mankind." The government had only limited powers, but it might, unless prohibited, abuse its discretion as to its choice of means under the necessary and proper clause; it might, for example, use general warrants in the enforcement of its revenue laws. In Britain, bills of rights merely erected barriers against the powers of the crown, leaving the powers of Parliament "altogether indefinite," and the British constitution left unguarded the "choicest" rights of the press and of conscience. The great objective he had in mind, Madison declared, was to limit the powers of government, thus preventing legislative as well as executive abuse, and above all preventing abuses of power by "the body of the people, operating by the majority against the minority." Mere "paper barriers" might fail, but they raised a standard that might educate the majority against acts to which they might be inclined.

To the argument that a bill of rights was not necessary because the states constitutionally protected freedom, Madison had two responses. One was that some states had no bills of rights, others "very defective ones," and that the states constituted a greater danger to liberty than the new national government. The other was that the Constitution should, therefore, include an amendment, that "no State shall violate the equal rights of conscience, or the freedom of the press, or the trial by jury in criminal cases." He argued that the states would more likely abuse their powers than would the national government "if not controlled by the general principle, that laws are unconstitutional which infringe the rights of the community." He thought that "every Government should be disarmed of powers which trench upon those particular rights" of press, conscience, and jury trial. The amendment was all the more needed, he asserted, because some of the states did not protect these rights in their own constitutions. As for those that did, a "double security" could not reasonably be opposed. When Congressman Thomas Tucker of South Carolina moved to strike the proposed restriction on state powers, Madison carried the House by a two-thirds majority after he argued that this was "the most valuable amendment in the whole list."

To the contention that an enumeration of rights would disparage those not protected, Madison replied that the danger could be guarded against by adopting a proposal of his composition that became the Ninth Amendment. If his amendments were "incorporated" into the Constitution, Madison said, "independent tribunals of justice will consider themselves in a peculiar manner the guardians of those rights; they will be an impenetrable bulwark against every assumption of power in the legislative or executive; they will be naturally led to resist every encroachment upon rights expressly stipulated for in the constitution."

Although many Federalists preferred to give the new government time to operate before amending the Constitution, supporters of Madison exulted, largely for political reasons. Hugh Williamson of North Carolina, a signer of the Constitution, informed Madison that the Anti-Federalists of that state did not really want a bill of rights. William R. Davie, who had been Williamson's colleague in the Convention, gleefully reported to Madison that his amendments had "confounded the Anties exceedingly." Edmund Pendleton of Virginia wrote of Madison's amendments that "nothing was further from the wish of some, who covered their Opposition to the government under the masque of uncommon zeal for amendments." Tench Coxe of Pennsylvania praised Madison for having stripped the Constitution's opponents of every rationale "and most of the popular arguments they have heretofore used."

Notwithstanding the support of correspondents, Madison's speech stirred no immediate support in Congress. Indeed, every speaker who followed him, regardless of party affiliation, either opposed a bill of rights or believed that the House should attend to far more important duties. Six weeks later Madison "begged" for a consideration of his amendments, but the House assigned them to a special committee instead of debating them. That committee, which included Madison, reported in a week. It added freedom of speech to the rights protected against state abridgment, deleted Madison's reference to no "unreasonable searches and seizures," and made some stylistic revisions, but otherwise it recommended the amendments substantially as he had proposed them. The committee's report was tabled, impelling Madison on August 3 to implore its consideration.

On August 13 the House finally began to consider the reported amendments, and in the course of debate it made some significant changes. Madison had proposed to "incorporate" the amendments within the text of the Constitution at appropriate points. He did not recommend their adoption as a separate "bill of rights," although he had referred to them collectively by that phrase. Members objected, however, that to incorporate the amendments would give the impression that the Framers of the Constitution had signed a document that included provisions not of their composition. Another argument for lumping the amendments together was that the matter of form was so "trifling" that the House should not squander its time debating the placement of the various amendments. Ironically, Roger Sherman, who had insisted that the amendments were unnecessary, deserves the credit for insistently arguing that they should be appended as a supplement to the Constitution instead of being interspersed within it. Thus, what became the "Bill of Rights" achieved its significant collective form over the objections of its foremost proponent, Madison, and because of the desire of its opponents in both parties to downgrade its importance.

The House recast the free exercise of religion clause and its allied clause banning establishments of religion, improving Madison's original language. The House also confined to criminal cases Madison's broad phrasing that no person should be compelled to give evidence against himself. By contrast, the House restored the extremely important principle against unreasonable searches and seizures, which had been dropped by the committee. In another major decision the House decisively defeated Elbridge Gerry's motion, on behalf of the Anti-Federalists, to consider not just the committee's report but all amendments that the several states had proposed; the Anti-Federalists thus failed to intrude crippling political amendments. Finally, the House added "or to the people" in the recommendations by Madison that the powers not delegated to the United States be reserved to the states. On the whole, the House adopted Madison's amendments with few significant alterations during the course of its ten-day debate on the Bill of Rights.

In the midst of that debate Madison wrote a letter to a fellow Federalist explaining why he was so committed to "the nauseous project of amendments" that some of the party supported reluctantly. Protecting essential rights was "not improper," he coolly explained, and could be of some influence for good. He also felt honor-bound to redeem a campaign pledge to his constituents, mindful that the Constitution "would have been certainly rejected" by Virginia without assurances from its supporters to seek subsequent amendments. Politics, moreover, made proposing the amendments a necessity in order to beat the Anti-Federalists at their own game. If Federalists did not support the amendments, Anti-Federalists would claim that they had been right all along and gain support for a second convention. And, Madison wrote, the amendments "will kill the opposition everywhere, and by putting an end to disaffection to the Government itself, enable the administration to venture on measures not otherwise safe."

Madison had, in fact, upstaged and defeated Anti-Federalists. That is why Congressman Aedanus Burke of South Carolina cried sour grapes. During the debate on what became the First Amendment, he argued that the proposals before the House were "not those solid and substantial amendments which the people expect; they are little better than whip-syllabub, frothy and full of wind. . . . Upon the whole, I think . . . we have done nothing but lose our time, and that it will be better to drop the subject now, and proceed to the organization of the Government." The private correspondence of Senators Richard Henry Lee and William Grayson of Virginia reveals the explanation for the attitude of their party toward a bill of rights. A few days after Madison had introduced his amendments, Grayson complained to his mentor, Patrick Henry, that the Federalists meant to enact "amendments which shall effect [sic] personal liberty alone, leaving the great points of the Judiciary, direct taxation, &c, to stand as they are." Lee and Grayson had failed in their effort to have the Senate amend the House's proposals by adopting the Virginia ratifying convention's recommendations on direct taxation and the treaty and the commerce powers. Lee then regretted the original Anti-Federalist strategy of opposing the Constitution unless revised by the addition of a bill of rights and other amendments. He sorrowfully informed Henry that "the idea of subsequent amendments, was little better than putting oneself to death first, in expectation that the doctor, who wished our destruction, would afterwards restore us to life." Later, after the Senate had approved of the amendments that became the Bill of Rights, Grayson reported, "they are good for nothing, and I believe, as many others do, that they will do more harm than benefit."

The Senate, which kept no record of its debates, had deliberated on seventeen amendments submitted by the House. The Senate killed the one proposal Madison thought "the most valuable": protection against state infringement of speech, press, religion, or trial by jury. The motion to adopt failed to receive the necessary two-thirds vote, though by what margin is unknown. The Senate also weakened the House's ban on establishments of religion. Otherwise, the Senate accepted the House proposals, although the Senate combined several, reducing the number from seventeen to twelve. The first of the twelve dealt with the relation of population to the number of representatives from each state, and the then second would have prevented any law going into effect increasing the salaries of members of Congress until after the next election.

The House adamantly refused to accept the Senate's version of its ban on establishments of religion. A conference committee of both houses met to resolve their differences. The committee, which included Madison, accepted the House's ban on establishments but otherwise accepted the Senate's version of the amendments. On September 24, 1789, the House voted for the committee report; on the following day, the Senate concurred, and the twelve amendments were submitted to the states for ratification.

Within six months nine states ratified the Bill of Rights; of the twelve amendments submitted for approval, the first and second were rejected. The four recalcitrant states by mid-1790 were Virginia, Massachusetts, Connecticut, and Georgia. The admission of Vermont to the Union raised the number of states needed for ratification to eleven. Connecticut and Georgia refused to ratify. Georgia's position was that amendments were superfluous until experience under the Constitution proved a need. Connecticut believed that any suggestion that the Constitution was not perfect would add to the strength of Anti-Federalism.

In Massachusetts, Federalist apathy to the Bill of Rights was grounded on a satisfaction with the Constitution as it was, and the Anti-Federalists were more interested in amendments that would strengthen the states at the expense of the national government. Nevertheless, the Massachusetts lower house adopted all but the first, second, and twelfth amendments, and the upper house adopted all but the first, second, and tenth. Thus both houses of the Massachusetts legislature actually approved what became our First through Seventh and Ninth Amendments. However, a special committee dominated by Anti-Federalists urged that all amendments recommended by Massachusetts should be adopted before the state concurred in any amendments. As a result, the two houses never passed a bill promulgating ratification of eight amendments. Jefferson, the secretary of state, believed that Massachusetts, "having been the 10th state which has ratified, makes up the threefourth [sic] of the legislatures whose ratification was to suffice." He wrote to a Massachusetts official, asking for clarification. The reply was, "It does not appear that the Committee ever reported any bill." In 1939 Massachusetts joined Connecticut and Georgia when they belatedly ratified on the sesquicentennial anniversary of the Constitution.

Ratification of the Bill of Rights by Vermont, in November 1789, left Virginia the last state to act. Its ratification as the eleventh state was indispensable, although the hostility of its Anti-Federalist leaders presaged a doubtful outcome. Senators Grayson and Lee reported to the Virginia legislature that they transmitted the recommended amendments "with grief." They still hoped for a new constitutional convention that would devise "real and substantial Amendments" to "secure against the annihilation of the state governments." Patrick Henry moved in vain to postpone consideration of the Bill of Rights. The victims of a dilemma of their own making, the Anti-Federalists sought to sabotage the Bill of Rights. The Federalists of Virginia, however, eagerly supported the Bill of Rights in the knowledge that its adoption would appease public fears and stymie the amendments supported by the Anti-Federalists. Virginia's lower house, controlled by the Federalists, acted quickly, but the opposition dominated the state senate. Not all Anti-Federalists were implacably opposed. Some respected George Mason's opinion. When he had first heard of Madison's amendments he had called them "Milk and Water Propositions," not "important & substantial Amendments." But Mason changed his mind, saying that they gave "much satisfaction," though he still wanted other amendments, including one that prevented commercial regulations by mere majority vote of Congress.

Virginia's senate, as Edmund Randolph reported to Washington, postponed consideration of the amendments, "for a majority is unfriendly to the government." As a member of the lower house reported to Madison, the senate inclined to reject the Bill of Rights, not because of opposition to its guarantees, but from an apprehension "that the adoption of them at this time will be an obstacle to the chief object of their pursuit, the amendment on the subject of direct taxation." For that reason, Randolph reported to Washington, the Federalists meant to "push" the Bill of Rights; passage would "discountenance any future importunities for amendments."

At the close of 1789 Virginia's senate rejected what became the First, Sixth, Ninth, and Tenth Amendments, at least until the next session, thereby allowing time for the electorate to express itself. The Anti-Federalists still hoped to drum up support for "radical" amendments, as Lee called them. The senators in the majority also issued a statement grossly misrepresenting the First Amendment (then the third). Madison confidently believed that this Anti-Federalist tactic would backfire, and it did. For the senators' statement was not only inaccurate on its face; it came from men who with a single exception had opposed separation of church and state. Madison expected the ratification of the Bill of Rights, which he believed would eliminate the opposition to the new government and would give it a chance to operate with the confidence of the public. Jefferson made his influence felt on behalf of the Bill of Rights, and the Anti-Federalists grudgingly gave ground before public opinion. On December 15, 1791, after two years of procrastination, the Virginia senate finally ratified without record vote, thereby completing the process of state ratification and making the Bill of Rights part of the Constitution.

The history of the framing and ratification of the Bill of Rights indicates slight passion on the part of anyone to enshrine personal liberties in the fundamental law of the land. We know almost nothing about what the state legislatures thought concerning the meanings of the various amendments, and the press was perfunctory in its reports, if not altogether silent. But for Madison's persistence the amendments would have died in Congress. Our precious Bill of Rights, at least in its immediate background, resulted from the reluctant necessity of certain Federalists to capitalize on a cause that had been originated, in vain, by the Anti-Federalists for ulterior purposes. The party that had first opposed the Bill of Rights inadvertently wound up with the responsibility for its framing and ratification, whereas the people who had at first professedly wanted it discovered too late that it not only was embarrassing but disastrous for their ulterior purposes. The Bill of Rights had a great healing effect, however; it did, as Mason originally proposed, "give great quiet" to the people. The opposition to the Constitution, Jefferson informed Lafayette, "almost totally disappeared," as Anti-Federalist leaders lost "almost all their followers." The people of the United States had had the good sense, nourished by traditions of freedom, to support the Constitution and the Bill of Rights.

CHAPTER TWO

Habeas Corpus

THE WRIT OF HABEAS CORPUS—a writ to "have the body"—goes back in English history to time immemorial. The writ is even older than Magna Carta and may have originated in the courts of chancery. For centuries it served a variety of purposes; for example, it enabled the royal courts to command the presence of a person so that a suit might commence or continue. At an early stage of its development the writ applied not only to law enforcement officers but to private persons as well, compelling them to produce in court the person whose presence they might control. Courts frequently issued the writ to enhance their jurisdiction. Rival courts used it to make the king's justice a means of augmenting their authority. The writ also once operated as a means of extraditing a person, thus allowing a court to require an individual to appear before it so that justice could be done in the locale where a crime had been committed.

Almost always the writ ensured the presence in court of a party to litigation, civil or criminal. By the fifteenth century the writ functioned to allow a sheriff to produce the party in court. As the writ developed, the courts required not only the presence of a party but an explanation of the reasons for his having been detained by royal officers. That explanation was called the "return" to the writ. If the return did not satisfy the judges, they discharged the prisoner. If the return was sufficient, they remanded him.

The writ could develop only because judicial functions eventually became differentiated from legislative and executive ones. Separation of powers was centuries in the making, and once courts obtained some independence, the writ of habeas corpus became an instrument of their operation. Separation of powers also intensified the efforts of common-law courts to settle various legal disputes between parties. The common-law courts aggrandized their jurisdiction over chancery courts and ecclesiastical courts by effective use of the writ; in the process the writ became a means of liberating the unjustly imprisoned and also those who were imprisoned by a court that the common-law judges considered as lacking the power to imprison. In 1577, for example, the Court of Common Pleas, a common-law court, learned from the return on its writ of habeas corpus that the Court of High Commission, the supreme ecclesiastical court, had imprisoned a man named Hinde for religious reasons. The common-law court held that the commitment was illegal because the return to it failed to certify the cause of commitment with sufficient detail to allow the court to determine for itself the lawfulness of the commitment. The court added, however, that a commitment on the king's authority need not be justified by a showing of reasons, "because it may concern the state of the realm, which ought not to be published."

The common-law courts soon showed greater independence. In 1587, when confronted by a return to its writ revealing merely that the chief officer of the Privy Council had ordered an imprisonment, the Court of Common Pleas ruled that the return was insufficient and discharged the prisoner. But when the entire Privy Council rather than just one member of it commanded an imprisonment, the court decided in 1588 that no cause had to be stated. In 1592 the court summarized the law of the matter by observing that if the queen or her Privy Council ordered commitment, or in a case of high treason if one member of the council had made the order, a general return not specifying causes would suffice. In 1593, James Morice, a Puritan lawyer and member of Parliament, introduced a bill providing that because many subjects had been imprisoned without adequate cause, no person should be committed contrary to Magna Carta without warrant and any common-law judge might award a writ of habeas corpus to deliver anyone so imprisoned. But the Commons tabled the bill, showing that the writ had not yet become a routine liberty document.

In 1605 the Court of Common Pleas issued the writ for one Thomlinson, a prisoner who had been committed by the Court of Admiralty for his refusal to answer questions. Common Pleas ruled that the return, which stated only that he had been imprisoned for contempt, was insufficient. It was too general because it did not stipulate the reason for Thomlinson's examination by the Admiralty. The case showed that the writ of habeas corpus was becoming more respected. Fifty years earlier, the Admiralty had haughtily refused to obey writs of habeas corpus issued in one case by the lord chief justice and in another by the Court of Exchequer.

Nicholas Fuller, a Puritan lawyer, applied in 1607 to the King's Bench, the highest common-law criminal court, for a writ of habeas corpus on behalf of his clients, Thomas Ladd, a merchant, and Richard Mansel, a Puritan minister. Both had been imprisoned by the High Commission for having attended outlawed religious meetings and for contumacious behavior. Fuller's argument that Ladd and Mansel had been illegally imprisoned took two days, and its publication in pamphlet form popularized Magna Carta as a liberty document. Fuller relied on Magna Carta and habeas corpus to combat the inquisitorial procedures of ecclesiastical courts, but his intemperate language got him imprisoned. He applied to the King's Bench for a writ of habeas corpus, which the court awarded, thereby freeing him and requiring his jailers to defend their commitment of him.

Because the writ raised questions about the royal prerogative, James I summoned an extraordinary meeting of the members of the Privy Council and all members of the three common-law supreme courts—King's Bench, Common Pleas, and Exchequer. Edward Coke, the lord chief justice of Common Pleas, confronted by a royal assertion of divine rule, quoted Magna Carta to James I, suggesting that even the king was under the law. Coke remained prodigal in his issuing of various kinds of writs that challenged the royal prerogative, including writs of habeas corpus.

In 1608 in the case of Roper, who had been imprisoned by the High Commission, the King's Bench freed Roper on habeas corpus because the commission did not have authority to punish by imprisonment. In 1610 the King's Bench issued a writ of habeas corpus resulting in a return that stated that the lord chancellor of England had ordered the warrant of commitment "for matters concerning the King." To its credit the court held that the return was inadequate because it did not show the causes of the person's imprisonment, "for it might be a cause which would not hinder him of his privilege." In 1612 in Chancey's case, the King's Bench issued another writ of habeas corpus releasing a High Commission prisoner who had been committed for adultery. The King's Bench claimed that the commission lacked authority to imprison for that offense. In 1615 in Hodd's case, Coke for the court freed another prisoner of the High Commission because he had been committed for his contemptuous language. Coke declared that "it did not appear by the return what the words were which he spake, and they may be such as ought to be determined by the common law; for this cause the return is not good." Coke deserves honor for his role in making the writ a liberty document, but even he occasionally buckled under executive powers.

In the next year, for example, the court decided the case of Burrowes and several others, all Puritan laymen committed for holding private conventicles. When their case came before the King's Bench on habeas corpus, Coke delivered an unusual opinion. He gave three reasons for sustaining the writ of habeas corpus and releasing the prisoners, and then he failed to do so. First he reasoned that because the statute used by the High Commission to imprison the petitioners was a penal law, the commissioners could not exact from the prisoners an oath whereby they might accuse themselves. Second, the prisoners had been denied a copy of the charges, to which they were entitled. "A third reason," said Coke, "may be drawn from the liberty of the subject, the which is very great as to the imprisonment of the body, and therefore before commitment, the party ought to be called to make his answer, and if he be committed, yet this ought not to be perpetually; if one shall have a remedy here for his land and goods, *a multo fortiori*, he shall have a remedy here for his body, for delivery of him out of prison, being there detained without just cause." Yet Coke inexplicably balked at issuing the writ after having explained why he should. He resolved the case by bailing the prisoners yet advising them that they should submit themselves to the High Commission. At the next session of the court, Burrowes and several others again applied for discharge on the writ of habeas corpus, but Coke ruled that the High Commission could imprison them for obstinate heresy and schism; he remanded the prisoners to the custody of the commission.

So stood the law of the matter: the writ of habeas corpus was ineffective if the imprisoning agency had lawful authority and followed appropriate procedure. Then Thomas Darnel's case arose in 1627. He was one of five knights who refused to make the forced "loan" that Charles I sought to exact after having dissolved Parliament, thus having no way of raising taxes. Imprisoning those who did not comply caused "great murmuring," but the king was adamant. From prison, Darnel sought a habeas corpus from the King's Bench. Chief Justice Nicholas Hyde, a new appointee of Charles I, granted the writ but on its return remanded the prisoners to jail. The return specified that Darnel had been committed "by special command of his Majesty." Attorney General Robert Heath argued that such a return was sufficient in a case involving a matter of state because the king could imprison anyone by his own authority without being obliged to explain.

On behalf of Darnel, his counsel contended that the return, which had not offered any reason for his imprisonment, conflicted with Magna Carta's requirement that no one be imprisoned "unless by the lawful judgment of his peers or by the law of the land." If, counsel added, the court deemed the return to be valid, then the king might imprison a man forever and "by law there can be no remedy for the subject." Counsel continued: "The Writ of Habeas Corpus is the only means the subject hath to obtain his liberty, and the end of this Writ is to return the cause of the imprisonment, that it may be examined in this court, whether the parties ought to be discharged or not; but that cannot be done upon this return; for the cause of the imprisonment of this gentleman at first is so far from appearing particularly by it, that there is no cause at all expressed in it." The argument by Darnel's counsel won "wonderful applause" from the people in the crowded courtroom.

The attorney general replied that in a matter of state no man could question the king's judgment. That was comparable to stating that in a time of national crisis or when national security is involved, the laws are silent. Theoretically, justice is supposed to be available though the heavens should fall. But as Justice Oliver Wendell Holmes, speaking for the Supreme Court, once said, in *Moyer v. Peabody* (1909), "Public danger warrants the substitution of executive process for judicial process." The Constitution's habeas corpus provision therefore allows for the suppression of the writ "when in cases of rebellion or invasion the public safety may require it." Abraham Lincoln's conduct during the Civil War is an appropriate illustration.

Thus, when told that a "matter of state" was involved, the King's Bench remanded Darnel and the others to their jailers. One of the judges declared, "This is the greatest cause ever I knew in this court," and another judge asked how any person could be "delivered" by the court if it did not respect Magna Carta. Chief Justice Nicholas Hyde added, "This is a case of very great weight and expection" and spoke of the possibility of "a perpetual imprisonment." He noted that the court had to decide whether, if a person is committed by the king's authority and the return to the writ of habeas corpus does not declare the cause of commitment, the court must deliver him. If no cause was stated, he ruled, "it is presumed to be for matter of state, which we cannot take notice of." And on such reasoning, the king's authority superseded the great writ.

Parliament agreed. One of its resolutions, which the king was obliged to affirm in the Petition of Right of 1628, was that habeas corpus must be available in any case of imprisonment so that a court could examine the cause even if the king or Privy Council had ordered the commitment. But if they claimed reason of state, the court canceled the writ. The king lost only his authority to imprison without declaring the cause for his order on the return to the writ. Commons also stated, inaccurately, that the writ of habeas corpus derived from Magna Carta. Such an error resonated the writ's association with liberty. Although the link between the writ of habeas corpus and Magna Carta lacked historical fact, it became historical fact as popular belief developed the conviction that the two were tied together. In the same way Magna Carta, once a feudal document protecting only the nobility, had become a constitutional guarantee of due process of law and fair procedure.

The Petition of Right of 1628 ended the last vestige of government by divine right of kings. Parliament declared that the commitment of those like Darnel who had refused to "loan" money to the king had violated Magna Carta, and "when for their deliverance they were brought before your justices by . . . habeas corpus," the returns showed no cause of commitment. Yet they "were returned back to several prisons, without being charged with any thing to which they might make answer according to the law." Consequently, the Petition of Right promised that without authorization by Parliament, no person could be forced to make a loan to the king or be imprisoned for his refusal.

In 1629 Charles I betrayed the principle of the Petition of Right. He imprisoned six opponents, members of Parliament, "for notable contempt, stirring up sedition against us." That was the language of the return to the writ. Counsel for the prisoners observed that according to the Petition of Right the return was insufficient. Attorney General Heath responded that the Petition of Right was not a law, meaning not an enactment or statute with force of law. Accordingly, Heath concluded, its language should not be stretched. It merely had reconfirmed the ancient liberties of the subject without adding anything new. In Chamber's case, moreover, also in 1629, the King's Bench rejected the argument that the Court of Star Chamber had no authority to imprison for mere words. Not until 1641, when Parliament abolished the Star Chamber and passed the Habeas Corpus Act, did the writ again become effective. The new measure guaranteed that the writ should be issued without delay to anyone imprisoned by command of the king or his councillors; it also obliged the officer in charge to certify the imprisonment's cause, and it required the court to decide within three days whether the commitment was "just and legal, or not." Anyone who failed to obey the act was liable for triple damages to the offended party.

A statute of 1649 authorized habeas corpus for anyone whose imprisonment resulted from breach of contract or bad debt. But Oliver Cromwell defied laws not of his making or liking; he authorized his officers not to honor writs of habeas corpus in cases in which imprisonment resulted from violation of various public policies of his administration. And in 1653, when one John Streater, a critic of Cromwell, was imprisoned by the government because of his seditious publications, the high court of the Commonwealth acknowledged that the return to its writ was insufficient because it did not mention the titles of Streater's publication; still the court refused to challenge the government and remanded the prisoner. After Parliament's dissolution, Streater had another hearing before the same court on habeas corpus and won a dismissal. The next year, the court heard a case on habeas corpus involving one Cony, who had refused to pay a tax that he regarded as illegal. Cromwell summoned the judges, reprimanded them for opposing the safety of the Commonwealth, and cursed Magna Carta; he also advised the judges not to suffer lawyers who prated what they should not hear. When Cony's lawyers persisted in defending him, Cromwell sent them to the Tower of London, where they languished until they submitted to his will.

During Richard Cromwell's reign, some prisoners were sent to islands beyond England. Parliament resolved that such imprisonments were "illegal, unjust and tyrannical," because the "sending of prisoners beyond the reach of the writ of habeas corpus and of the courts was, in effect, a banishment," and no Englishman could be lawfully banished except by Parliament. But Cromwell dissolved Parliament before it could liberate these prisoners. When the Stuarts were restored, the writ of habeas corpus worked effectively except, as before, in cases of political prisoners. Supporters of the writ sought to correct its defects but could not muster a majority.

After a mass meeting of Quakers in 1670, the Quaker leaders William Penn and William Mead were tried for unlawful assembly. When the jurors were asked for their verdict they would only say, "Guilty of preaching in Grace Church Street." Prompted to add "unlawful assembly," the jury refused. The court threatened to hold the jurors in confinement "without meat, drink, fire, and tobacco," and even without "so much as a chamber-pot," but they remained obstinate until finally, in outright defiance of the court, they acquitted the prisoners. Rejecting the verdict as contrary to the evidence, the court fined both prisoners and jurors and imprisoned them all for nonpayment.

One of the jurors was Edward Bushell, who appealed his conviction to the Court of Common Pleas, which issued a writ of habeas corpus for him. The court declared: "The Writ of Habeas Corpus is now the most usual remedy by which a man is restored again to his liberty, if he have been against law deprived of it. Therefore the writ commands the day," and the return to it must certify the reason for the imprisonment "as specifically and certainly as possible" in order to permit the court to judge whether the commitment conformed to the law; if the return was insufficient the prisoner would be discharged. In Bushell's case the court said, it could not know from the evidence whether his commitment was justified; the return to the writ did not say that the jurors had acquitted him even though they knew from the evidence that he was guilty. The judge could not direct a verdict of guilty without making the jury superfluous. Incidentally, nowadays a judge may set aside a guilty verdict if he or she believes that the evidence does not warrant it, but as a result of Bushell's case judges cannot reverse a verdict of not guilty. The case established the principle that a jury may render a verdict in accord with its convictions, regardless of the evidence. Thus, guilty persons may be acquitted because the jury may not wish to punish their crimes. That happened in 1735 in a celebrated case involving John Peter Zenger.

In the Jenckes case of 1676, the prisoner was arrested for his supposedly "seditious and mutinous manner" because at a public meeting in London he had called for a new Parliament to be elected. The sitting Parliament had been elected fifteen years earlier and Jenckes had respectfully recommended a public petition to the king that he order new elections; instead, the Privy Council, headed by Charles II, ordered Jenckes's commitment. The chief justice refused to grant a writ of habeas corpus because the court was on vacation; the lord chancellor also refused to grant the writ. Jenckes rotted in prison throughout the hot summer. No inferior judge would grant him the writ in defiance of the lord chancellor, though under the Petition of Right the prisoner was entitled to it for the purpose of getting a judicial hearing to determine whether his commitment was lawful. Counsel for Jenckes vainly sought the writ in one court after another. Finally the lord chancellor, feeling guilty about having denied the writ in violation of law, informed Charles II that Jenckes was entitled to it, and the king relented.

The Jenckes case revealed some of the defects in the procedures by which the writ was obtained. In 1679, when a new Parliament finally met, a bill was introduced "for the better securing of the liberty of the subject, and the prevention of imprisonment beyond the seas." Such imprisonment stymied the writ. Parliament passed the great Habeas Corpus Act of 1679, which tightened procedures by dealing with every possible evasion or trick of the king, his ministers, and jailers. Neglect in obeying the statute resulted in a fine of one hundred pounds and for the second offense double that amount. The act also specified that no one was to be imprisoned beyond England out of reach of the writ and that the writ had to be issued even during vacation periods. After the enactment of 1679, habeas corpus became routine, and few cases merit reporting.

One important case occurred in 1763 because of John Wilkes's studied insult to the king, published in Wilkes's *North Briton*, No. 45. After he was convicted for seditious libel, his friends secured a writ of habeas corpus for him from the Court of Common Pleas but at an hour too late in the day for the writ to be processed. The delay allowed Wilkes's jailer to move him to another prison—and then another. All persons who tried to see him, including a brother, were denied admission. When his jailers finally returned the writ of habeas corpus, they stated that Wilkes was no longer in their custody. Wilkes's counsel insisted that they should acknowledge when he was taken from their custody and by what authority. The matter was left unresolved, even though the court agreed with the defense attorneys. They obtained a second habeas corpus that was directed to the head of the Tower of London. Although Wilkes's counsel sought his discharge, all their arguments failed but one. When they informed the court that Wilkes was a member of Parliament and "privileged from being arrested" unless for treason or felony, Lord Chief Justice Charles Pratt decided in Wilkes's favor and ordered his release. Wilkes's crime was only a misdemeanor. Nevertheless, Parliament resolved that the exemption of its members from arrest did not extend to seditious libelers and expelled Wilkes, but he was already free thanks to the writ of habeas corpus.

A few years after the Wilkes case, Sir William Blackstone published his influential *Commentaries,* in which he described the writ of habeas corpus as "the most celebrated writ in the English law," one that is "a high prerogative writ" issuable at any time and in any of the king's dominions. It was, Blackstone said, a writ "grantable of common right" and available to "every subject of the kingdom" that superseded all other proceedings and should not be evaded or delayed.

The writ was triumphant and had great consequences in the case of James Sommersett, a black man held in slavery, in 1772. While he was aboard a ship docked in London, which awaited orders to sail to Jamaica, antislavery supporters secured the writ on his behalf from Lord Chief Justice William Murray Mansfield. The return to the writ revealed that Sommersett was claimed as a slave by a man who had purchased him in Virginia, had a contract to prove it, and had taken him along on a trip to England. Counsel for Sommersett, making an argument that the court endorsed, declared that English air "is too pure for a slave to breathe." Mansfield observed that "the person of the slave himself" was the "object of enquiry," not the contract for his purchase. In Virginia and

Jamaica he might be chattel, but the return to the writ of habeas corpus raised the question whether claiming him as a slave was a sufficient reason for his being held involuntarily in England. Slavery, Mansfield declared, could exist only if positive, local law allowed and protected it, but England had no law "so odious." Consequently no legal basis existed for keeping a person as a slave. Sommersett was freed, and thereafter sojourner slaves were emancipated in England—and in the United States where northern judges emulated Mansfield. The law of habeas corpus led them to emancipation.

In America little is heard about the writ until the later seventeenth century, perhaps because legislative, executive, and judicial powers were scarcely distinguished, and lawyers, even law books, were scarce. The early colonies, moreover, did not rely on imprisonment; they preferred the whipping post, the stocks, and fines. Thus, the writ of habeas corpus had no history for much of the 1600s in America. It first appeared in 1664 in the New York case of Waddel Cunningham, but no other reference to the writ seems to appear until 1683 in the Beverley case in Virginia. Robert Beverley, the clerk of the Virginia House of Burgesses, refused to provide copies of the house's journals to the governor and his executive council, without permission of the house. The council jailed him, and when he applied for a writ of habeas corpus the council intervened to prevent its issuance because the matter had been referred to England. The writ was equally futile in New York, where it first surfaced in 1679, when one Fransa was arrested on order of the lieutenant governor for breach of the peace. However, a court liberated Fransa on a writ of habeas corpus on learning that he had been arrested under the wrong statute.

New York's 1683 charter provided that government should be according to the laws of England. New Yorkers therefore assumed that they had a right to the writ, yet in 1684 the Privy Council in England disallowed the provision for the writ because "this privilege is not granted to any of His Majesties Plantations where the Act of Habeas Corpus and all other such bills do not take place." In 1689, however, the common law writ freed Philip French after he was imprisoned for protesting a tax "in a most insolent manner." When a court denied bail, French's counsel obtained the writ, but the lieutenant governor successfully defied it, and French was released only after making a deferential submission to him. In 1707 New York arrested Francis Makemie and John Hampton, Presbyterian ministers accused of preaching their "pernicious doctrine" without a license. The two applied for release from imprisonment by seeking the writ, which Chief Justice Roger Mompesson granted. At their trial the jury acquitted them.

The writ also featured in the celebrated case of John Peter Zenger, the printer who was prosecuted for seditious libel of Governor William Cosby of New York. Zenger's counsel, knowing that under the law he was guilty of having published criminal material, appealed to the jury to acquit him even though the law was against him. If the jury had behaved in an orthodox manner, it would have rendered a verdict only on the question whether Zenger had in fact published the matter specified in the indictment and would have left to the court a decision on the question whether he had violated the law. Cosby's flunkies kept Zenger incommunicado for three days until his counsel obtained a writ of habeas corpus, and he was freed on bail. In the 1770 case of the American propagandist Alexander McDougall, the prisoner was arrested on order of the speaker of the house, who threatened to throw McDougall out of the window; the speaker acted, however, only after a vote of the house condemned the prisoner for having breached parliamentary privilege. When McDougall secured the writ of habeas corpus, the sheriff who held him refused to free him because the legislature had ordered the sheriff not to recognize the writ. Once again the legislature's will triumphed over habeas corpus.

The writ was unavailable for a time in Massachusetts. Under

Governor Edmund Andros, the executive council in 1687 levied town taxes without consulting the legislature. A town meeting in Ipswich, led by the Reverend John Wise, regarded the new taxes as illegal and refused to pay them. Governor Andros ordered Wise's arrest and imprisoned him and five supporters. When the prisoners applied for a writ of habeas corpus, the chief judge of the province, Joseph Dudley, denied it, declaring that they must "not think the Laws of England follow [them] to the ends of the earth or whither [they] went." Contemptuously dismissing the argument that the imprisonment violated Magna Carta, the judge remarked that the only privilege that the prisoners possessed was "not to be sold as a slave." The prisoners were tried by a packed jury, which found them guilty and fined them heavily. Thus, neither the writ of habeas corpus nor Magna Carta had any force when confronted by a court that either feared or followed a powerful executive. Later that year, however, the Massachusetts legislature authorized defendants to remove cases by habeas corpus to the supreme judicial court of the province and empowered that court to exercise powers comparable to those of the courts at Westminster, in effect granting them power to issue the writ of habeas corpus as a common law writ. Cotton Mather no longer had to complain that the people of Massachusetts were "slaves."

In 1692, under a new governor, the Massachusetts legislature enacted one law providing that its consent was necessary before any tax could be exacted and another law modeled on England's Habeas Corpus Act of 1679. The Massachusetts act made the writ available even to persons imprisoned for treason and felony until they were indicted at the next term of court. The Privy Council vetoed both measures, saying of the second one, as it had said in 1684 of New York's protection of habeas corpus, that the writ "has not yet been granted to any of His Majesty's Plantations." But the common law writ was available for prisoners whose friends or lawyers were savvy enough to invoke it. The statutory efforts of

Pennsylvania and South Carolina to make the writ available were also voided in England. The writ had briefly become available to South Carolinians as a result of an act by their legislature in 1692, which copied the provisions of the Habeas Corpus Act of 1679. The proprietors in England vetoed the measure on ground that it was unnecessary because Carolinians were subject to the laws of England. The facts showed otherwise. In 1700 South Carolina recommended to the Board of Trade "that, it being the practice for governors to imprison the subjects without bail, the habeas corpus act should be extended as fully as possible to the colonies as it is in England." The Board of Trade rejected the recommendation. In 1706 Queen Anne ordered the royal governors not to endorse any assembly bills "wherein our prerogative . . . may be prejudiced." In 1710 Governor Alexander Spotswood received orders from the queen to extend the writ of habeas corpus to Virginia, which he did in all cases not involving treason or felony. A statute of 1712 again extended the English act of 1679 to every Carolinian, north and south, "as if he were personally in the said Kingdom of England." In 1721 when an edition of Henry Care's *English Liberties, or the Free Born Subject's Inheritance* was published in Boston, it contained a copy of the act of 1679 together with copies of Magna Carta, the Petition of Right, and the Bill of Rights. In 1730 the governors of both Carolinas were instructed to proclaim the availability of the writ, and in 1749 North Carolina added statutory protections of the writ.

Earlier, in 1719, Delaware had authorized the state's high court to issue writs of habeas corpus, and in 1722, Pennsylvania's legislature had passed an act that empowered its courts to issue the writ. However, anyone accused of breach of parliamentary privilege discovered that the writ of habeas corpus meant nothing to an affronted assembly. Parliamentary privilege referred to a bundle of rights that each house claimed and exercised. Among these were freedom from arrest, access to the executive, passing upon the credentials of members, freedom of speech, and the power of punishing anyone for violations of privilege. No assembly condoned freedom of speech for nonmembers. The unauthorized reporting of legislative proceedings and reflections on either house or any of their members, or on the government generally, were regarded as seditious libels, subject to prosecution by the legislature as breach of privilege. Guilty parties were summoned, examined, and summarily tried, their publications burned, and the parties humiliated, usually on their knees, begging forgiveness before the bar of the offended house. Anyone found guilty could be imprisoned for the life of the assembly's session.

Habeas corpus remained ineffective for political prisoners, as the Cooper case illustrated. In 1732 the South Carolina legislature ordered the imprisonment of one Thomas Cooper who had filed a petition that insulted some members. Chief Justice Robert Wright granted Cooper's request for a habeas corpus, thereby provoking the anger of legislators who believed that the court had breached parliamentary privileges. They ordered that the court's writ be ignored and arrested Cooper's attorneys. In vain the lawyers petitioned the governor and council for their release. The chief justice, who was a member of the council, criticized the legislature; he believed that the council's insistence that its parliamentary privilege took precedence over the writ of habeas corpus was "extraordinary." It tended, he said, "to the subversion of all government by disallowing his Majesty's undoubted prerogative, removing all obedience to his writ of habeas corpus, and assuming to themselves power to abrogate and make void the known laws of the land by arbitrarily imprisoning their fellow subjects." But Wright spoke only for a minority of the council. The majority endorsed the actions of the legislature, holding that it could authorize the imprisonment of anyone breaching parliamentary privilege and that in such cases the writ of habeas corpus should not be granted.

Thus, the legislative will superseded the writ in South Carolina, a fact emphasized in the 1732 passage of an act granting to members of the legislature and to judges who supported them immunity against any person seeking to sue them for refusing or not obeying a writ of habeas corpus. Although Chief Justice Wright defended the writ as a guarantee of the liberty of the subject, the governor supported the legislature and sought the additional support of the Council of Trade and Plantations in London. But the lawyer who advised the council called the suspension of the writ in South Carolina an illegal infringement of the liberty of the subject that the writ protected. The council therefore reinstated the writ in South Carolina. In New York in 1735, counsel for John Peter Zenger, who was imprisoned for seditious libel, sought to free him by applying for the writ, but Chief Justice James DeLancey set bail so high, at four hundred pounds, that Zenger languished in jail until his trial ended eight months later. The writ of habeas corpus is ineffective if bail is excessive.

In Georgia, the last of the original thirteen states to be founded, the writ encountered no problems because the royal governor introduced it on instructions of the crown. But in New Jersey, an unusual situation developed because of judicial hostility to the prisoner. When Thomas Gordon, the speaker of the house, was committed for political differences with the executive council, Judge William Pinhorne of the state supreme court simply refused to issue a writ of habeas corpus for him. Even though the assembly accused the lieutenant governor of subverting the liberties of the people, Gordon would have remained in prison but for the fact that he hired as his counsel the judge's son, who managed to get him bailed.

The writ was impotent when confronted by an irate legislature in Pennsylvania in 1757. William Moore, the Anglican chief judge of the court of common pleas of Chester County, Pennsylvania, criticized the Quaker assembly's war policies. The assembly imprisoned and tried him for seditious libel. Upon his conviction, the hangman burned his offensive publications, and the assembly ordered the sheriff to hold him in prison until such time as the assembly might authorize his discharge. The assembly also ordered the sheriff that "he do not obey any Writ of *Habeas Corpus,* or other Writ whatsoever, that may come to his hands for bailing and discharging" Moore. The assembly's flagrant contempt of the writ, especially in a case of mere misdemeanor in the form of breach of privilege, comported more with the conduct of a Stuart despot than with the principles of law.

Because the Reverend William Smith, one of the colony's most prominent Anglicans and president of the college that became the University of Pennsylvania, openly supported Moore, he, too, was imprisoned in 1758. Before Smith's trial began, the assembly voted that he was guilty of publishing a libel. On conviction, he was condemned to imprisonment until he should give "satisfaction" to the assembly for his offense. Smith's defense of himself roused people in the courtroom to applause, resulting in their imprisonment for breach of privilege and Smith's commitment for an indefinite period. The assembly commanded the sheriff that he should not, on his peril, obey a writ of habeas corpus. Smith and Moore petitioned the chief judge of the province's highest court for the writ, but he ruled that the petitioners, having been committed by the house for breach of privilege, could not be granted the writ nor be bailed during the sitting of the house. The governor also refused to intercede on their behalf. They were released only after the house adjourned, but when it reconvened it sought their reimprisonment. Moore could not be found.

Smith, having fled to England to plead his case before the Privy Council, confronted Benjamin Franklin, the assembly's official agent in England. Franklin, who characterized Smith as a "Scribbler of Libels," vigorously championed the power of the assembly to imprison for libels and breaches of privilege. The Privy Council agreed with Franklin that Smith and Moore had libeled the house but ruled that "these inferior assemblies in America" could not imprison anyone for breach of privilege, nor could they suspend the writ of habeas corpus. Smith and Moore were finally free, no thanks to the writ, which lacked efficacy when confronted by an outraged legislature intent on punishing its critics.

In New York, in 1764, Waddell Cunningham, who was imprisoned for assault and battery, received a writ of habeas corpus, freeing him until his case came up for trial at the next term of court. Six years later, in the case of Alexander McDougall, a feisty critic of the provincial assembly, the writ was of little avail because the prisoner could not make the extremely high cost of bail. McDougall's was a political case, as Zenger's was, with the result that a hostile court fixed bail as a means of thwarting the writ.

Before the American Revolution, the writ of habeas corpus was known in all the colonies, though it was not obeyed by officials in some and was not often invoked in others. In some, such as New York, the writ seems to have a spotty and infrequent history. But colonial Americans sufficiently valued it so that its denial could be used as a propaganda point. When, for example, the colonies sought to attract Quebec to their cause, they criticized the British for not having extended the writ to Quebec. Congress said of the residents of Quebec, "They are now the subjects of an arbitrary government, deprived of trial by jury and when imprisoned, cannot claim the benefits of the *habeas corpus* act, that great bulwark and palladium of English liberty."

The American Revolution generated the most creative constitutional achievements in history, including the world's first written constitutions and bills of rights. North Carolina, the first state to protect the writ of habeas corpus constitutionally, did so by a generous provision that, oddly, did not include an exception for suspension during emergencies: "That every freeman restrained of his liberty, is entitled to a remedy, to enquire into the lawfulness thereof, and to remove the same, if unlawful; and that such remedy

ought not to be denied or delayed." Only four other states—
Georgia, Pennsylvania, Massachusetts, and New Hampshire—
constitutionally guaranteed the writ; Rhode Island did so by statute; and Vermont, which joined the Union before the federal Bill
of Rights was adopted, was the seventh state to do so. All but
North Carolina allowed for suspension of the writ during emergencies. All fourteen states in 1791 respected the writ in judicial practice, if not by their constitutions or statutes, because all
adopted the English common law.

Constitution-writing at the time was pretty much a haphazard
affair anyway. Of the twelve states that had written constitutions
(all but Rhode Island and Connecticut), only two, Pennsylvania
and Vermont, constitutionally protected freedom of speech. One
cannot assume that constitutional protection was regarded as unnecessary simply because the writ was so highly respected. Trial
by jury ranked as high in American opinion yet was constitutionally protected, rather than taken for granted, more than any
other right; indeed, all twelve state constitutions protected it.
There is no rational explanation why four states did not constitutionally protect freedom of the press; or why the Virginia Declaration of Rights of 1776 omitted a ban on bills of attainder, double
jeopardy, and ex post facto laws and failed to include the right to
counsel, grand jury proceedings, and separation of church and
state, as well as the writ of habeas corpus. There is no explanation
either why eleven states with written constitutions were silent on
double jeopardy; or why nine ignored grand jury proceedings; or
why seven had no ban on general search warrants and six permitted establishments of religion; or why five failed to protect the
rights of assembly, petition, representation by counsel, and jury
trial in civil cases; or why four said nothing about excessive fines,
excessive bail, and compulsory self-incrimination.

Habeas corpus fared better in Congress. The Northwest Ordinance of 1787, passed by the Congress of the Confederation for

the governance of the Northwest Territory, provided that the inhabitants of the territory should "always be entitled to the benefits of the writs of habeas corpus and the trial by jury," but the Articles of Confederation had no such protection.

At the Philadelphia Constitutional Convention, Charles Pinckney proposed: "The privileges and benefits of the writ of habeas corpus shall be enjoyed in this government in the most expeditious and ample manner: and shall not be suspended by the Legislature except upon the most urgent and pressing occasion and for a time period not exceeding" an unspecified number of months. The phrase "in this government" meant that in proceedings before federal authorities, the writ would be available to federal prisoners. Pinckney had substantially followed the provision of the Massachusetts constitution of 1780. During the course of debate on Pinckney's motion, he urged that no suspension of the writ should be for more than twelve months. John Rutledge of South Carolina responded that he did not think a suspension would ever be necessary "at the same time through all the States," but Gouverneur Morris of New York moved that the writ could be suspended "where in cases of Rebellion or invasion the public Safety may require it." James Wilson of Pennsylvania, like Rutledge, doubted whether a suspension would ever be necessary, and he endorsed the discretionary authority of judges to decide whether to issue the writ or keep a prisoner in jail. The Convention adopted Morris's motion, and the Committee on Style placed the habeas corpus provision in the article of the Constitution dealing with Congress.

In *The Federalist*, Alexander Hamilton vainly sought to defend the Constitution from its attackers who urged against ratification because it lacked a bill of rights. Hamilton observed that the Constitution protected trial by jury in criminal cases and provided for habeas corpus "in the most ample manner." Jefferson, from Paris, had a good deal more to say about the habeas corpus provision of the proposed Constitution. Writing to Madison, he asked why the writ should be suspended during insurrections and rebellions in view of the fact that insurrectionists, like any persons charged with public crimes, would be arrested; if the public safety required, he thought, a person could be imprisoned on less evidence than showed probable cause. The history of England, Jefferson believed, showed "how few of the cases of suspension of the Habeas corpus act have been worthy of that suspension." Those cases had involved treason, whether real or sham. In the "few" cases in which the suspension of the writ had "done real good, that operation is now become habitual, and the minds of the nation almost prepared to live under it's [sic] constant suspension."

A few days later, in another letter to Madison, Jefferson made explicit his recommendations for improving the habeas corpus clause in the proposed Constitution: "No person shall be held in confinement more than —— days after they shall have demanded and been refused a writ of Hab. Corp. by the judge appointed by law nor more than —— days after such writ shall have been served on the person holding him in confinement and no order given on due examination for his remandment or discharge, nor more than —— hours in any place at a greater distance than —— miles from the usual residence of some judge authorised to issue the writ of Hab. Corp. nor shall that writ be suspended for any term exceeding one year nor in any place more than —— miles distant from the station or encampment of enemies or of insurgents." Madison, who prepared amendments constituting a bill of rights, failed to make use of Jefferson's recommendation. When the First Congress established a system of federal courts, it empowered them to grant the writ of habeas corpus "for the purpose of inquiry into the cause of commitment." In 1807 in the case of *Ex Parte Bollman* the Supreme Court ruled that the authority to issue the writ was an essential characteristic of judicial power, appropriately provided for by act of Congress and supported by precedent. Chief Justice John Marshall for the Court said of the habeas corpus provision in the Constitution that Congress felt its "peculiar force" by sensing an obligation to establish "efficient means whereby this great constitutional privilege should receive life and activity; for if the means be not in existence, the privilege itself would be lost, although no law for its suspension should be enacted. Under the impression of this obligation, they give to all courts the power of awarding writs of habeas corpus." Thus, the Court completed the reception of the writ into American law.

CHAPTER THREE

Bills of Attainder

THE CONSTITUTION denies to both Congress and the states the power to enact bills of attainder, which are legislative findings that a named individual or an identifiable one is guilty of a crime and must suffer death as punishment. Bills of attainder wholly circumvent the judicial system. In effect they are egregious violations of due process of law and specimens of unfairness. Parliament devised bills of attainder as a means of retaliating against individuals whom it regarded as objectionable or hostile. Bills of attainder punished their victims by authorizing their execution and the forfeiture of all their properties, both real and personal, to the crown. The legislative infliction of a punishment short of death was called a bill of pains and penalties.

We know that the last bill of attainder passed by Parliament occurred in 1798, but we do not know the date of the first one. One of the earliest was the attainder of the earl of Lancaster, who was executed in 1322. In 1397 Thomas Haxey, a prominent clergyman, had the audacity to protest against royal extravagance. King Richard II urged that Haxey be attainted, and Parliament complied with a far-fetched enactment that anyone who sought to induce the legislature to reform or remedy a situation pertaining to the king or his governance should be deemed guilty of treason. Haxey escaped the death sentence only because he was a clergyman and benefited from the intervention on his behalf by Thomas Arundel, archbishop of Canterbury. Richard II finally pardoned Haxey, and when Henry IV succeeded to the throne, Parliament persuaded the new king to restore Haxey to his rank and properties. The episode involving him showed that an opponent of the crown or of the legislature risked attainder and its terrible penalties.

A more formidable person whom Parliament attainted was Jack Cade of Kent, an experienced soldier who boasted of royal descent. In 1450, following Henry VI's loss of Normandy to the French, Cade marched on London at the head of four thousand men, forcing the king to flee. After occupying London for several days Cade was forced to retreat. The king's council granted a general amnesty to his followers but offered a price of one thousand pounds for Cade, dead or alive. He was soon captured and killed. Even after his death Parliament revenged itself on him by passing a bill of attainder whose only purpose was to cause the forfeiture of all his properties and to corrupt his blood—that is, to prevent any heirs from enjoying an inheritance from him.

As time passed, Parliament found that impeachment was an effective means of eliminating undesired officers of state, but attainders possessed merit as a way of retaliating against strong ministers. Henry VIII found attainders useful, too, in eliminating some of his unwanted wives. Attainders had the attractiveness of preventing their victims from presenting a defense, but because the king might veto a bill of attainder, impeachments ultimately became more attractive; a crown favorite could not benefit from his influence at court in an impeachment case. Bills of attainder fell into a state of desuetude until the sensational case of Thomas Wentworth, the earl of Stratford, a confidant of Charles I. Parliament not only impeached him; it found him guilty of high treason and attainted him in 1641. His beheading was a spectacle witnessed by stupendous crowds. Bills of attainder also brought down Archbishop William Laud in 1645 and the regicides in 1660. In 1667 the earl of Clarendon was impeached for high treason and fled the country. Parliament banished him after passing a bill of pains and penalties against him. The duke of Monmouth, the illegitimate son of Charles II, also suffered from a bill of attainder. Sir John Fenwick, who had been mainly responsible for Monmouth's attainder, was himself the victim of an attainder in 1692 by the House of Commons.

Because kings enjoyed considerably greater personal security after the Stuarts, attainders became extremely scarce. Jonathan Swift's ridicule of the House of Lords resulted in a bill of pains and penalties against him. In 1798 Lord Edward Fitzgerald, who led an Irish rebellion, was attainted and died in prison of wounds incurred in his capture. The last bill of pains and penalties was enacted in 1820 against Queen Caroline, the wife of George IV, who, despite his own infidelities, sought her punishment by Commons for adultery. The prosecution against her was tainted and failed, and since then no Parliament has resorted to a statute in order to declare the guilt and punishment of an individual. When Blackstone had codified the law of the matter, he emphasized the consequences of attainder: the forfeiture of properties and corruption of the blood or the incapacity of the guilty party to possess or transmit property.

Bills of attainder were rare in American history except during the Revolution. None were employed by provincial legislatures during the earlier colonial period. When Maryland framed its state constitution in 1776 it was the first state to prohibit bills of attainder by providing that "no law to attaint particular persons of treason or felony ought to be made in any case, or at any time hereafter." Only three other states—New York, Massachusetts, and Vermont—followed suit in their original constitutions. But

New York's ban on attainders made an extraordinary exception by explicitly permitting the legislature to enact them for the purpose of confiscating the estates of Tory landowners, especially those of Lords Tryon and Dunmore, former royal governors. New York also suspended the right of Tory members of the bar from practicing their profession.

Several states attainted Tories and confiscated their lands during the Revolution. Bills of pains and penalties were fairly common wartime practices. What passed as a war measure, however, also benefited Whigs who coveted Tory real estate and even sought to escape from competition with them. New Jersey closed its courts to Tory lawyers. In 1776 Pennsylvania attainted no fewer than 490 individuals by name for high treason as a means of expelling them from its borders. Pennsylvania also extended its bill of pains and penalties to clerks, druggists, chemists, and notaries as well as attorneys, and even provided that Tory sympathizers could be additionally punished for pursuing their professions. Doctors and surgeons suffered like disabilities and penalties. Pennsylvania enacted one of the most egregious bill of pains and penalties when it named some 200 persons who were to be seized and either imprisoned or deported. Several states banned or burned some Tory publications, a species of literary attainder. Eight states banished particular Tories. Sometimes the condemnation of a person was rather casual. Town selectmen in Massachusetts, for example, compiled lists of people suspected of Tory sentiments, and any suspects found guilty at a trial risked deportation out of the country. In 1778 Massachusetts named about 260 Tories, subjecting them to imprisonment or expulsion, under threat of death if any returned. In 1779 New York added another 60 names to those whose persons and properties were seized for the offense of having "voluntarily been adherent to George III." Indeed, that state convicted more than 1,000 individuals during the years of the Revolution by means of bills of attainder or bills of pains and penalties.

John Jay, the chief justice of New York, believed that the state "is disgraced by injustice too palpable to admit even of palliation."

The most notorious bill of attainder in American history was the handiwork of Thomas Jefferson and involved Josiah Philips, reputed to be a Tory cutthroat. Philips used a British commission as a shield for plundering and terrorizing the Virginia countryside. On May 1, 1778, the governor's council learned that Philips, "the noted Traitor has again made an insurrection in Princess Anne Country at the head of fifty Men." At his council's authorization, Governor Patrick Henry summoned one hundred militiamen and offered a reward of five hundred dollars for the capture of Philips, dead or alive. By the end of the month word arrived from the local commander that the "cowardly" militia had failed miserably in locating the desperadoes; the only hope lay in flushing them from "their secret places in the swamp" by removing their relations and friends from the vicinity. Henry placed the matter before the assembly. He also consulted Jefferson, then its most influential member, who later recalled, "We both thought the best proceeding would be by a bill of attainder, unless he [Philips] delivered himself up for trial within a given time."

The assembly, without debate, promptly adopted a bill of attainder written by Jefferson, providing for the conviction of Josiah Philips for having levied war against the commonwealth, committed murder, burned houses, and wasted farms. Alleging that "the usual forms and procedures of the courts of law" would leave the people exposed to further crimes, the bill provided that if Philips and his confederates did not surrender to some lawful authority within one month, they "shall stand and be convicted and attainted of high treason, and shall suffer the pains of death, and incur all forfeitures [of all property, real and personal]. . . . And that the good people of this commonwealth may not in the meantime be subject to the unrestrained hostilities of the said insurgents. Be it further enacted, That from and after the passing of this act, it shall be lawful for any person, with or without orders, to pursue and slay the said Josiah Philips, and any others who have been of his associates for the period of the revolutionary war." Perhaps the most sinister aspect of the bill of attainder was its declaration of an open hunting season on the unnamed men whose guilt for treason and murder was legislatively assumed. Any of Philips's associates might be killed on the mere supposition that he shared his leader's guilt. Guilt by association constituted a patent outrage on civil liberties.

Within the month Philips and several of his followers were captured after a battle in which one of his men was killed. Because the bill of attainder had not yet by law become operative, the prisoners were regularly indicted and tried. But the crime charged against them was not high treason, not even murder or arson; it was robbery—the theft of twenty-eight men's felt hats and five pounds of twine, valued at forty-five shillings. Robbery, however, was a capital felony, so that the convicted men were executed.

Jefferson later explained the reason that Edmund Randolph, then the attorney general of Virginia, pressed only the robbery charge. Randolph expected Philips to plead that he was a British subject taken in arms, under a commission from Lord Dunmore, in support of his sovereign, and that he was therefore a prisoner of war entitled to the protection of the law of nations. Philips, as a matter of fact, did make this plea, but it was rejected by the court on the ground that a citizen's crimes cannot be justified by a commission from the enemy. The court might have made the same ruling had the charge been high treason or any of the capital felonies specified in the legislature's bill of attainder. That only a charge of robbery was pressed suggested that the evidence of treason and murder might not stand up in court, making the legislature's assumption of Philips's guilt rather arbitrary, as well as violative of Article VIII of the Virginia Declaration of Rights, which had been adopted two years earlier. That article provided that in any criminal prosecution a person had a right to confront his accusers, call for evidence in his favor, and enjoy a speedy trial by an impartial jury without whose unanimous consent he cannot be found guilty. Article VIII also genuflected to Magna Carta by providing that no person should be deprived of liberty "except by the law of the land or the judgment of his peers." The reputations of the legislature and of Jefferson, already stained by the attainder of Philips, were still further blotched, as were the names of Randolph and Patrick Henry, because all quickly forgot that the criminals, despite the attainder, had been executed after receiving due process of law. What was remembered without shame was the abhorrent fact that Virginia had employed a bill of attainder.

In 1788, for example, when the Virginia ratifying convention debated the proposed national constitution, Randolph was irked beyond endurance by Henry's demagogic complaint that liberty was being sacrificed in the absence of a federal bill of rights. Rising to declare that parchment guarantees were no insurance against legislative violation, Randolph reminded the convention:

> There is one example of this violation in Virginia, of a most striking and shocking nature—an example so horrid, that, if I conceived my country would passively permit a repetition of it, dear as it is to me, I would seek means of expatriating myself from it. A man, who was then a citizen, was deprived of his life thus: from a mere reliance on general reports, a gentleman in the House of Delegates informed the house that a certain man [Josiah Philips] had commited several crimes. And was running at large, perpetrating other crimes. He therefore moved for leave to attaint him. He was attained very speedily and precipitately, without any proof better than vague reports. Without being confronted with his accusers and witnesses, without the privilege of calling for evidence in his behalf, he was sentenced to death, and was afterwards actually executed. . . . I cannot contemplate it without horror.

Randolph later added that Philips "had a commision in his pocket at that time. He was, therefore, only a prisoner of war."

Randolph had given the impression that the execution of Philips was the result of the bill of attainder against him. Amazingly, Patrick Henry endorsed the misinformation as fact. Philips, he argued, had been no Socrates. "He was a fugitive murderer and outlaw. . . . Those who declare war against the human race may be struck out of existence as soon as they are apprehended. He was not executed according to those beautiful legal ceremonies, which are pointed out by the laws in criminal cases. The enormity of his crimes did not entitle him to it." The enormity of Patrick Henry's crime was that he did not believe that bad men were entitled to the benefits of the Virginia Declaration of Rights.

Of the several rejoinders to Henry's defense of the bill of attainder, John Marshall's was the most incisive. "Can we pretend to the enjoyment of political freedom or security," he asked, "when we are told that a man has been, by an act of Assembly, struck out of existence without being confronted with his accusers and witnesses, without the benefits of the law of the land? Where is our safety, when we are told that this act was justifiable because the person was not a Socrates? What has become of the worthy member's maxims? Is this one of them? Shall it be a maxim that a man shall be deprived of life without the benefit of law. Shall such a deprivation of life be justified by answering, that the man's life was not taken . . . because he was a bad man?" Marshall's remarks demonstrated the profound repugnance with which a bill of attainder was regarded by fair-minded men and provided a standard by which to measure Jefferson's subsequent defense of his handiwork in Philips's case.

In 1815, thirty-seven years after the case, on receiving the proof sheets of Louis Girardin's continuation of John Burk's *History of Virginia*, Jefferson commented at length on the Philips case. Objecting to quotations from the Virginia debates and from St. George Tucker's edition of Blackstone, Jefferson recommended that "the whole of the quotations from Tucker, Randolph and

Henry be struck out" and that his own version of the case, running to two pages, be inserted in their place. According to Jefferson, Tucker had written a "diatribe" against bills of attainder, instead of having defined their "occasion and proper office." Legislative outlawry and attainder were justifiable, Jefferson contended, when a person charged with a crime withdrew from justice or forcibly resisted it. In such a case the legislature should give him sufficient time to appear for trial and declare that his refusal be taken as a confession of guilt.

Bills of attainder, Jefferson acknowledged, had been abused in England, but "what institution is insusceptible of abuse in wicked hands?" As for Philips, he had been tried by common law, though he had "not come in before the day prescribed." Indeed, had Philips been denied jury trial, confrontation, and the right to produce evidence in his own behalf, "I would have asked of the Attorney General," he claimed, "why he proposed or permitted it?" Jefferson preferred the bill of attainder, which declared the guilt and fixed the punishment of Philips without court and common-law process.

Continuing his attack on Randolph, Jefferson declared that if the former attorney general had meant that Philips had been denied constitutionally guaranteed procedures on the passage of the attainder, "how idle to charge the legislature with omitting to confront the culprit with his witnesses, when he was standing out in arms and in defiance of their authority." The observation by Jefferson was sophistical, because it would have been even more idle to have expected the culprit to surrender when his guilt had already been explicitly determined and announced by the legislature. That body had also declared that "the usual forms and procedures of the courts of law," being insufficient, would not be followed. Jefferson's position was baldly exposed when he added:

> No one pretended then that the perpetrator of crimes who could successfully resist the officers of justice, would be protected in the

continuance of them by the privileges of his citizenship, and that baffling ordinary process, nothing extraordinary could be rightfully adopted to protect citizens against him. No one doubted that society had a right to erase from the roll of its members any one who rendered his own existence inconsistent with theirs; to withdraw from him the protection of laws, and to remove him from among them by exile, or even by death if necessary.

In forwarding to Patrick Henry's apologetic biographer a copy of this lengthy letter to Girardin, Jefferson concluded: "I was then [1778] thoroughly persuaded of the correctness of this proceeding, and am more and more convinced by reflection. If I am in error, it is an error of principle. I know of no substitute for the process of outlawry, so familiar to our law, or to it's [sic] kindred process by act of attainder, duly applied, which could have reached the case of Josiah Philips." Thus, Jefferson in the end agreed fundamentally with Patrick Henry's statement of 1788 on the propriety of attainders in certain cases, notwithstanding John Marshall's incisive answer. Jefferson's position was all the more surprising because he himself, in 1783, had proposed a new constitution for Virginia that explicitly denied to the legislature any power "to pass any bill of attainder, (or other law declaring any person guilty) of treason or felony." But on careful reflection, Jefferson in 1815 strongly endorsed outlawry and the bill of attainder against Philips.

Outlawry never had more than a slight foothold in America. New York resorted to outlawry on a few occasions between 1702 and 1710 but not thereafter. In 1774 a New York act referred to the fact that outlawry "is not used in this Colony," yet the legislature proclaimed the guilt of Ethan Allen and others for a riot, requiring their surrender to the civil authorities on pain of being attainted for felony. Allen and his followers denounced outlawry and attainders as unconstitutional.

In 1784 Pennsylvania enacted a bill of attainder against the robber Aaron Doane. The state supreme court sustained the attainder, which was not prohibited by the state constitution, and sentenced

Doane to be executed. However, John Dickinson, then the "president" of the state, withheld the warrant necessary to complete the sentence until he should receive from the court satisfactory answers to a series of questions posed by Dickinson. Those questions revealed his implacable hostility to outlawry as a "menacing part of jurisprudence," "so dangerous a practice," and contrary to the "liberality of spirit" with which the law should be enforced. The judges of the supreme court, in *Respublica v. Doane*, answered Dickinson's questions and defended their use of outlawry and attainder. But Dickinson and his council rebuked the court for "establishing a precedent in a capital case, altogether new . . . [and] so dangerous." Dickinson refused to issue the warrant, thereby preventing the death sentence from being carried out.

When enacting the Northwest Ordinance in 1787, Congress outlawed bills of attainder. At the Constitutional Convention of the same year, no discussion was required for approval of the clauses in Article I, sections 9 and 10, banning bills of attainder by Congress and the state legislatures. Article III, section 3, of the Constitution declared: "No attainder of treason shall work corruption of blood or forfeiture except during the life of the person attainted."

CHAPTER FOUR

The First Amendment:
The Establishment Clause

LTHOUGH the Framers of the Bill of Rights did not rank the rights in order of importance, some are more precious than others. A right that has no superior is the first mentioned: freedom from a law respecting an establishment of religion. The First Congress recommended twelve amendments to the states, which failed to ratify the first two: as a result, the proposal that originally stood in the third place became the first, a fact swollen with symbolic significance. At the very least, establishments of religion summon historical memories associated with religious persecution. Equality for all opinions on the subject of religion and for the free exercise of religious conscience cannot exist in the presence of an establishment of religion. The classic establishment of religion denoted a legal union between a state and a particular church that benefited from numerous privileges not shared by other churches or by the nonchurched or unbelievers. An uncontested and incontestable fact that stands out from the establishment clause is that the United States cannot constitutionally enact any law preferring one church over others in any manner whatever.

Does the establishment clause permit government aid to religion? Do the views of Chief Justice William H. Rehnquist have any historical validity? In 1985, he declared in dissent in *Wallace v. Jaffree* that the "well accepted meaning" of the establishment clause is that it merely prohibited the establishment of a "national religion," which he defined as the official designation of any church as a national one. The clause also "forbade preference among religious sects or denominations." But it created no wall of separation between government and religion, not even between church and state. "The Establishment Clause," Rehnquist wrote, "did not require governmental neutrality between religion and irreligion, nor did it prohibit the federal government from providing non-discriminatory aid to religion."

The language of the establishment clause provides few sure conclusions. If, taken literally, the clause creates no wall of separation, neither does it refer to a national religion or to the concept of preference; it does not permit government preference for religion over irreligion, let alone of one religion or church over others. It does not even restrict itself to laws banning establishments of religion, because it applies, more broadly, to laws "respecting" establishments of religion. Therefore, a law that falls short of creating an establishment, whatever that might be, comes within the constitutional prohibition if it concerns an establishment or is a step in that direction. But the clearest proposition about the establishment clause is that it limits power by placing an absolute restriction on the United States: "Congress shall make no law . . . ." Reading an empowerment from that is about as valid as reading the entrails of a chicken for the meaning of the establishment clause or for portents of the future.

The clause was added to the Constitution because the unamended text not only placed religious liberty in jeopardy; it seemed to allow for the implication that Congress might exercise powers not prohibited and might, therefore, create an establishment of religion—or so the Constitution's opponents claimed. To the supporters of the Constitution, such reasoning was specious because the proposed new national government would possess merely limited powers, and none had been granted on any subject that would be the concern of a bill of rights. If no power existed, it could neither be exercised or abused. Of the many statements of this argument, the best known is that of Alexander Hamilton in *The Federalist,* where he concluded simply: "For why declare that things shall not be done which there is no power to do? Why, for instance, should it be said that the liberty of the press shall not be restrained, when no power is given by which restrictions may be imposed?" Thus, James Wilson of Pennsylvania, in response to the contention that the rights of conscience had no security, asserted: "I ask the honorable gentleman, what part of this system puts it into the power of Congress to attack those rights? When there is no power to attack, it is idle to prepare the means of defense." Similarly, Edmund Randolph of Virginia declared that "no power is given expressly to Congress over religion," and he added that only powers "constitutionally given" could be exercised. James Madison said, "There is not a shadow of right in the general government to intermeddle with religion." And Richard Dobbs Spaight of North Carolina maintained: "As to the subject of religion . . . . [n]o power is given to the general government to interfere with it at all. Any act of Congress on this subject would be a usurpation." Wilson, Randolph, Madison, and Spaight had attended the Philadelphia Convention. Their remarks show that Congress was powerless *even in the absence of the First Amendment,* to enact laws on the subject of religion, whether in favor of one church or all of them, impartially and equally. In 1790, before the ratification of the First Amendment, Madison opposed the inclusion of ministers in a list of occupations to be covered in the first census bill. He reasoned that "the general government is proscribed from interfering, in any manner whatever in matters respecting religion; and it may be thought to do so in ascertaining who, and who are not ministers of the gospel."

The ratification controversy yielded no evidence that reveals the understanding at the time of the term "establishment of religion." Some states, however, proposed amendments that included a ban on establishments. New Hampshire, the ninth state to ratify, was the first to urge an amendment on the subject: "Congress shall make no laws touching Religion, or to infringe the rights of Conscience." That proved to be as concise and perfect a statement of the matter as could be devised, and indeed, it most clearly revealed the meaning of what would become the equivalent clauses of the First Amendment. Virginia, New York, North Carolina, and Rhode Island also recommended an amendment on the subject. Virginia, copied verbatim by North Carolina and Rhode Island, urged that "no particular religious sect or society ought to be favored or established, by law, in preference to others," and New York expressed the same thought. In each of these four states, opponents of ratification urged amendments as a price of Union. The Constitution nearly failed to be ratified because it had no bill of rights. New Hampshire, the necessary ninth state, ratified by a vote of 57–47, but the votes of Virginia and New York were still indispensable. Virginia ratified by 89–79, New York by 30–27. North Carolina at first rejected the Constitution, and Rhode Island barely ratified, 32–30, even after Congress had recommended the Bill of Rights to the states. The point is, in part, that advocates of ratification necessarily swallowed recommendations for amendments whose language they did not necessarily approve.

Moreover, the language of Virginia and New York by no means implied that Congress should have power to favor religion so long as no sect received preference over others. A page of history is worth a volume of logic here. Parsing the nonpreferential language of the proposed amendments on establishments holds no key to understanding. In the first place, Patrick Henry and his followers in Virginia, who were responsible for the language of the amendment, had no intention of augmenting the powers of Congress; they opposed any federal authority over the subject of religion, which they believed to be exclusively within state jurisdiction. They surely did not favor an expansion of the tax powers of Congress, and they did not want Congress to enact an assessment on behalf of religion generally. Virginia had defeated a proposal of 1784 that authorized a state tax for the benefit of religion, allocating each person's money to the Christian church of his choice. Virginia did not intend for the United States a power that it denied even to itself. Its proposal of 1788 against laws preferring one sect above others did not represent the state's position, which is best found in its great Statute for Religious Freedom of 1786. It placed religion wholly on private, voluntary support. Virginia, like New York, had no religious test for office-holding.

The constitutions of Pennsylvania, New Jersey, North Carolina, Delaware, and New York used the language of no preference, yet all five, including the three that had never supported an establishment of religion, relied on private support of religion. In other words, they believed that a constitutional provision insuring no subordination of one sect to another, or providing no preference of one over others, banned government aid to religion. Rhode Island, which failed to frame a state constitution, never had an establishment of any kind, and as a stronghold of the Baptists, most vehemently opposed government aid to religion, state or federal; yet Rhode Island expressed that position in the language of no preference of one above others. Massachusetts, by contrast, maintained an establishment of religion by its constitution of 1780 yet endorsed the principle of no preference. Several towns that opposed an establishment of religion believed that the principle of no preference required private support of religion. When the Baptist leaders of Massachusetts sought to separate church and state, they relied on the language of no preference, oblivious to the possibility that a subsequent generation, ignorant of history, might twist that language to make it yield government support of religion on a nonpreferential basis. No one in the United States during the generation of the Framers advocated a federal power to promote, assist, or support religion. Religion was a topic that only the arts of voodoo might transmogrify from exclusive state jurisdiction into the subject of a federal power. And no state that banned laws preferring one sect over others ever regarded its ban against preference as an authority to enact laws assisting religion generally or all sects without preference to any.

The history of the drafting of the establishment clause by the First Congress will not make sense to anyone who fails to understand Madison's objective in introducing the amendments that became the Bill of Rights. Its "great object," he said, was to "limit and qualify the powers of Government" to prevent legislation in such forbidden fields as religion. He declared that the goal of "restraining the Federal Government" could be achieved by ensuring that "the abuse of the powers of the General Government may be guarded against in a more secure manner" than in the unamended Constitution. As Madison succinctly informed Jefferson, the Bill of Rights was not framed "to imply powers not meant to be included in the enumeration."

When Madison introduced his amendments, the clauses on religion read that no one's civil rights should be abridged "on account of religious belief or worship, nor shall any national religion be established, nor shall the full and equal rights of conscience be in any manner, or on any pretext, infringed." In one respect that constituted a vast improvement over the final version of the First Amendment's clause on religious liberty, which merely guarantees against a law "prohibiting the free exercise thereof." A literal interpretation destroys the original intent, which was to preserve religious liberty from diminution. But the reference to no prohibition in the free exercise clause and to no abridgment in the free press clause gives the impression that the Framers deliberately allowed for the infringement of religious liberty and sought only to prevent its abolition. The point is that the clauses of the First

Amendment cannot be taken literally. They do not mean what they say nor say what the Framers meant.

The establishment clause as introduced by Madison surely did not mean that the United States could pass laws on religion short of creating a national religion—that is, short of a federal preference of one religion or church over others. By "national" Madison meant any act of the national government. His next proposal safeguarded the rights of conscience against state acts, which the Senate defeated. In any case, a House select committee omitted the word "national." It is not part of the First Amendment, and it should not be construed, à la Rehnquist, as if it were still a part and as if the ban against a "national religion" authorized nonpreferential assistance to all faiths. Madison nevertheless continued to employ the phrase "national religion," raising the question of whether he favored nonpreferential aid to religion.

He did not. He had led the fight in Virginia against the "general assessment" bill of 1784, which would have imposed taxes to subsidize religion. Madison did not oppose that bill because it referred, too narrowly, to Christianity, and no one for or against the bill thought that its extension to Hinduism, Islam, Judaism, and other religions would remedy any defects. Madison opposed the bill because he opposed any kind of establishment of religion, no matter how inclusive or exclusive. Proponents of the bill declared themselves to be on the side of God because they praised religion and its many benefits. Madison replied that the question was not whether religion was a good thing but whether establishments of religion were good for religion, and he decidedly thought not. He did not believe that religion needed government support any more than government needed religious support. He argued, in his famous "Memorial and Remonstrance against Religious Assessments," that religion was not an "engine of civil society," that the establishment contemplated by the bill differed from the Inquisition "only in degree," not in principle, and that any establishment violated freedom of religion, injured religion, corrupted government, and threatened public liberty.

Madison, in fact, had an exquisite sense of the separate jurisdictions of religion and government, and he shared Jefferson's belief in a high wall of separation between the two. He spoke of a "perfect separation" and believed that "religion and Government will exist in greater purity, without . . . the aid of Government." As for the phrase "national religion," he used it to describe federal use of public funds for the support of interfaith invocations and benedictions, congressional and military chaplains, and a law incorporating a church in the District of Columbia, all of which he believed to be unconstitutional. His antagonism to government-assisted religion was extreme, even as to trifling matters.

Madison rarely used the phrase "establishment of religion." He almost always misquoted the First Amendment as if it outlawed "religious establishments," a revealing usage. A religious establishment is a church, a church school, or any religious institution, and such an establishment implies no government aid or involvement with religion, as does establishment of religion. That Madison, father of the Constitution and of the Bill of Rights, misquoted the establishment clause as he did, even in official documents when he was president, shows that he understood it to mean that the government had no authority to legislate on the subject of religion or on matters concerning religion.

Madison's influence notwithstanding, he did not compose the establishment clause by himself or determine its meaning. When his proposed amendments emerged from a House select committee, the religion clauses stated: "No religion shall be established by law, nor shall the equal rights of conscience be infringed." The House briefly debated these recommendations without clarifying their meaning. No one suggested that the United States had the constitutional power to pass laws about religion. Disagreement existed about the best way to say that it had no such power; saying so in some way would satisfy the popular clamor for an amendment that specifically opposed establishments of religion and favored religious liberty. Samuel Livermore of New Hampshire recommended that "Congress shall make no laws touching religion, or infringing the rights of conscience." The Committee of the Whole adopted this motion, but it apparently did not accommodate those who believed that something specific had to be said on the subject of establishments of religion. When, therefore, the House took up the report of the Committee of the Whole, a motion made by Fisher Ames of Massachusetts passed, with the result that the proposal that went to the Senate said: "Congress shall make no law establishing religion, or to prevent the free exercise thereof, or to infringe the rights of conscience."

The Senate conducted its debate without reporters present and left a record of only motions and their disposition. On one day the Senate defeated three motions phrased in the language of no preference. One said that Congress should not establish "one religious sect or society in preference to others," another that it should not establish "any religious sect or society," and the third that it should not establish "any particular denomination of religion in preference to another." These narrowly phrased motions allowed the semantic implication, however baseless, that nonpreferential federal aid to religion seemed to be the object of those who supported such motions. Such a view, which has no historical backup, ignores the fact that the Senate defeated these motions. It was seeking a way to limit a nonexistent power, not a way to enhance or even vest power. Moreover, the language of no preference often seemed appropriate to those who believed that religion should rest on merely voluntary support. Elder John Leland, the great Baptist minister who was the only person to fight establishments of religion in Virginia, Connecticut, and Massachusetts, strongly believed that because Christ's kingdom is not of this world, government should have no jurisdiction over it. When he sought to frame an amendment terminating the establishment in Massachusetts, he used the language of no preference; he would have been astonished to learn that such language could be stretched to allow government assistance to all sects without preference to any. The Senate, when drafting the amendment that became the First, consistently defeated no preference motions and adopted the House motion.

Six days later, however, the Senate changed its mind and substituted for the House version one that read: "Congress shall make no law establishing articles of faith or a mode of worship, or prohibiting the free exercise of religion." This was overly narrow language, because South Carolina was the only state that had an establishment of religion prescribing articles of faith; in five other states whose laws as of 1789 authorized establishments of religion, public taxation for religion, rather than articles of faith, constituted the principal feature of an establishment. The South Carolina provision of 1778 was scrapped when a new state constitution of 1790 omitted all reference to an establishment of religion and guaranteed free exercise for everyone.

Despite the narrow language of the Senate, the complexity of the matter demands recognition of the fact that a Baptist memorial of 1774 had used similar language, opposing prescribed articles of faith or forms of worship, in order to achieve, in the minds of its Baptist sponsors, endorsement of the idea that government and religion should be kept separated. As a matter of fact, the foremost Baptist champion of religious liberty in Massachusetts, Isaac Backus, supported ratification of the Constitution in the belief that the United States had no power at all in religious matters, and in his three-volume *History of New England*, he misquoted the First Amendment by stating, approvingly, that "Congress shall make no law, establishing articles of faith, or a mode of worship, or prohibiting the free exercise of religion." That is, he regarded the Senate's language as sufficient to condemn the establishments of religion then existing in Massachusetts and Connecticut. As Monsignor Thomas Curry has said in his analysis of the original meaning of the establishment clause, "Eighteenth-century American history offers abundant examples of writers using the concept of preference, when, in fact, they were referring to a ban on all government assistance to religion."

The House adamantly refused to accept the Senate's version of the religion clauses. Differences on several of the proposed amendments required a joint committee of the two houses to negotiate a compromise. A strong committee of three members from each house, including four men who had been influential Framers (Madison, Roger Sherman, Oliver Ellsworth, and William Paterson), drafted the language that we know as the First Amendment. Both houses adopted it and recommended its ratification by the states.

Several facts clearly emerge from the legislative history of the establishment clause. The United States had no authority before the First Amendment to enact laws about religion; only the states held that power. The amendment did not increase the legislative power of Congress. Congress seriously considered alternative readings of the establishment clause and rejected every phrasing that logic could construe as more narrow than the final version. The Livermore–New Hampshire alternative, the broadest restriction of power, failed because it did not mention an establishment. Another fact may be added: the meaning of an "establishment of religion" remains uncertain after an analysis of the legislative history. Whatever such an establishment was, the nation's legislature faced an absolute ban concerning it.

The states ratified the Bill of Rights but left nothing to clarify the meaning of an establishment of religion. We have no debates, newspaper coverage, tracts, or personal correspondence that provide clues, except in Virginia, where the evidence is utterly misleading. The state senate, narrowly dominated by Anti-

Federalists who took orders from Patrick Henry, voted 8–7 to postpone a decision on the recommended amendments. Virginia's Anti-Federalists understood that if the Bill of Rights became part of the supreme law, no chance would remain for a second constitutional convention or for the passage of the amendments crippling the national judicial, tax, and commerce powers. The eight state senators, who had consistently voted in support of taxes for religion, issued a patently false public statement contending that the proposed religion clauses neither protected freedom of religion from violation nor prevented Congress from levying taxes for the support of religion; they even alleged that it would benefit one particular sect over others. Their statement conflicted with the language of the amendment at issue. Finally, the Virginia senate, unable any longer to explain its opposition to a Bill of Rights, ratified.

What then was the understanding in 1789 of the meaning of the term *an establishment of religion?* Doubtless, any union of state and church comparable to the familiar European establishments of religion came within the prohibition of the First Amendment. Such establishments of religion had weak counterparts in the tidewater towns of the southern colonies before the American Revolution. Where such an establishment existed, attendance upon its services was supposed to be compulsory, unless the government indulged the open existence of dissenters. But only the official creed of the established church could be publicly taught, and only its clergy had civil sanction to perform marriage services and other sacraments or could allow them to be performed. Only clergymen of the established religion received stipends paid from religious taxes imposed on everyone, regardless of faith, and only the churches of the establishment were built and maintained by those taxes. Dissenters, even if tolerated, suffered from the imposition of various civil disabilities, such as exclusion from universities and disqualification for office, whether civil, military, or religious.

Their orphanages, schools, churches, and other religious institutions had no legal capacity to bring suits, hold or transmit property, or receive or bequeath trust funds.

According to William Tennent, a Presbyterian minister of South Carolina, in which the Church of England (Episcopal) had been established, Protestant dissenters were merely tolerated as if they stood "on the same footing with the Jews," unmolested but unequal. Except in Rhode Island, second-class citizenship also characterized non-Congregational Protestants in the New England colonies, where for all practical purposes the Congregational Church enjoyed the preferences of the established church. By banning laws respecting an establishment of religion, the First Amendment meant, indisputably, that Congress could make no law concerning the sort of establishment that characterized Lutheran Sweden, Anglican England, Roman Catholic Spain, or Presbyterian Scotland.

The question is whether an establishment of religion signified anything other than a church with preferred status or official privileges. In fact, Europe's post-Reformation model of an establishment of religion was barely known in America, if at all, by the time of the Revolution. The term *establishment of religion* came to have a far broader meaning in America than it had in Europe. To begin with, American establishments had never been as powerful or as discriminatory as their European counterparts. Tennent may have felt merely tolerated in Anglican Charleston, but further west in Carolina, Anglicans were few in number, their clergy was almost nonexistent, all churches were equal in fact, and discriminatory laws had no real operation. By the time of the Revolution, the interior of the southern colonies had been populated with Scotch-Irish Presbyterians and various German sects and denominations. A bewildering multiplicity of religions existed in the middle colonies, none of which had ever endured an establishment of religion. And in New England, outside of Rhode Island where state and church had always been separated, Congregationalists reaped the benefits of an establishment not because their church was by law established but because a nondescript establishment of Protestant ministers on a local town basis operated in favor of the overwhelmingly numerous Congregationalists. Nowhere in New England was the Congregational Church established by name.

The American experience with establishments of religion was unknown to eighteenth-century Europe. As a matter of fact, at the time of the framing of the Bill of Rights, every one of the six states that still maintained an establishment of religion in the United States had *multiple* or *general* establishments of religion. An establishment of religion had come to mean government support, primarily financial, for religion generally, without legal preference to any church. For all practical purposes, and surely for all legal purposes, the states that authorized establishments in 1789 established all the churches within their borders.

New York's colonial history of church-state relations provided the first example of an establishment of religion radically different from the European type, an establishment of religion in general—or at least of Protestantism in general—and without preference to one church over others. After the English conquered New Netherlands in 1664, the "Duke's Laws," named for the duke of York, later James II, fixed the governance of New York and made provisions for the regulation of churches in Long Island. Any church of the Protestant religion could become an established church. In a sense, of course, this was an exclusive establishment of one religion, Protestantism; but the system involved a multiple establishment of several Protestant churches, in sharp contrast to European precedents, which provided for the establishment of one church only.

Under the "Duke's Laws," every township was obliged publicly to support some Protestant church and a minister. The denomination of the church did not matter. Costs were to be met by a public tax: "Every inhabitant shall contribute to all charges both in Church and State." A local option system prevailed. On producing evidence of ordination "from some Protestant bishop or minister," the minister selected by a town was inducted into his pastorate by the governor representing the state. In other words, this was an establishment of religion in which there was a formal, legal, official union between government and religion on a nonpreferential basis and without the establishment of any individual church. In 1683 the New York Assembly enacted a "Charter of Liberties" that adopted the Long Island system of multiple establishments and extended it to the whole colony.

Following the Glorious Revolution of 1688, the English government instructed its governors of New York to implement an establishment of Anglicanism there. In 1693 a recalcitrant legislature, composed almost entirely of non-Anglicans, passed "An Act for Settling a Ministry & raising a Maintenance for them" in the four southern counties. The law called only for "a good and sufficient Protestant Minister" and nowhere mentioned the Church of England. The royal governors and most Anglicans asserted that the statute had established their church; but non-Anglican New Yorkers disagreed. Thus, in 1695 the legislature declared that the 1693 act allowed the selection of a "Dissenting Protestant Minister," that is, a non-Anglican one, although the governor refused to permit this. A few years later, Lewis Morris, a prominent Anglican, wrote: "The People were generally dissenters [and] fancied they had made an effectual provision for Ministers of their own persuasion by this Act."

In 1703 and 1704 Anglicans, assisted by the governor of the colony, gained possession of the church and parsonage in the town of Jamaica, Long Island. These buildings had been erected at public expense, and the town had chosen a Presbyterian minister. The Anglicans' action set off a long and bitter controversy. The Presbyterians refused to pay the salary of the Anglican minister because, as the Church of England townspeople reported, "they [the Presbyterians] stick not to call themselves the Established Church." In 1710 the Presbyterians managed to seize and retain the parsonage, and in 1727 they brought suit for the recovery of the church, which the provincial court, in an unreported decision, awarded them. For much of the remainder of the colonial period, Anglicans managed to pry a minister's salary out of the reluctant inhabitants, but not without constant complaints and a further attempt, defeated by the courts in 1768, to withhold the minister's salary. Elsewhere on Long Island, the inhabitants supported the non-Anglican town ministers chosen by the majority. Brookhaven certainly supported such a minister, and given the scarcity of Anglicans and Anglican ministers in the colony, most towns had to reach their own accommodations with the ministers of their choice.

In the 1750s the organization of King's College (later Columbia) provoked a controversy over the nature of New York's establishment. Anglicans demanded that they control the new school because they enjoyed "a preference by the Constitution of the province." Non-Anglicans rejected both claims. A young lawyer, and a future framer of the Federal Constitution, William Livingston, denied that the Anglican Church was exclusively established in the colony. He insisted that the establishment "restricted no particular Protestant Denomination whatsoever" and that the people were to choose which ministers to establish. Here again is evidence that the concept of a multiple establishment of religion was understood by inhabitants of colonial New York. Although New York Anglicans claimed an exclusive establishment of their church, a large number of the colony's population understood the establishment set up by the act of 1693, not simply as a state preference for one religion or sect over others, but as allowing public support for many churches to be determined by popular vote.

Massachusetts, the major New England colony, proclaimed no

establishment of the Congregational Church by name after 1692. That year the legislature provided for an establishment of religion on a town basis by simply requiring every town to maintain an "able, learned and orthodox" minister, to be chosen by the voters of the town and supported by a tax levied on all taxpayers. By law several denominations could benefit from the establishment. Because Congregationalists constituted the overwhelming majority in nearly every town, they reaped the benefits of the establishment of religion. Except in Boston, where all congregations were supported voluntarily, the law in effect made the Congregational Church the privileged one, which unquestionably was the purpose of the statute, and non-Congregationalists, chiefly Episcopalians, Baptists, and Quakers, were for a long time taxed for the support of Congregationalism. However, in the few towns dominated by a non-Congregational denomination, as Baptists did in Swansea, the official established church represented that denomination.

The growing number of dissenters, however, forced Congregationalists to make concessions. In 1727 Episcopalians won the statutory right of having their religious taxes applied to the support of their own churches. Connecticut passed a similar act on behalf of the Episcopal churches in the same year. In 1728 Massachusetts exempted Quakers and Baptists from taxes for the payment of ministerial salaries. Thereafter, each denomination was respectively exempted from sharing the taxes for building new town churches. Tax exemption statutes on behalf of Quakers and Baptists were periodically renewed, so that members of these denominations were not supposed to pay religious taxes for the benefit of either Congregational churches or their own.

Because of complicated legal technicalities, as well as outright illegal action, frequent abuses occurred under the system of tax exemption, which also prevailed in Connecticut. In Massachusetts and Connecticut many Quakers and Baptists were unconscionably forced to pay for the support of Congregational churches, and even Episcopalians who lived too far from a church of their own denomination to attend its services were taxed for support of Congregational ones. Abuses of both the letter and the spirit of the law did not alter the basic fact that after 1728 the establishments of religion in both colonies meant government support of two churches, Congregational and Episcopal, without specified preference to either.

Prominent Congregational spokesmen understood that they did not constitute an exclusive establishment. Cotton Mather wrote that "the Person elected by the Majority of the Inhabitants . . . is . . . the King's Minister," and, he continued, the minister elected by each town was the official minister and as such was entitled to its taxes. Benjamin Colman declared: "If any Town will chuse a Gentleman of the Church of England for their Pastor . . . he is their Minister by the Laws of our Province as much as any Congregational Minister." In 1763 Jonathan Mayhew explained that Massachusetts had established not a single church but rather "protestant churches of various denominations." He understood that "an hundred churches, all of different denominations . . . might all be established in the same . . . colony, as well as one, two, or three." Thus, three of the most prominent New England ministers of the eighteenth century specified that in Massachusetts an establishment of religion was something other than an exclusive preference for one church. Massachusetts, and Connecticut to a lesser extent, maintained not an exclusive but a dual establishment of religion.

New Hampshire's law allowed a multiple establishment. Down to the middle of the eighteenth century, the town system of establishment operated to benefit the Congregational Church exclusively. But New Hampshire did not systematically require the payment of rates by dissenters nor concern itself with the support of their ministers. Quakers, Episcopalians, Presbyterians, and Baptists were exempt from supporting the local established church, which was usually Congregational. In some towns, however, Episcopalians and Presbyterians were authorized to establish parishes and to use town authority to collect taxes for their churches. By the eve of the Revolution, the pattern of establishment had become bewilderingly diverse. Some towns maintained dual establishments, others multiple establishments, with free exercise for dissenters.

In the wake of the Revolution the exclusive establishments of religion inherited from the colonial period collapsed. States that had never had establishments renewed their barriers against them, except for Rhode Island, which did not adopt a new state constitution. New York, denying that it ever had a preferential establishment, placed religion on private, voluntary support, as did New Jersey, Delaware, and Pennsylvania. Nowhere in America after 1776 did an establishment of religion restrict itself to a state church or to a system of public support of one sect alone; instead, an establishment of religion meant public support of several or all churches, with preference to none. The six states that continued to provide for public support of religion were careful to make concessions that extended their establishments to embrace many sects.

Three of these six states were in New England. Massachusetts adopted its constitution in 1780. Article III of its Declaration of Rights commanded the legislature to authorize the "several towns, parishes, precincts, and other bodies politic, or religious societies, to make suitable provision, at their own expense, for the institution of the public worship of God, and for the support and maintenance of public Protestant teachers of piety, religion, and morality." The same article empowered the legislature to make church attendance compulsory, and it authorized the towns and parishes to elect their ministers. In addition, the article stated: "And all moneys paid by the subject to the support of public worship, and all the public teachers aforesaid, shall, if he require it, be uniformly applied to the support of the public teacher or teachers of his own religious sect or denomination, provided there be any on whose instructions he attends; otherwise it may be paid towards the support of the teacher or teachers of the parish or precinct in which the said moneys are raised." A final clause provided that "no subordination of any one sect or denomination to the other shall ever be established law." That clause against preference proves that constitutionally speaking the several churches of the establishment were on a nonpreferential basis. Clearly an establishment of religion in Massachusetts meant government support of religion and of several different churches in an equitable manner. Congregationalists continued to be the chief beneficiaries of the establishment, because they were the most numerous and resorted to various tricks to fleece non-Congregationalists out of their share of religious taxes. But the fact remains that Baptist, Episcopal, Methodist, Unitarian, and even Universalist churches were publicly supported under the establishment after 1780. Massachusetts did not separate church and state until 1833.

In New Hampshire the state constitution of 1784 also created a statewide multiple establishment with the guarantee that no sect or denomination should be subordinated to another. As in Massachusetts, all Protestant churches benefited. The multiple establishment in New Hampshire ended in 1819. Connecticut, like Rhode Island, did not adopt a constitution during the Revolution. Its establishment of religion was regulated by the Act of Toleration of 1784, which was in force when the Bill of Rights was framed. The statute empowered each town to choose which minister to support and guaranteed that no sect was to be subordinated to any other. Those who did not belong to the church representing the majority were exempt from paying toward its support as long as they could prove membership in a different church and that they contributed to the support of their church. Baptists protested against the system but participated in it and benefited from it. The establishment lasted until 1818.

In Maryland, Georgia, and South Carolina, "an establishment of religion" meant much what it did in the New England states that maintained multiple establishments. In Maryland, where the Church of England had been exclusively established, the constitution of 1776 provided that no person could be compelled "to maintain any particular place of worship, or any particular ministry," thus disestablishing the Episcopal Church. But the same constitution provided for a new establishment of religion: "Yet the Legislature may, in their discretion, lay a general and *equal tax*, for the support of the Christian religion; leaving to each individual the power of appointing the payment over of the money, collected from him, to the support of any particular place of worship or minister." "Christian" rather than "Protestant" was used in Maryland because of the presence of a large Catholic population, thus ensuring nonpreferential support of all churches existing in the state. In 1785 the Maryland legislature sought to exercise its discretionary power to institute nonpreferential support, but "a huge uproar arose against the measure," and it was denounced as a new establishment and decisively beaten. In 1810 the power to enact a multiple establishment was taken from the legislature by a constitutional amendment providing that "an *equal* and *general* tax or any other tax . . . for the support of any religion" was not lawful.

Georgia's constitution of 1777 tersely effected the disestablishment of the Church of England while permitting a multiple establishment of all churches without exception: "All persons whatever shall have the free exercise of their religion; . . . and shall not, unless by consent, support any teacher or teachers except those of their own profession." "This, of course, left the way open for taxation for the support of one's own religion," says Reba C. Strickland, a historian of eighteenth-century church-state relations in Georgia, "and such a law was passed in 1785," although similar bills had failed in 1782 and 1784. According to the 1785 law, all Christian sects and denominations were to receive tax support in proportion to the amount of property owned by their respective church members, but it is not clear whether this measure went into operation. What is clear is that an establishment of religion meant government tax support to all churches, with preference to none. The state constitution in effect at the time of the framing of the Bill of Rights was adopted in 1789. Its relevant provision declared that no persons should be obliged "to contribute to the support of any religious profession but their own," thereby permitting a multiple establishment as before. In the state constitution adopted in 1798, however, Georgia separated church and state by a guarantee against any religious taxes and by making the support of religion purely voluntary.

South Carolina's constitution of 1778 was the sixth state constitution providing for a multiple establishment of religion. Article XXVIII elaborately spelled out the details for the maintenance of the "Christian Protestant religion" as "the established religion of this State." Adult males forming themselves into any religious society of a Protestant denomination were declared to be "a church of the established religion of this State," on condition of subscribing to a belief in God, worshipping him publicly, regarding Christianity as "the true religion," and accepting the divine inspiration of Scripture. Pursuant to this law, Baptists, Independents, Methodists, and Anglicans qualified as "Established" churches. The state also specifically guaranteed that "no person shall, by law, be obliged to pay towards the maintenance and support of a religious worship that he does not freely join in, or has not voluntarily engaged to support." In 1790 South Carolina adopted a new constitution with no provisions whatever for public support of religion.

The constitutions of North Carolina and Virginia did not provide for an establishment of religion of any kind. In 1776 North Carolina banned state support for religion and disestablished the Church of England. By contrast, Virginia's constitution of 1776 was noncommittal on the subject of an establishment. At the close of 1776, the Church of England was for all practical purposes disestablished in Virginia. But the statute of 1776 that initiated the end of the exclusive establishment expressly reserved for future decisions the question of whether religion ought to be placed on a private, voluntary basis or be supported on a nonpreferential basis by a new "general" assessment. The indecision continued until 1785, when public opinion turned against a general assessment. Madison's "Memorial and Remonstrance" became a catalyst for the political opposition to the assessment bill, but the religious opposition to it from evangelicals was decisive, resulting in the election of a legislature with an overwhelming majority against it. The new legislature let the bill die unnoticed and by a vote of 67–20 enacted instead Jefferson's bill for religious freedom with its provision against government support of religion. Had the assessment bill in Virginia been enacted, it would simply have increased the number of states maintaining multiple establishments from six to seven. Indeed, there were seven states with multiple establishments as a result of the admission of Vermont to the Union in 1791, whose vote was counted to determine whether enough states had ratified the Bill of Rights.

Clearly the provisions of these seven states show that to understand the American meaning of "an establishment of religion" one cannot adopt a definition based on European experience. In every European precedent of an establishment, the religion established was that of a single church. Many churches, or the religion held in common by all of them—that is, Christianity or Protestantism— were never simultaneously established by any European nation. Establishments in America, by contrast, in both the colonial and the early state periods, were not limited in nature or in meaning to state support of one church. An establishment of religion meant government aid and sponsorship of religion, principally by impartial tax support of the institutions of religion, the churches.

In no state or colony, of course, was there ever an establishment of religion that included every religion without exception. In three of the seven multiple establishments existing in 1791, the establishment included only Protestant churches, and in the other four, all Christian churches. In effect all Christian churches of each of the seven states were establishments of religion. Christianity or

Protestantism may signify one religion in contrast with Judaism, Buddhism, Hinduism, or Islam. But no European establishment of religion included all the churches within national boundaries; all European establishments of religion denoted a single state church—that is, the church of one denomination. No member of the First Congress came from a state that supported one church or an exclusive establishment of religion; no such example could have been found in the America of 1789. Their experience told the legislators in 1789 that an establishment of religion meant not just state preference for one religion but also nonpreferential support for many or all. At the time of its ratification in 1791 the establishment clause prevented the United States from doing what half the fourteen states then permitted—giving government aid to religion on a nonpreferential basis. From a broader standpoint, the establishment clause was also meant to depoliticize religion, thereby defusing the potentially explosive condition of a religiously heterogeneous society. By separating government and religion the establishment clause enables such a society to maintain some civility among believers and unbelievers as well as among diverse believers. Above all, the establishment clause functions to protect religion from government, and government from religion.

CHAPTER FIVE

The First Amendment:
The Free Press Clause

ALMOST two months after the Constitutional Convention had begun its deliberations, Charles Pinckney of South Carolina recommended "sundry propositions" to supplement a partial list of rights that had been prepared by the Committee of Detail. One of Pinckney's propositions urged that the liberty of the press should be "inviolably preserved." He offered no explanation, as if the meaning of "liberty of the press" was self-evident.

The Convention adopted Pinckney's proposal for a ban on religious tests as a qualification for office and his guarantee of the writ of habeas corpus, but it did nothing about liberty of the press or his other propositions. On September 12, 1787, when the convention was drawing to a close, a motion to include a bill of rights was defeated. A couple of days later, Pinckney renewed his earlier proposal for a free press clause. Sherman replied, "It is unnecessary. The power of Congress does not extend to the Press." Pinckney's motion lost, and three days later the Convention adjourned.

The Convention had made a massive mistake by having proposed a Constitution that protected a few rights but omitted most. Moreover, Roger Sherman to the contrary, the Constitution empowered the United States to make laws that might infringe upon particular liberties. The power to tax, implemented by the ominous necessary and proper clause, could even be used to destroy a free press and might be enforced by general warrants enabling the government to ransack homes and businesses for evidence of criminal evasion of the revenue laws. Some opponents of ratification, who were either fools or demagogues, wildly hinted at abuses of the treaty power. They predicted that the United States would make a deal with the pope, establish a national church, revive the Inquisition, and torture suspects.

Equally absurd were arguments by ratificationists as sophisticated as James Wilson, Alexander Hamilton, James Madison, and Oliver Ellsworth to the effect that a bill of rights would be un-American, because government here derived from the people who retained everything not surrendered, and would be "dangerous," because any right omitted was lost. Throughout the nation, freedom of the press became a topic for grand declamation, but nowhere was the insistent demand for its constitutional protection accompanied by a reasoned consideration of what it meant, how far it extended, and whether any circumstances justified its limitation. The rhetorical effusions of Anti-Federalists yield no definition of any freedoms, later protected under the First Amendment, and the newspapers, pamphlets, and state ratification conventions offer as little illumination.

The remarks of the members of the Constitutional Convention who either decamped or refused to sign are representative. Of the fourteen, Elbridge Gerry, George Mason, Robert Yates, John Lansing, Luther Martin, and Edmund Randolph published explanations of their rejection of the Constitution. None showed any serious concern for the omission of a bill of rights or the guarantee of a free press. Not one of them endorsed the principles of the Zenger case—namely, that truth should be a defense to a charge of libel and that the jury, not the court, should judge the criminality of the statements made by the defendant. Not one person who refused or failed to sign the Constitution argued the value of a broad scope for political discussion or rejected restrictions on the press that existed in the common law or state laws. Mason, for example, regretted not only the absence of a bill of rights but also the absence of benefits of the common law, which allowed prosecutions for harsh criticism of the government, its policies, or its officials. Yates, the likely author of the "Brutus" essays, a major Anti-Federalist series, failed to mention liberty of the press.

The ratification controversy in Pennsylvania, where the Anti-Federalist press published voluminously against ratification, reveals how stunted was the thinking about a free press. Opponents of the Constitution frequently urged a guarantee that liberty of the press "ought never to be restrained," which echoed verbatim the language of the state's constitution. Those words should not be taken as a guarantee of a broad freedom, because even Sir William Blackstone, the oracle of the common law, had declared that the absence of "previous restraints upon publications" ensured that "neither is any restraint hereby laid upon freedom of thought or enquiry." He added that publicizing "bad sentiments destructive of the needs of society is the crime which society corrects." In Pennsylvania, too, the language of no restraints meant no prior restraints: one could publish without fear of censorship but might be criminally convicted for aspersions on the government. The 1782 case of Eleazar Oswald, the rambunctious Philadelphia printer, showed that the state supreme court believed that the state constitutional guarantee of a free press was compatible with prosecution for seditious libel, and in 1788, Chief Justice Thomas McKean of Pennsylvania sentenced Oswald to a month in prison plus a fine, after holding that Blackstone's views controlled the meaning of the free press clause. In 1797 McKean ruled: "The liberty of the press is, indeed, essential to the nature of a free State, but this consists in laying no previous restraints upon public actions, and not in freedom from censure for criminal matter, when published. Every freeman has an undoubted right to lay what sentiments he pleases before the public . . . but take the consequences." Thus, in Pennsylvania, whose constitutional provisions of 1776 and 1790 were the most libertarian in the nation as to freedom of speech and press, the crux of the common law on criminal libels remained in force.

Anti-Federalists reiterated that the United States would have the power to legislate against libels of the government or prosecute such libels under common law even if Congress had not enacted a statute. Yet they merely proposed a free press guarantee, even though the state's free press clause accommodated Blackstone's views. Similarly, the Anti-Federalists urged a free press clause to prevent a tax on the press, even though in Massachusetts a free press clause had not prevented enactment of a stamp tax on newspapers or prosecutions for seditious libel. At the Pennsylvania ratifying convention, Wilson insisted that although Congress had no power to pass laws against the press, liberty of the press meant "no antecedent restraint on it," that "every author is responsible" if he attacked the government, and that the proper proceedings would be by a criminal prosecution in a federal court. No one argued that a free press clause would thwart such prosecution or supersede the common law of criminal libels, and no one urged that truth should be a defense to a charge of libel or that the jury should have the power to return a general verdict in libel prosecutions. Nevertheless, the Anti-Federalist members of the Pennsylvania convention urged the addition of a free press clause in language that improved on the state's version. The Pennsylvania minority substituted "shall" for the namby-pamby "ought" that had been conventional ("shall not be restrained by any law of the United States") and used phrasing broad enough to preclude federal prosecution, because "any law" applied to common as well as statutory law.

Richard Henry Lee of Virginia and Melancthon Smith of New York shared the belief that a federal free press clause would prevent Congress from taxing the press. Lee, the likely author of an Anti-Federalist tract that was probably the most widely read in the country, also shared with Smith the remarkable view that Great Britain provided a model for the legal protection of freedom of the press. Patrick Henry had an even more complaisant view of the matter. Although he raged frenetically against all sorts of imagined oppressions that would result from ratification, he told the Virginia ratifying convention that as to liberty of the press, he need say nothing, because members of Congress would not infringe the "palladium of our liberties." That he was sarcastic does not alter the fact that he contributed nothing to an understanding of freedom of the press.

On the ratificationist side, almost no Framers had yet revealed their understanding of the meaning of freedom of the press. Ben Franklin was one. In 1758 he managed Pennsylvania's case before the Privy Council when two men appealed their conviction by the provincial assembly for "highly reflecting" on the government by the publication of seditious libels. In 1789, in an essay on the licentiousness of the press, Franklin urged the use of the cudgels to break the heads of those who used the press for libels. He did not then endorse prosecutions for criminal publications, but he never in his long, active life criticized the law governing the press. William Livingston, a signer from New Jersey, had been the author of a youthful essay in which he wrote that anyone who published "any Thing injurious to his Country" should be convicted for "high Treason against the State." In 1784, however, he criticized the doctrine that truth magnified a libel, but not the doctrine that words can criminally attack a free government. Roger Sherman framed a bill of rights in 1789, with a provision that safeguarded the right to express one's sentiments "with decency," a conventional formulation of the time that ruled out libels—

personal, obscene, blasphemous, or seditious. Similarly, Sherman's proposal that the government should have no power to "restrain the Press" was straight out of Blackstone and meant no prior censorship. James Wilson supported truth as a defense but otherwise endorsed Blackstone's views on the press. Hugh Williamson of North Carolina was the only other Framer who troubled to indicate his understanding of freedom of the press when, in 1788, he invoked England as a model for that freedom. Williamson's friend, James Iredell, who had not been at the Convention, masterminded ratification strategy in their state. Iredell, soon to become a member of the original Supreme Court, agreed with Williamson. Before the ratification of the Bill of Rights, Madison never indicated his dissent from prevailing views. His libertarian interpretations of freedom of the press came later, at the earliest in 1794 and then, fully, during the Sedition Act controversy.

Jefferson, also an advocate of ratification but not a Framer, thought about freedom of the press more than most of his contemporaries. His opinions on the meaning and scope of the freedom of the press reveal the limitations of his time. He once remarked that he did not care whether his neighbor said that there are twenty gods or no God, because "it neither picks my pocket nor breaks my leg." But in drafting a constitution for Virginia in 1776 he considered proposing that freedom of religion "shall not be held to justify any seditious preaching or conversation against the authority of the civil government." And in the same year he helped frame a statute on treasonous crimes, punishing anyone who "by any word" or deed defended the British cause. Apparently, political opinions could break his leg or pick his pocket. What, then, did Jefferson mean by freedom of the press? He, like his contemporaries, supported an unrestricted public discussion of issues, but "unrestricted" meant merely the absence of censorship in advance of publication; although no one needed a government license to express themselves, everyone was accountable under the criminal law for abuse of the right to speak or publish freely.

Jefferson never protested against the substantive law of seditious libel, not even during the later Sedition Act controversy. He directed his protests at that time against national as opposed to state prosecution for verbal crimes. He accepted without question the dominant view of his generation that government could be criminally assaulted merely by the expression of critical opinions that allegedly tended to subvert it by lowering it in the public's esteem. His consistent recognition of the concept of verbal political crimes throughout the Revolution continued in the period of peace that followed.

Jefferson's draft constitution for Virginia in 1783 proposed that the press "shall be subject to no other restraint than liableness to legal prosecution for false facts printed and published." He wrote this as an amendment to the state's free press clause. His amendment explicitly opened the door to criminal prosecutions. Yet he framed that amendment after considering the contrary opinion of his neighbors and constituents, who favored exempting the press from prosecution for any signed opinion or news. Jefferson singled out for prosecution "false facts," or "falsehoods," as he initially phrased his provision, in the face of a more liberal recommendation.

He endorsed prosecution again in 1788 when urging Madison to support amendments to the new federal Constitution, including a guarantee for freedom of the press. "A declaration that the federal government will never restrain the presses from printing anything they please, will not take away the liability of the printers for false facts printed. The declaration that religious faith shall be unpunished," he offered as added assurance, "does not give impunity to criminal acts dictated by religious error." Publication of false facts on political matters seemed the equivalent of an overt crime resulting from a misguided religious conscience. Unlike Blackstone, however, Jefferson implicitly opposed the prosecution of accurate information.

Jefferson received a copy of Madison's proposed amendments

to the Constitution in 1789. He was disappointed not to see the adoption of his recommendation on the press. He liked the proposal on the press, he said, but would be pleased to see the following revision: "the people shall not be deprived or abridged of their right to speak or write or otherwise to publish anything but false facts affecting injuriously the life, liberty, property, or reputation of others or affecting the peace of the confederacy with foreign nations." One can imagine how free the press would have been during the controversies over Jay's Treaty or the Louisiana Purchase had Jefferson's recommendations prevailed and been taken seriously.

Significantly, neither Jefferson nor anyone else in the United States, before 1798, extended their "overt acts" test to freedom of political opinion. Jefferson had devised that test when seeking a way to ensure the free exercise of religion. In his Statute of Religious Freedom, which became law in Virginia in 1786, he declared that

> to suffer the civil magistrate to intrude his powers into the field of opinion, and to restrain the profession or propagation of principles, on supposition of their ill tendency, is a dangerous fallacy, which at once destroys all religious liberty, because he being of course judge of that tendency, will make his opinions the rule of judgment, and approve or condemn the sentiments of others only as they shall square with or differ from his own; that it is time enough for the rightful purposes of civil government for its officers to interfere when principles break out into overt acts against peace and good order.

The overt-acts test applied, in Jefferson's words, only to "opinions in matters of religion," although its principle should have been as relevant in cases of political opinion and had been specifically extended to such cases by many English theorists.

Virginia's legislature did not extend the overt-acts test to proscribed political utterances. In the same year that it enacted the Statute of Religious Freedom, 1786, the legislature passed a law that penalized advocacy that a new state be carved out of the state's boundaries without the legislature's consent. The statute did not bespeak broad understanding in Virginia that freedom of political speech and press included a right to express any principle that did not "break out into overt acts." On the contrary, Virginia embodied the bad-tendency test of utterances by failing to distinguish mere words from the overt criminal act of attempting by unconstitutional means to erect a new government within the state's territory.

Virginia reenacted the same statute in 1792 when it passed an "Act Against Divulgers of False News." The new act of 1792, which covered printers and others who misinformed the people, showed that the legislature believed that it could regulate the press without restraining it in violation of the state's free press clause. Virginia's public law accepted prosecutions for criminal words, and in the later words of a member of the Assembly, "it is known to the people that in a prosecution for libel in Virginia, under the state laws, you can neither plead nor give in evidence the truth of the matter contained in the libel." In other words, Virginia even rejected the bedrock of the Zenger case, that truth is a defense.

No state got rid of the common-law concept of seditious libel. No state gave statutory or constitutional recognition to the overt-acts test embodied in the preamble of Virginia's 1786 statute. No state adopted truth as a defense during the period 1776–1789. If an objective of the Revolution was to repudiate Blackstone's exposition of the common-law restrictions on freedom of expression, how very strange that Americans of the revolutionary generation did not say so. Excepting a few dissident reactions to the Oswald prosecution in Pennsylvania in 1782, Americans accepted the justice of punishing false opinions or malicious scandals against the government.

The history of the reception of the common law during the Revolution tends to establish the acceptance of the Blackstonian definition of liberty of press and speech. Twelve states, including all nine guaranteeing a free press, provided by constitution or statute that the common law of England before the Revolution was to operate with full force unless inconsistent with or repugnant to some other statutory provision. New York, the home of Zenger's case, repudiated its principles. The state constitution of 1777 expressly adopted the common law as of the date of the outbreak of the war with England. In the states where no protection to freedom of speech or press was afforded, there is not even the basis of an implication that it was the intention to get rid of the idea that a republican government may be criminally assaulted by the opinions of its citizens.

In 1787 Massachusetts, which had a free press clause, indicted several people who encouraged and supported Shays's Rebellion; among the defendants were George Brock and Gideon Pond, accused of having published "scandalous, seditious" libels against the government. Although their cases never came to trial, the state did convict Captain Moses Harvey of "seditious and inflammatory words" because he called the legislature "thieves" and urged the closing of the courts. In April 1787 the most important of these cases was tried. A jury convicted Dr. William Whiting before the Supreme Judicial Court sitting in Great Barrington, which was the scene of Whiting's crime. No ordinary libeler, Whiting was chief justice of the Court of Common Pleas of Berkshire County. Shortly before the fall term of his court in 1786, he had written an article, signed Gracchus, in which he censured the government for unjust laws and recommended that a virtuous people who lacked redress of grievances should "disturb the government." When Shays's Rebellion broke out, armed men with whom he sympathized closed his court. After the defeat of Shays at Petersham, the government began its arrests. Whiting was dismissed from his judicial post and convicted of writing a seditious libel; his prison sentence was suspended, but he had to pay a one-hundred-pound fine and post sureties for good behavior for five years. No one claimed that the free press clause of the state constitution stood in the way of a prosecution for seditious libel.

In 1791 Edmund Freeman, a newspaper editor, for having grossly libeled the private life of a member of the legislature, was criminally prosecuted on the theory that his words tended to breach the public peace of the Commonwealth. Attorney General James Sullivan, later Jeffersonian governor of the state, maintained that the constitutional guarantee of a free press meant only the absence of a licensing act; he quoted Blackstone at length to prove the point and urged that licentiousness must be distinguished from liberty. The defendant's attorneys did not challenge Sullivan's principles. Although they did not ask for a ruling that truth was a defense, they denied licentiousness or breach of peace on the part of Freeman and sought to prove the accuracy of his publication. Of the three judges who presided at the trial, none accepted truth as a defense. The jury's verdict was not guilty, but as historian Clyde A. Duniway concluded in *The Development of Freedom of the Press in Massachusetts:* "A judicial construction of liberty of the press in the state had been announced, differing in no wise from the opinions of Chief Justice Hutchinson in 1768 or of the Superior Court of Judicature in 1724. In effect, it was affirmed that the constitutional provision of 1780 was merely declaratory of the law as it had existed for nearly sixty years, with an added prohibition of any possible reestablishment of censorship." This observation has the substantiation of the prosecutions for seditious libel against the editor of the Boston *Independent Chronicle* and the paper's clerk and bookkeeper.

Two states, in the midst of affording a constitutional guarantee to freedom of religion, provided that its exercise could not justify libeling the government. North Carolina's article on religious liberty (1776) contained this qualification: "Provided, that nothing herein contained shall be construed to exempt preachers of treasonable or *seditious discourses*, from legal trial and punishment." If preachers were not exempt from the law of seditious libel, others were not either. South Carolina's equivalent clause (1778) stated: "No person whatever shall speak anything in their religious assembly irreverently or *seditiously* of the government of this State." If people could not speak seditiously of the state in church, they could not do so elsewhere. To the same effect, though not as explicitly, are the qualifying clauses of the religious freedom provisions in the first constitutions of New York, New Hampshire, Massachusetts, Georgia, and Maryland. The last, for example, provided (1776) that no one "under colour of religion . . . shall disturb the good order, peace, or safety of the State, or shall infringe the laws of morality." At common law, an utterance tending to disturb the peace of the state was seditious. New York, New Hampshire, Massachusetts, and Georgia used similar language, prohibiting exercises of religion repugnant to the public peace or safety.

Before 1798, the avant-garde among American libertarians staked everything on the principles of the Zenger case, which they thought beyond improvement. They believed that no greater liberty could be conceived than the right to publish without restriction, if only the defendant could plead truth as a defense in a criminal prosecution for libel, and if the criminality of his words might be determined by a jury of his peers rather than by a judge. The substantive law of criminal libels was unquestioned. But libertarians who accepted Zengerian principles painted themselves into a corner. If a jury returned a verdict of "guilty" despite a defense of truth, due process had been accorded and protests were groundless, because the substance of the law that made the trial possible—criminal responsibility for abuse of the press—had not been challenged.

American acquiescence in the common-law definition of a free press was so widespread that even the frail Zengerian principles seemed daring and novel and had few adherents. Not until 1790 did the first state, Pennsylvania, take the then radical step of adopting those principles, which still left the crux of common law of seditious libel intact. The Pennsylvania provision was drafted by James Wilson, who endorsed Blackstone's definition of liberty of the press. The state constitutional provision of 1790 reflected this proposition, as did state trials before and after 1790.

Delaware and Kentucky followed Pennsylvania's lead in 1792, but elsewhere the status quo prevailed. In 1789 William Cushing and John Adams worried about whether the guarantee of a free press in Massachusetts ought to mean that truth was a good defense to a charge of criminal libel, but they agreed that false publications against the government were punishable. In 1791, when a Massachusetts editor was prosecuted for a criminal libel against a state official, the Supreme Judicial Court divided on the question of truth as a defense but agreed, like the Pennsylvania judges, that the state constitutional guarantee of a free press accommodated common-law crimes of libel.

State pronouncements show no greater enlightenment. None of the first nine states to ratify the Constitution recommended an amendment guaranteeing freedom of speech or press. Indeed, the Pennsylvania ratifying convention, led by Wilson and Thomas McKean, rejected the minority's proposal for such an amendment, and the Maryland convention took no action on any of the amendments recommended by its committee on amendments, one of which declared, "That the freedom of the press be inviolably preserved." The committee had added this explanation: "In prosecutions in the federal courts for libels, the constitutional preservation of the great and fundamental right may prove invaluable." The necessary implication of this is that prosecutions for criminal libel might be maintained in the federal courts under common if not statutory law, and that the free press guarantee would provide some advantage to the defendant—possibly truth as a defense or a general verdict by a jury.

Of the twelve states to ratify the Constitution before Congress drafted the First Amendment in 1789, only the last three, Virginia, North Carolina, and New York, sought to safeguard the expression of political opinion from violation by the new national government. Virginia urged that "among other essential rights the liberty of Conscience and of the Press cannot be cancelled abridged restrained or modified by any authority of the United States." Virginia sought to prevent a concurrent jurisdiction in the national government on the subject of criminal libels. State sovereignty probably dominated Virginia's concern. New York accompanied its ratification of the Constitution in 1788 with the recommendation for an amendment worded "That the Freedom of the Press ought not to be violated or restrained," although no comparable provision existed in that state's constitution. In 1799 a New York court imprisoned a printer, David Frothingham, for four months and fined him for the crime of having copied from another newspaper the criminal innuendo that Alexander Hamilton opposed the republican form of government and worked with the British government to undermine it by trying to buy out the Philadelphia *Aurora*. Hamilton himself instigated the indictment on the theory that the calumny against him had the "dangerous tendency," he said, of destroying the confidence of the people in the leading defenders of the administration. At Frothingham's trial the court refused to allow evidence to prove the truth of his accusation, even though the prosecution consented to permit truth as a defense. Hamilton, the star witness for the state, testified that the Philadelphia *Aurora*, the source of the seditious libel and the country's foremost Jeffersonian newspaper, was hostile to the government of the United States.

As for the states that constitutionally protected freedom of speech or press, the evidence for the period 1776–1791 does not show an understanding that the crime of seditious libel and government by consent of the governed contradicted each other.

State recommendations that a free press clause be annexed

to the Constitution did not signal a different theory about the compass of freedom of political expression. Whatever the Anti-Federalists meant in recommending a bill of rights with a free press clause, they transformed political opinion in the nation. In 1787 a consensus had existed to strengthen the national government. In 1788 a new consensus existed: ratify the Constitution with the understanding that a bill of rights be added to it. A failure to fulfill public expectations could easily have aborted the Constitution by turning public opinion in favor of a second constitutional convention that would have scrapped the Constitution and merely modified the Articles of Confederation. Madison prevented that. He saved the new system and his own political career by his successful struggle in the First Congress for the amendments that became the Bill of Rights.

He described freedom of the press as one of the "choicest" of the "great rights of mankind" and sought vainly to secure it against violation by the states as well as by the United States. But he said nothing in 1789, or earlier, that revealed what he meant by a free press clause. Although he remarked that freedom of the press was unguarded by the British constitution, he meant only that none of the great freedom documents, such as the English Bill of Rights of 1689, mentioned the press. Had he meant more than that and in any way implied a novel view, proof would have appeared in his private correspondence, if not his public speeches. He capitalized on existing public opinion; when he proposed his amendments he did not intend to reshape either the legal or the popular mind. He sought, rather, to satisfy the widespread clamor for protection of rights, rather than provoke fresh controversy. He said explicitly that Congress should "confine" itself to "an enumeration of simple, acknowledged principles." The entire history of the framing and ratification of the free press clause, from 1789 through 1791, suggests nothing new about its meaning or how it was understood. Madison did, however, contribute a crucial verb to the free press clause by providing that it "shall" be inviolable. The Pennsylvania minority had used "shall" but no state constitution and no state ratifying convention had used the imperative voice; previously the weaker "ought" prevailed.

What import did the free press clause possess at the time of its adoption? Its meaning was surely not self-evident. The controversy in the states over the ratification of the Constitution without a bill of rights had revealed little about the substance and scope of a free press, and the debates by the First Congress, which framed the free press clause, illumined even less. Congress debated the clauses on religion, but on the remainder of the First Amendment it considered only whether the right of peaceable assembly vested the people with the power to instruct their representatives on how to vote. In the course of that discussion, Madison made the only recorded statement on the subject of speech or press. If by peaceable assembly, he said, "We mean nothing more than this, that the people have a right to express and communicate their sentiments and wishes, we have provided for it already. The right of freedom of speech is secured; the liberty of the press is expressly declared to be beyond the reach of this Government." Any interpretation of the meaning and compass of the free press drawn from this vague statement would strain credulity.

The state legislatures that ratified the First Amendment offer no enlightenment either. Without the records of their legislative debates, we do not know what the state legislatures understood the free press clause to mean. Other contemporary materials do not help either. Most people undoubtedly cared about protecting freedom of the press, but no one seems to have cared enough to clarify what he meant by the subject upon which he lavished praise. If definition were unnecessary because of the existence of a tacit and widespread understanding of "liberty of the press," only the received or traditional understanding could have been possible. To assume the existence of a generally accepted latitudinarian under-

standing that veered substantially from the common-law definition is warrantless, given the absence of evidence. Any novel definition expanding the scope of free expression or repudiating, even
altering, the concept of seditious libel would have been the subject
of public debate or comment. Not even the Anti-Federalists offered the argument that the clause on speech and press was un-
satisfactory because it was insufficiently protective against prosecutions for criminal defamation of the government. Not even
they urged the truth could be no libel.

Even if we assume that the Framers really intended to impose
upon the national government "an absolute, unqualified prohibition"—there shall be *no* law abridging freedom of the press—we
should recognize that the Framers cared less about giving unqualified immunity to all discourse than they cared for states'
rights and the federal principle. Granting, for the moment, an
intention to render the national government utterly powerless to
act in any way against oral, written, or printed utterances, the
Framers meant the clause to reserve to the states an exclusive
legislative authority in the field of speech and press. Thus, no
matter what the Framers meant or understood by freedom of
speech or press, the national government even under the unamended Constitution could not make speech or press a legitimate
subject of restrictive statutory action. The Framers intended the
First Amendment as an added assurance that Congress would be
limited to the exercise of its enumerated powers, and therefore
they phrased it as an express prohibition against the possibility that Congress might use those powers to abridge freedom of
speech or press. It goes without saying that an express prohibition
on power did not vest or create a new power, previously nonexistent, to abridge speech or press, because, as Madison declared,
the Bill of Rights was not framed "to imply powers not meant to
be included in the enumeration." Because the Senate rejected
the House-approved amendment to prohibit state abridgment of

freedom of speech, the First Amendment left the states free to act against individual expression, subject only to such restraints as might be laid down in state constitutions. The big question persists, however: Even had Congress passed, and the states ratified, an amendment imposing upon the states the same prohibition laid by the First Amendment upon the national government, what did the Framers understand by freedom of speech and freedom of press?

No one can say for certain what the Framers had in mind because there is not enough evidence to justify cocksure conclusions, even though all the evidence points in one direction. Whether the Framers themselves knew what they had in mind is uncertain. At the time of the drafting and ratification of the First Amendment, few among them clearly understood what they meant by the free press clause, and we cannot know that those few represented a consensus. Considerable disagreement existed, for example, on the question of whether freedom of expression meant the right to print the truth about government measures and officials if the truth was defamatory or was revealed for unworthy motives. Disagreement existed, too, about the function of juries in trials for criminal libel. Zengerian principles had few open advocates.

What is clear is that no evidence suggests an understanding that the concept of a free press conflicted with prosecutions of seditious utterances. Freedom of speech and press was not understood to include a right to broadcast sedition by words. The security of the state against libelous advocacy or attach outweighed any social interest in open expression, at least through the period of the adoption of the First Amendment. The thought and experience of a lifetime, indeed the taught traditions of law and politics extending back many generations, supplied an a priori belief that freedom of political discourse, however broadly conceived, stopped short of seditious libel.

The Sedition Act, passed less than seven years after the ratification of the First Amendment, suggests that the generation that framed the amendment did not consider the suppression of seditious libel to be an abridgment of freedom of speech or press. Yet the Framers themselves, whatever they understood freedom of the press to mean, had given the public specific assurances again and again that neither speech nor press could be the subject of repressive legislation by a government bereft of authority on that subject.

The injunction of the First Amendment, therefore, did not imply that a sedition act might be passed without abridging the freedom of the press. Even if a sedition act might not be an abridgment, that was not the main point of the amendment. To understand the Framers' intentions, the amendment should not be read with the focus only on the meaning of "the freedom of the press." It should also be read with the stress on the opening clause: "Congress shall make no law . . . ." In part, the injunction was intended and understood to prohibit any congressional regulation of the press, whether by means of censorship, a licensing law, a tax, or a sedition act. The Framers meant Congress to be totally without power to enact legislation respecting the press, excepting copyright laws. They intended a federal system in which the central government could exercise only specifically enumerated powers or powers necessary and proper to carry out the enumerated ones. Thus, no matter what was meant or understood by freedom of the press, the national government, even in the absence of the First Amendment, could not make the press a legitimate subject of regulation. The objective of the amendment was to quiet public apprehension by offering further assurance that Congress would be limited to the exercise of its delegated powers. The First Amendment could not possibly have enhanced the powers of Congress; it did not add to them a previously nonexisting power.

The amendment protected the *freedom* of the press, not the press. The freedom of the press and of political discourse generally had so widened in scope that seditious libel had become a rather narrow category of verbal offenses against government, government officials, and government policies. To be sure, the legal definition of seditious libel remained what it had been from the time of Sergeant William Hawkins, author in 1716 of a major treatise on criminal law, to Lord Chief Justice William Murray, earl of Mansfield: malicious, scandalous falsehoods of a political nature that tended to breach the peace, instill revulsion or contempt in the people against their government, or lower their esteem for their rulers. But prosecutions for criticism of government were infrequent, and the press was habitually scurrilous. Governments forbore, realizing that prosecutions might fail or backfire because critics represented strong factions and, often, influential men. Moreover, public opinion, except in times of crisis like Shays's Rebellion, tended to distrust an administration that sought to imprison its critics. The press could not have endured as aspersive and animadversive as it was without public support. For the most part people understood that scummy journalism unavoidably accompanied the benefits to be gained from a free press. People seem also to have understood that critics vented unfavorable opinions in order to excite a justifiable contempt for the government; to prosecute those critics seemed to immunize from criticism public officials who had probably deserved to be disliked or distrusted.

The actual freedom of the press bore slight relation to the fact that, as a legal concept, freedom of the press was a cluster of constraints. The law threatened repression; yet the press conducted itself as if the law scarcely existed. In 1799 Madison observed that in England, despite the common law on the press and "the occasional punishment of those who use it with a freedom offensive to the government," all knew that "the freedom exercised by the press, and protected by the public opinion far exceeds the limits prescribed by the ordinary rules of law." The English press, said Madison, criticized the ministry "with peculiar freedom," and during elections for the House of Commons the calumnies of the press raged. The American press enjoyed at least as much freedom.

When the Framers of the First Amendment provided that Congress shall not abridge the freedom of the press, they could only have meant to protect the press they knew and as it operated at the time. In effect, they constitutionally guaranteed the freedom of the press as it existed and was then practiced. They did not adopt the limited conception of it found in the law or in the views of libertarian theorists. By freedom of the press, the Framers meant a right to engage in rasping, corrosive, and offensive discussions on all topics of public interest. The English common-law definition had become unsuitable, and American libertarian theory had not caught up with press practice. Government in the United States derived from the people, who reserved a right to alter it, and the government was accountable to the people. That required a broader legal concept of freedom of the press than existed in England, where the monarch was a hereditary ruler not accountable to the people and the House of Lords was also not elected or accountable. Glimmerings of a broader libertarian theory existed but did not systematically emerge until 1798.

In a sense, the constitutional guarantee of freedom of the press signified nothing new. It did not augment or expand freedom of the press. It recognized and perpetuated an existing condition. Freedom of the press meant, in part, an exemption from prior restraints and continued to mean that. The practical problem faced by writers and printers dealt with subsequent punishment for licentious use of the right to publish without prior restraint. The press remained subject to the common law despite a constitutional guarantee, but the threshold of public tolerance had significantly widened. Thus freedom of the press meant more than just freedom from prior restraint. It meant the right to criticize harshly the government, its officers, and its policies as well as to comment on matters of public concern. The right to criticize and comment no longer implied a decent or temperate fashion. It meant a free-dom for foul-tempered, mean-spirited expression. For practical purposes what the law called malice did not signify just a nasty disposition; it signified ill-will, an intention to provoke readers or listeners to hope for damage to the public weal or to the government. But this broad view of the matter rests on inference. Within a decade of the ratification of the First Amendment, merely mild criticism, certainly not scorching billingsgate, resulted in convictions under the Sedition Act, showing a wholly different understanding of freedom of the press. The public revulsion that shortly manifested itself in Jefferson's election suggests, however, that the Federalists of 1798–1800 misread the free press clause.

Freedom of the press signified not only freedom from prior restraints; if politics allowed, it also meant responsibility under the law for damaging publications. It meant, too, that the press enjoyed a preferred position in the American constitutional scheme because of its special relation to popular government. The electoral process would have been a sham if voters did not have the assistance of the press in learning what candidates stood for and what their records showed about past performance and qualifications. A free press was becoming indispensable to the existence of a free and responsible government. Even Blackstone conceded, "The liberty of the press is indeed essential to the nature of a free state." Its essentiality derived also from the fact that the press had become the tribune of the people by sitting in judgment on the conduct of public officials. A free press meant the press as the Fourth Estate or, rather, in the American scheme, an informal or extraconstitutional fourth branch that functioned as part of the intricate system of checks and balances that exposed public mismanagement and kept power fragmented, manageable, and accountable. Freedom of the press had accrued still another function that intimately associated it with a free state, meriting its constitutional protection. The cliché that it was the bulwark of liberty, "essential," as the Massachusetts constitution asserted, "to the security of freedom in a state," meant that the existence of various personal liberties depended at least in part on the vigilance of the press in exposing unfairness, inequality, and injustice. Freedom of the press had become part of the matrix for the functioning of popular government and the protection of civil liberties.

It does not necessarily follow that the Framers desired to give the utmost latitude to expression. The First Amendment did not embody an absolute because not all speech is free speech, or, to put it another way, there are several classes of speech or of publication, some of which were not intended to be categorized under the rubric of "freedom of speech" or freedom of the press. Did the Framers intend that the federal mails should be open to pornographic materials or that a speaker should be free to incite violence directly and immediately against the United States? Did they intend that knowingly false, malicious, and damaging calumnies against the government should be free? Madison himself was "inclined to think that absolute restrictions in cases that are doubtful, or where emergencies may overrule them, ought to be avoided." If the Framers did not intend that all speech, without exception, should be free, the crucial question is, where did they intend to draw the line between speech that was constitutionally protected and speech that was not? The eighteenth century did not provide answers.

In 1798, however, a sudden breakthrough occurred in American libertarian thought on freedom of political expression. The change was abrupt, radical, and transforming. The Sedition Act, which was a thrust in the direction of a single-party press and a monolithic party system, triggered a libertarian surge among the Republicans. The result was the emergence of a new body of libertarian thought.

The Federalists in 1798 believed that true freedom of the press would benefit if truth—*their* truth—were the measure of freedom.

Their infamous Sedition Act was, in the later words of Gilbert and Sullivan, the true embodiment of everything excellent. It was, that is, the very epitome of libertarian thought since the time of Zenger's case. Everything that the libertarians had ever demanded was incorporated in the Sedition Act: a requirement that criminal intent be shown; the power of the jury to decide whether the accused's statement was libelous as a matter of law as well as of fact; and truth as a defense, which was an innovation not accepted in England until 1843. By every standard the Sedition Act was a great victory for libertarian principles of freedom of the press—except that libertarian standards abruptly changed.

The Sedition Act provoked the Republicans to develop a new libertarian theory. It began to emerge in 1798 when Congressmen Albert Gallatin, John Nicholas, Nathaniel Macon, and Edward Livingston argued against the enactment of the sedition bill. It was further developed by defense counsel, most notably George Blake, in Sedition Act prosecutions. It reached its most reflective and systematic expression in tracts and books that unfortunately became rare and little known. The main body of original Republican thought on the scope, meaning, and rationale of the First Amendment was expressed in George Hay's tract *An Essay on the Liberty of the Press;* in Madison's *Report* on the Virginia Resolutions for the Virginia House of Delegates; in the book *A Treatise Concerning Political Enquiry, and the Liberty of the Press*, by Tunis Wortman of New York; in John Thomson's book *An Enquiry, Concerning the Liberty and Licentiousness of the Press;* and in St. George Tucker's appendix to his edition of Blackstone's *Commentaries*, a most significant place for the repudiation of Blackstone on the liberty of the press. Of these works, Wortman's philosophical book is preeminent as the only equivalent on this side of the Atlantic to John Milton and John Stuart Mill.

The new libertarians abandoned the straitjacketing doctrines of Blackstone and the common law, including the recent concept of a federal common law of crimes. They scornfully denounced the no-prior-restraints definition. Said Madison: "this idea of the freedom of the press can never be admitted to be the American idea of it," because a law inflicting penalties would have the same effect as a law authorizing a prior restraint. "It would seem a mockery to say that no laws shall be passed preventing publications from being made, but that laws might be passed for punishing them in case they should be made." As Hay put it, the "British definition" meant that a man might be jailed or even put to death for what he published, provided that no notice was taken of him before he published.

The old yardstick for measuring the scope of freedom was also rejected by the new libertarians. "Liberty" of the press, for example, had always been differentiated from its "licentiousness," which was the object of the criminal law's sanctions. "Truth" and "facts" had always divided the realm of lawfulness from "falsehoods," and a similar distinction had been made between "good motives" and "criminal intent." All such distinctions were now discarded on the grounds that they did not distinguish and therefore were not meaningful standards that might guide a jury or a court in judging an alleged verbal crime. The term "licentiousness," wrote Thomson, "is destitute of any meaning"; it was used, according to him, by those who wished "nobody to enjoy the Liberty of the Press but such as were of their own opinion." The term "malice," in Wortman's view, was invariably confused with mistaken zeal or prejudice. It was merely an inference drawn from the supposed evil tendency of the publication itself, and just a further means of punishing the excitement of unfavorable sentiments against the government even when the people's contempt of the government was richly deserved. The punishment of "malice," or intent to defame the government, concluded Madison, necessarily struck at the right of free discussion, because critics intended to excite unfavorable sentiments. Finding criminality in the tendency of words was merely an attempt to erect public "tranquility . . . upon the ruins of Civil Liberty," wrote Wortman.

The wholesale abandonment of the common law's limitations on the press was accompanied by a withering onslaught against the constrictions and subjectivity of Zengerian principles. The Sedition Act, Hay charged, "appears to be directed against false hood and malice only; in fact . . . there are many truths, important to society, which are not susceptible of that full, direct, and positive evidence, which alone can be exhibited before a court and a jury." If, argued Gallatin, the administration prosecuted a citizen for his opinion that the Sedition Act itself was unconstitutional, would not a jury, composed of the friends of that administration, find the opinion "ungrounded, or, in other words, false and scandalous, and its publication malicious? And by what kind of argument or evidence, in the present temper of parties, could the accused convince them that his opinions were true?" The truth of opinions, the new libertarians concluded, could not be proved. Allowing "truth" as a defense and thinking it to be a protection for freedom, Thomson declared, made as much sense as letting a jury decide which was "the most palatable food, agreeable drink, or beautiful color." A jury, he asserted, could not give an impartial verdict in political trials. Madison agreed, commenting that the "baleful tendency" of prosecutions for seditious libel was "little diminished by the privilege of giving in evidence the truth of the matter contained in political writings."

The renunciation of traditional concepts reached its climax in the assault on the idea that there was such a thing as a crime of seditious libel. That crime, Wortman concluded, could "never be reconciled to the genius and constitution of a Representative Commonwealth." He and the others constructed a new libertarianism, genuinely radical because it broke sharply with the past and advocated an absolute freedom of political expression. One of the major tenets of this new libertarianism was that a free government cannot be criminally attacked by the opinions of its citizens. Hay, for example, insisted that freedom of the press, like chastity, was either "absolute" or did not exist. Abhorring the very concept of verbal political crimes, he declared that a citizen should have a right to "say everything which his passions suggest; he may employ all his time, and all his talents, if he is wicked enough, to do so, in speaking against the government matters that are false, scandalous and malicious," and yet he should be "safe within the sanctuary of the press" even if he "condemns the principle of republican institutions . . . censures the measures of our government, and every department and officer thereof, and ascribes the measures of the former, however salutary, and conduct of the latter, however upright, to the basest motives; even if he ascribes to them measures and acts, which never had existence; thus violating at once, every principle of decency and truth."

In brief, the new libertarians advocated that only "injurious conduct," as manifested by "overt acts" or deeds, rather than words, should be criminally redressable. They did not refine this proposition except to recognize that the law of libel should continue to protect private reputations against malicious falsehoods. They did not even recognize that under certain circumstances words may immediately and directly incite criminal acts.

This absolutist interpretation of the First Amendment was based on the now familiar, but then novel and democratic, theory that free government depends for its very existence and security on freedom of political discourse. The scope of the amendment, according to this theory, is determined by the nature of the government and its relation to the people. Because the government is the people's servant, exists by their consent and for their benefit, and is constitutionally limited, responsible, and elective, it cannot, said Thomson, tell the citizen: "You shall not think this or that upon certain subjects; or if you do, it is at your peril." The concept of seditiousness can exist only in a relation based on inferiority, when people are subjects rather than sovereigns and their criticism implies contempt of their master. "In the United States," Madison declared, "the case is altogether different." Coercion or abridgment of unlimited political opinion, Wortman explained, would violate the very "principles of the social state"—by which he meant a government of the people. Because such a government depended upon popular elections, all the new libertarians agreed that the widest possible latitude must be maintained to keep the electorate free, informed, and capable of making intelligent choices. The citizen's freedom of political expression had the same scope as the legislator's, and had the same reasons behind it. That freedom might be dangerously abused, but the people, if exposed to every opinion, would decide on men and measures wisely.

This brief summary of the new libertarianism barely does justice to its complexity and sophistication but suggests its boldness, originality, and democratic character. The new libertarianism developed, to be sure, as an expediency of self-defense on the part of a besieged political minority that was struggling to maintain its existence and its right to function unfettered. But the new libertarians established, virtually all at once and in nearly perfect form, a theory justifying the rights of individual expression and of opposition parties. That the Jeffersonians in power did not always adhere to their new principles does not diminish the enduring nobility and rightness of those principles. It proves only that Jeffersonians set the highest standards of freedom for themselves and posterity. Their legacy was the idea that there is an indispensable condition for the development of free people in a free society: the state must be bitted and bridled by a bill of rights that is to be construed in the most generous terms and whose protections are not to be the playthings of momentary majorities. That legacy deepened and enriched American libertarian theory, but it did not surmount the resistance of the law. Ultimate victory in the courts and statutes belongs to Alexander Hamilton's restatement of Zengerian principles.

Hamilton, a supporter of the Sedition Act and of prosecutions for criminal libel, believed that the law of libel should be governed by the principles of the Zenger case, in order to protect the legitimate freedom of the press. In 1804 he was permitted by his Jeffersonian opponents in New York, who were then in power, to make political capital and legal history by advocating these old principles. The state indicted Harry Croswell, an obscure Federalist editor, for the common-law crime of seditious libel against President Jefferson. Croswell's crime was his publishing of the accusation that Jefferson had paid to have George Washington denounced as a traitor and John Adams as an incendiary. Chief Justice Morgan Lewis, a Jeffersonian, refused Croswell the opportunity of introducing evidence to prove the truth of his statements. In instructing the jury, Lewis told the jurors that their only duty was to determine whether the defendant had in fact published the statements as charged; that they must leave the court, as a matter of law, the determination of the statements' libelous character. Lewis, in other words, charged the jury that the law of New York was the law as laid down by Chief Justice James DeLancey in the Zenger case.

On the appeal of Croswell's conviction, before the highest court of the state, Alexander Hamilton championed the cause of freedom of the press. That freedom, he said (in words that were even more restrictive than those of the Sedition Act), "consists in the right to publish, with impunity, truth, with good motives, for justifiable ends, though reflecting on government, magistracy, or individuals." The Sedition Act itself did not require proof of "good motives, for justifiable ends," but Hamilton's position seemed a shining standard of libertarianism when compared with the reactionary views of Chief Justice Lewis—or of the prosecutor, Attorney General Ambrose Spencer, another Jeffersonian. Spencer argued from Blackstone (not Tucker's version) and declared that a libel, even if true, was punishable because of its dangerous tendency. The former prosecutor had become a member of the Supreme Court of

Judicature by the time it decided the case. Had Spencer not been ineligible to participate in the decision, the repressive opinion reexpressed by Chief Justice Lewis would have commanded a majority. Instead, the court divided evenly, two against two. The opinion of Judge James Kent expressed Hamilton's position.

In the following year, 1805, the state legislature enacted a bill that allowed the jury to decide the criminality of an alleged libel and that permitted truth as a defense, if published "with good motives and for justifiable ends." That standard, which prevailed in the United States until 1964, effectively protected freedom of the press.

CHAPTER SIX

The Right to Keep and Bear Arms

THE Second Amendment is the only provision of the Bill of Rights that has a preamble. The amendment states: "A well regulated Militia, being necessary to the security of a free State, the right of the people to keep and bear Arms, shall not be infringed." Does the amendment vest a personal right to keep and bear arms? If it had no preamble it would undoubtedly vest such a right. But the preamble is present, and it creates problems about the amendment's meaning. Some scholars mistakenly believe that the function of the preamble is to restrict the keeping and bearing of arms to members of the militia. If that were so, the preamble signifies that the amendment refers to a collective right of the people rather than a personal right of individuals. But the amendment does protect individuals.

The theory that the amendment vests only a collective right to bear arms interprets the Second Amendment as if it protects the power of the states to maintain militias. Of course, the collective right also supports the powers of the national government, for Congress has the authority to provide for the calling forth of the militia to execute the laws of the Union. Moreover, Congress has the power to provide for organizing, arming, and disciplining the militia, while the president is commander-in-chief of the militia of the states when called "into the actual Service of the United States." Nevertheless, a substantial scholarly literature maintains that those militias exist, at least in part, as a shield against tyranny by the national government. That notion is bizarre, even loony, in character; the Constitution does not authorize the state militias to make war against the national government. However, a right to insurrection theoretically exists to correct intolerable and systematic abuses. Americans embrace the doctrine that a right of revolution is a natural right; some state constitutions even endorse that right. The Constitution nevertheless brands as treason overt acts or the levying of war against the United States. Militia members do not possess firearms for the purpose of committing treason, not even under the collective right theory of the Second Amendment.

According to the collective right theory, militia members may bear arms, but the possession of firearms by persons other than the police or military has no constitutional warrant. The collective right suggests, too, that the maintenance of militias is the prime reason for constitutionally allowing an armed public. Under this antiquated view of the Second Amendment, individuals have a right to bear arms only so that they may serve in the militia. Many influential authorities, including the American Bar Association and the American Civil Liberties Union, believe that the amendment does not vest a personal right or, rather, that it endorses a collective right. As the President's Commission on Law Enforcement and Administration of Justice declared in 1967, "The U.S. Supreme Court and lower Federal courts have consistently interpreted this Amendment only as a prohibition against Federal interference with State militias and not as a guarantee of an individual's right to keep or carry firearms."

Believing that the amendment does not authorize an individual's right to keep and bear arms is wrong. The right to bear arms is an individual right. The military connotation of bearing arms does not necessarily determine the meaning of a right to bear arms. If all it meant was the right to be a soldier or serve in the military, whether in the militia or the army, it would hardly be a cherished right and would never have reached constitutional status in the Bill of Rights. The "right" to be a soldier does not make much sense. Life in the military is dangerous and lonely, and a constitutionally protected claim or entitlement to serve in uniform does not have to exist in order for individuals to enlist if they so choose. Moreover, the right to bear arms does not necessarily have a military connotation, because Pennsylvania, whose constitution of 1776 first used the phrase "the right to bear arms," did not even have a state militia. In Pennsylvania, therefore, the right to bear arms was devoid of military significance. Moreover, such significance need not necessarily be inferred even with respect to states that had militias. Bearing arms could mean having arms. Indeed, Blackstone's *Commentaries* spoke expressly of the "right to have arms." An individual could bear arms without being a soldier or militiaman.

The right to bear arms is by no means unlimited. Public regulation may specify the kinds of weapons that are lawful and the conditions under which those weapons may be kept; but no regulation may subvert the right itself. The very language of the amendment is evidence that the right is a personal one, for it is not subordinated to the militia clause. Rather the right is an independent one, altogether separate from the maintenance of a militia. Militias were possible only because the people were armed and possessed the right to be armed. The right does not depend on whether militias exist.

To say that the Supreme Court does not endorse a personal right to bear arms misleads, although the Court has a restrictive view of the Second Amendment. In 1939, in *United States v. Miller*, the Court asserted an interpretation that does not fully endorse the right to keep and bear arms and falls short of fulfilling the intentions of the amendment's Framers. The Court ruled that individuals may justify reliance on the amendment in keeping only such arms as a member of a militia might use—shotguns, rifles, and handguns, but not a short-barreled or sawed-off shotgun (under eighteen inches in length), a machine gun, a bazooka, a cannon, or assault rifles. As a G.I. in World War II, I can recall having to qualify on a variety of weapons, including short-barreled shotguns; the Court was not well informed on government-issued weapons. And the leading text writer on constitutional law, Laurence Tribe, has wrongly endorsed the Court's 1939 decision as a correct interpretation of the Second Amendment.

The right to have arms is an inheritance from England, as are so many American rights. In 1689, when England adopted its Bill of Rights, which endorsed the right to bear arms, that right was already centuries old. In the twelfth century Henry II had obligated all freemen to possess certain arms, and in the next century Henry III required every subject aged fifteen to fifty, including even landless farmers, to own a weapon other than a knife. Crown officers periodically inspected subjects to be certain that they were properly armed. The reason for this requirement was that in the absence of a regular army and a police force, which was not established until 1829, every man had to do his duty at watch and ward, standing guard by day and night in order to confront and capture suspicious persons. Every subject also had an obligation to protect the king's peace and assist in the suppression of riots. In the event of a crime, every man had to join in the "hue and cry"—summoning aid and joining the pursuit of anyone who resisted arrest or escaped from custody.

In 1671 Parliament for the first time enacted a statute that deprived almost all Englishmen of the right to have arms. The new measure was a game act that so steeply raised the property qualifications on the right to hunt that possession of firearms became illegal except for the wealthy few. Charles II undertook further measures to disarm his Whig opposition, and in 1686 his successor, James II, favored Catholic subjects and infuriated Protestants by banning their firearms. Royal attempts to control weapons convinced Englishmen that they must have a right to possess firearms. As a result, they resolved to take steps necessary to ensure their right to keep and bear arms. The gentry were in the vanguard of the movement for that right. The martyr Algernon Sydney stated a cliché when declaring that "swords were given to men that none might be slaves, but such as know not how to use them." So, too, political theorists John Trenchard and Walter Moyle believed that the surest way to preserve the liberties of the people is to arm them.

In 1689 the Glorious Revolution deposed James II and installed as his successor William of Orange, who pledged to protect the right of Protestants to have their firearms. Parliament demanded that protection for individuals by initially recommending: "It is necessary for the publick Safety, that the Subjects which are Protestants, should provide and keep Arms for their common Defence. And that the Arms which have been seized, and taken from them, be restored." A revised version more concisely recommended: "That the Subjects, which are Protestants, may provide and keep Arms, for their common Defence." The final version, which became law, stated: "That the Subjects which are Protestants may have Arms for their defence suitable to their Conditions, and as allowed by Law." England, incidentally, was about 98 percent Protestant. The qualification concerning what the law allowed was intended to prevent the king from ever again disarming subjects, because Parliament determined what was allowed by law. Parliament had made clear the fact that the right belonged to individuals.

On the eve of the American Revolution, English authorities reaffirmed the right of individuals to have firearms. Blackstone's *Commentaries*, the work most frequently cited by Americans, stated that the right "to have" arms was indispensable "to protect and maintain inviolate the three great and primary rights of personal security, personal liberty, and private property." James Burgh, whose *Political Disquisitions* of 1774 was probably more influential in America than John Locke's work, wrote most elaborately about the right to be armed. More than one hundred pages of Burgh's two-volume work focus on the history and values of an armed public in preference to a standing army. He spoke in the accustomed hyperbole when declaring that subjects without arms were no better off than slaves. "A militia-man," he observed, "is a free citizen; a soldier, a slave for life." He quoted Andrew Fletcher, the Scottish Whig, when arguing that ownership of firearms distinguished a free individual from a slave; arms, he wrote, "are the only true badges of liberty." Burgh explicitly supported the right of Americans to be armed in order to preserve their freedoms.

In 1780 the recorder of London, a judge who was the mayor's legal adviser, responded authoritatively to a query from a military group asking for his legal opinion on their right to keep firearms and parade with them. He declared:

> The right of his majesty's Protestant subjects, to have arms for their own defence, and to use them for lawful purposes, is most clear and undeniable. It seems, indeed, to be considered, by the ancient laws of this kingdom, not only as a right, but as a duty; for all the subjects of the realm, who are able to bear arms, are bound to be ready, at all times, to assist the sheriff, and other civil magistrates, in the execution of the laws and the preservation of the public peace. And that right, which every Protestant most unquestionably possesses, *individually*, may, and in many cases, must, be exercised *collectively*, is likewise a point which I conceive to be most clearly established by the authority of judicial decisions and ancient acts of parliament, as well as by reason and common sense. [emphasis added]

In 1782 Granville Sharp, who also supported the American cause, denied the loyalty of any Englishman who failed to defend the right of individuals to have arms. Richard Price, another pro-American Englishman, writing in 1784, expressed his belief that the prevalence of arms in America accounted for its strength. "Free states," he wrote, "ought to be bodies of armed citizens, well regulated and well disciplined, and always ready to turn out, when properly called upon, to execute the law, quell riots, and to keep the peace. Such, if I am rightly informed, are the citizens of America." Price admired the "hardy yeomanry" of America, "all nearly on a level—trained to arms,—instructed in their rights." The right of Englishmen to keep and bear arms was treasured. It was not a pro forma right; it was both an individual and a collective one.

Colonial charters and enactments guaranteed English settlers in the New World the rights of Englishmen, indeed, "all the rights of natural subjects, as if born and abiding in England." If the charter of a colony neglected to make such a provision, colonial laws like the Massachusetts Body of Liberties of 1641 remedied the deficiency. In 1720 Richard West, counsel for the Board of Trade, said that the English common law and all statutes enacted before the settlement of a colony were part of its law, and he added, "Let an Englishman go where he will, he carries as much of law and liberty with him, as the nature of things will bear." That law included, of course, the English Bill of Rights of 1689, which protected the right of Protestants to have weapons.

New World conditions also encouraged the keeping and use of firearms. Hunting was necessary for meat. Strangers could be dangerous. In some areas, foreign enemies, especially the Spanish and French, might attack frontiers, and Indians presented another widespread menace, requiring colonists to be armed.

Every American colony enacted laws that necessitated both militia service and guard duty by all able-bodied men. Excepting conscientious objectors, slaves, and clergymen, all men aged sixteen to fifty or sixty (depending on the colony) were subject to service in the militia. Men who were disabled were obligated to hire substitutes in their places. Several colonies required not only those eligible for militia service but all men, including indentured servants, to provide firearms for themselves and for members of their households. Several towns and a few colonies required subjects to go about armed even on the way to church. Internal dangers and the possibility of insurrection, as well as foreign and Indian dangers, explain such legislation.

After Bacon's Rebellion of 1676 in Virginia, the royal governor, Sir William Berkeley complained, "How miserable that man is who governs a people when six parts of seaven [seven] at least are Poore Endebted Discontented and Armed [sic]." The right to have arms was so basic that regulation seeking to control it acknowledged it. For example, an act of the Virginia legislature noted that liberty had been granted to "all persons to carry their arms wheresoever they go." Because that liberty seemed "prejudicial to the peace," the legislature amended the statute, but the amendment simply showed how entrenched was the right to bear arms. The new act penalized assemblages of five or more armed men, and the governor conceded the right of an individual to keep and bear arms for his own protection and use.

Arms were common. An English minister, on the eve of the American Revolution, wrote: "Rifles, infinitely better than those imported, are daily made in many places in Pennsylvania, and all the gunsmiths everywhere constantly employed. In this country, my lord, boys, as soon as they can discharge a gun, frequently exercise themselves therewith, some a fowling and others a hunting. The great quantities of game, the many kinds, and the great privileges of killing making the Americans the best marksmen in the world." He added that a thousand of these American riflemen "would cut to pieces ten thousand of your best troops." In 1768, when the British reinforced their military in Boston, *A Journal of the Times*, a newspaper founded to popularize American grievances, urged Americans to retain their arms and reminded them that the English Bill of Rights had recognized the "privilege of possessing arms." The paper declared, "It is a natural right which the people have reserved to themselves, confirmed by the Bill of Rights, to keep arms for their own defence." So, too, John Adams quoted Serjeant-at-Law William Hawkins's *Pleas of the Crown*, a widely used and authoritative treatise of 1716 and often reprinted, regarding the right: "Here every private person is authorized to arm himself" for his own defense. Similarly, Samuel Adams quoted Blackstone on the personal right to bear arms.

Americans abhorred large standing armies. During the controversy with Britain, James Wilson condemned George III's use of the military in the colonies as part of a plan "of reducing the colonies to slavery." Jefferson scathed the king for having used "large bodies of armed forces" to carry out his policies, and in the Declaration of Independence, Jefferson indicted him for having kept "among us in time of peace, standing armies without the consent of our legislatures." Jefferson also proposed that his state constitution should stipulate, "No freeman shall be debarred the use of arms." Like Washington and others of his class, Jefferson had a large collection of rifles and pistols; he was an amateur gunsmith who invented interchangeable firearms parts. In a letter to a fifteen-year-old nephew, Jefferson praised the importance of "the gun" as contributing to "boldness, enterprise and independence of mind," concluding: "Let your gun therefore be the constant companion of your walks." Sentiments like these explain the intense American reaction to General Thomas Gage's appropriation of private arms in Boston. The Revolution began with the British effort to seize the arms and ammunition in Lexington, Massachusetts, and the gunpowder stored in Williamsburg, Virginia.

The Articles of Confederation (1777), our first national constitution, provided that every colony shall always keep up a well-regulated and disciplined militia but said nothing about the individual's right to be armed for his own purposes. Any such protection would therefore have to derive from state law. Several state constitutions provided for militias, but the Massachusetts constitution of 1780 protected the right "to keep and bear arms." That could have included a personal right as well as a right to bear arms to provide for the common defense. But only the Pennsylvania constitution of 1776 referred to the people's right to bear arms "for the defence of themselves." That reference to the people's right did not mean the people collectively or society at large. Both the First and Fourth Amendments, on the rights of free expression and freedom from unreasonable searches and seizures, refer to the people's right, meaning the right of individuals. Free speech is a personal right, not a collective one. So, too, Pennsylvania's reference to the right to bear arms meant that the right was a personal right. Pennsylvania, which was the first to employ the phrase "the right to bear arms," did not even have a militia clause in its constitution. Consequently, the right had to belong to individuals. The Pennsylvania provision rested cheek-by-jowl with the rights to free speech and press, also personal rights. Vermont a year later, in 1777, copied Pennsylvania's language in its constitution.

Virginia's Declaration of Rights of 1776, which was quite different, stated: "That a well-regulated militia, composed of the body of the people, trained to arms, is the proper, natural, and safe defense of a free State; that standing armies in time of peace, should be avoided, as dangerous to liberty; and that in all cases the military should be under strict subordination to, and governed by, the civil power." This provision notably lacked endorsement of an individual's right to possess arms, though Virginians were in fact armed and furnished their own weapons when serving in the militia. Moreover, the language of the Virginia provision allowed for the interpretation that the right to bear arms was connected with the maintenance of the militia. North Carolina constitutionally safeguarded the right to bear arms for the purpose of defending the state, while Massachusetts offered that protection on behalf of "the common defense."

Massachusetts in 1780 was the first to use the phrase "to keep and bear arms." John Adams was responsible for it; in his monumental two-volume defense of the constitutions of the states, he argued that arms in the hands of individual citizens are subject to their discretion to defend themselves. The town of Northampton in Massachusetts protected the individual's right when it resolved that the people have a right to keep and bear arms for their own defense as well as for the common defense. Other Massachusetts towns had similar provisions. Maryland failed to mention the right to bear arms but provided for a well-regulated militia in its constitution. That language allowed for the interpretation that the right to bear arms was connected with the maintenance of a militia. The other states had no declaration of rights until after the Revolution.

During the debate over the ratification of the Constitution, Anti-Federalists, who opposed ratification of the Constitution, maintained that Congress might fail to provide weapons for the militias, a strange argument in view of the fact that individual members of the militia possessed their own weapons. When, for example, Congress enacted the Uniform Militia Act of 1792, it referred to the militias as consisting of "every free able-bodied male citizen of the respective states" aged eighteen to forty-five, and it added that every militia member should provide his own arms: "That every citizen so enrolled . . . shall . . . provide himself with a good musket or firelock, a sufficient bayonet, belt, two spare flints, and a knapsack, a pouch with a box therein to contain not less than twenty-four cartridges . . . each cartridge to contain a proper quantity of powder and ball."

During the controversy over the ratification of the Constitution, however, Anti-Federalists expressed concern that Congress might neglect the militias. The minority at the Pennsylvania ratifying convention, drawing largely on their own state's constitution, proposed various amendments that constituted a bill of rights, one of which spoke to the issue of an individual's having arms: "That the people have a right to bear arms for the defense of themselves and their own State, or the United States, or for the purpose of killing game; and no law shall be passed for disarming the people or any of them, unless for crimes committed, or real danger of public injury from individuals." The remainder of the provision repudiated standing armies and demanded civil control over the military. Richard Henry Lee of Virginia wrote elaborately on the same theme in nationally circulated essays.

The proposal of the Pennsylvania minority expressed a common sentiment shared by Federalists as well. In Massachusetts, for example, Theodore Sedgwick argued that "a nation of freemen who know how to prize liberty and who have arms in their hands" could not be subdued. Samuel Adams urged that the Constitution should expressly provide that it could never be construed "to prevent the people from keeping their own arms." Lexicographer Noah Webster agreed, observing that the national government would not be able to enforce unjust laws because the "whole body of the people are armed" and could defeat any federal army. The right to bear arms has frequently been associated with romantic notions like Webster's. Still, the belief was widespread that the right of individuals to be armed was associated with personal liberties and the existence of a free society. As Zachariah Johnson informed the Virginia ratifying convention, the people's liberties were safe because they "are not to be disarmed of their weapons. They are left in full possession of them." Similarly John Dewitt, an Anti-Federalist writer, argued that a well-regulated militia "composed of the yeomanry of the country have ever been considered as the bulwark of a free people"—a characteristic American idea of English origin. Blackstone, for example, had earlier voiced the thought that tyranny had no chance where the people are armed.

When James Madison in 1789 proposed to the First Congress the amendments to the Constitution that became the Bill of Rights, he included one that drew on his own state's constitution: "The right of the people to keep and bear arms shall not be infringed; a well armed, and well regulated militia being the best security of a free country; but no person religiously scrupulous of bearing arms shall be compelled to render military service in person." Madison did not make the right to bear arms dependent on serving in a militia. In his notes for the speech in which he urged Congress to recommend constitutional amendments, he wrote of those amendments, "They related 1st to private rights," and he referred to the English Declaration of Rights, which protected the right of individual Protestant subjects to have arms. In his personal correspondence Madison referred to his proposals as "guards for private rights." The recommendation that he made concerning individual ownership of arms sprang from his belief that "the greater danger to liberty is from large standing armies." In *The Federalist*, No. 46, Madison alluded to "the advantage of being armed, which the Americans possess over the people of almost every other nation." Elsewhere, he said, rulers feared having an armed public.

Madison proposed to interlineate his amendments at the appropriate points in the Constitution, for example, inserting the right to bear arms not next to the militia clause but, rather, in "article 1st, Section 9, between clauses 3 and 4"—in other words, immediately after the guarantee of the writ of habeas corpus and the prohibition of bills of attainder, which respected personal liberty. He did not recommend his proposed amendments as a separate bill of rights, though he spoke of a "bill of rights" when referring to the amendments collectively.

Roger Sherman of Connecticut believed that amendments were unnecessary and opposed interspersing them within the main body of the Constitution because that would leave the mistaken impression that the Framers had signed a document that included provisions not of their composition. He and some other members of the House thought that the amendments should be lumped at the end of the document, and they also believed that the matter of form was so trifling that the House should not squander its time debating the placement of the amendments. Sherman therefore urged that the amendments should be appended as a supplement to the Constitution—and thus the Bill of Rights achieved its significant collective form, with the right to bear arms as the Second Amendment ratified by the states.

The Framers also recognized that the states' neglect of their militias required a dependable alternative, a professional army but one kept under strict control. Thus, the Constitution authorizes Congress to raise and support military forces, though no appropriation for them may last more than two years, and civil control over them is assured because the president is commander-in-chief and Congress has not only responsibility for the governance of the military but also the power to declare war. So, too, Congress provides for organizing, maintaining, and training the military, although the states retain control over the appointment of its officers. Madison expressed the Framers' view when he supported national control over state militias on the theory that only they, if effective, could make possible the avoidance of a standing army or minimize its size. George Mason agreed. Like Jefferson, he argued that to keep the army small the state militias should be well prepared for public defense under centralized federal authority. Thus, Congress was empowered to summon the militias "to put the laws of the Union in execution."

Soon after Madison had recommended constitutional amendments, Tench Coxe, a Federalist partisan, published an influential essay on proposed amendments to the Constitution. In the leading Philadelphia newspaper, he wrote that because civil rulers might be tyrannical and the military might abuse its powers, a bill of rights would be helpful. Coxe knew that one of Madison's recommendations was an amendment that authorized the right of the people to keep and bear "their private arms," and Coxe argued that the "powers of the sword are in the hands of the yeomanry of

America," whom he identified as the members of the state militias. "Who are the militia?" he asked, and responded that they were "ourselves." The sword was not in the hands of government, state or federal, but "in the hands of the people." All adult males were required to own arms and serve in the militia, which, as Elbridge Gerry of Massachusetts stated, existed "to prevent the establishment of a standing army, the bane of liberty."

Tench Coxe's reference to "the people" did not refer to them in a collective sense or as society at large. "The people" was a term commonly used to mean the right of individuals, and as indicated above, the First Amendment protects the right of the people to freedom of expression and the Fourth protects the right of the people to be free from unreasonable searches and seizures; and each clearly refers to a personal right.

Newspapers throughout the nation reprinted Coxe's essay. Sending a copy of it to Madison, Coxe wrote that he thought his remarks might have a good effect on public opinion. Madison, who agreed, expressed indebtedness for Coxe's cooperation. Federalists advanced arguments like Coxe's in part to claim that no bill of rights was necessary—that is, so long as the people were armed, no government could limit their freedom. Anti-Federalists nevertheless insisted that the Constitution should not be ratified unless its advocates pledged that the new government would present to the states amendments consisting of a bill of rights. The Anti-Federalists felt apprehensive because the Constitution provided for a standing army, causing them to demand that one amendment to it should stipulate that every man had a right to be armed. Patrick Henry argued in the Virginia ratifying convention that the only defense of the people against an army controlled by Congress was the militia. "The great object," he thundered, "is that every man be armed. . . . Every one who is able may have a gun." Henry appeared not to be arguing here for the right of individuals to be armed for their own protection, because in context his words showed that he was thinking of members of the militia. Neverthe-less, as a newspaper in Charleston, South Carolina, observed, a well-regulated militia is "composed of the freeholders, citizen and husbandman, who take up arms to preserve their property as *indi-viduals,* their rights as freemen" (emphasis added).

George Mason at the Virginia ratifying convention reminded his listeners that the British had sought to disarm the Americans as "an effectual way to enslave them," and to this end had ne-glected the militias. "Who are the militia?" he asked and, like both Coxe and Henry, replied, "They consist now of the whole people." In response to complaints such as those made by the Pennsylvania minority, Federalist partisans of ratification insisted that under the proposed Constitution the people could not be disarmed.

Of the states that recommended amendments to the Constitu-tion, four urged an amendment guaranteeing the right of individ-uals to bear arms. New Hampshire, the ninth state to ratify, was the first to make that recommendation with a proposal that said: "Congress shall never disarm any Citizen, unless such as are or have been in Actual Rebellion." New York followed suit with the proposition that the people "have a right to keep and bear arms" and that a well-regulated militia, including "the body of the people capable of bearing arms" is the "proper" defense of a free state. Two other states, Rhode Island and North Carolina, used similar language in recommending amendments to the Constitution.

The second amendment in effect prevents the national govern-ment from destroying the militias of the states and preserves a personal right that is centuries old. Joel Barlow, the Connecticut wit and writer, in 1792 sagely declared that a tyrant disarms his subjects to "degrade and oppress" them, knowing that to be un-armed "palsies the hand and brutalizes the mind," with the result that people "lose the power of protecting themselves." But arms privately held can be dangerous to society. President George Washington once reminded Congress that "a free people ought not only be armed but disciplined." He meant that the militias of his time had to be under military authority or, in the frequently used phrase, should be "a well-regulated" militia. However, we no longer depend on militias, a fact that in some respects makes the right to keep and bear arms anachronistic. An armed public is not the means of keeping a democratic government responsible and sensitive to the needs of the people. As the Supreme Court said in 1951, in *Dennis v. United States:* "That it is within the power of Congress to protect the government of the United States from armed rebellion is a proposition which requires little discussion." Whatever hypothetical value there might be, the Court said, in the notion that a "right" against revolution exists against dictatorial government "is without force where the existing structure of the government provides for peaceful and orderly change." The Court added, "We reject any principle of government helplessness in the face of preparations for revolution, which principle, carried to its logical conclusion, must lead to anarchy."

The right to keep and bear arms still enables citizens to protect themselves against law breakers, but it is a feckless means of opposing a legitimate government. The so-called militias of today that consist of small private armies of self-styled superpatriots are entitled to their firearms but deceive themselves in thinking they can withstand the United States Army. The Second Amendment as they interpret it feeds their dangerous illusions. Even so, the origins of the amendment show that the right to keep and bear arms has an illustrious history connected with freedom even if it is a right that must be regulated.

CHAPTER SEVEN

The Fourth Amendment:
Search and Seizure

BEFORE the American Revolution, the right to be secure against unreasonable searches and seizures had slight existence. British policies assaulted the privacy of dwellings and places of business, particularly when royal revenues were at stake. The right to be taxed only by the consent of representatives of one's choice was the great right whose violation helped cause the Revolution. British attempts to enforce tax measures by general searches also occasioned deeply felt resentments that damaged relations between England and the American colonies and provoked anxious concerns that later sought expression in the Fourth Amendment. That amendment repudiates general warrants by recognizing a "right of the people to be secured in their persons, houses, papers, and effects, against unreasonable searches and seizures." Any warrant that is vague about the persons, places, or things to be searched violates the specificity required by the command of the amendment that warrants shall issue only "upon probable cause, supported by oath or affirmation, and particularly describing the place to be searched, and the persons or things to be seized."

The Fourth Amendment would not have been possible but for

British legal theory, which Britons of North America inherited and cherished as their own. The Fourth Amendment emerged not only from the American Revolution; it was a constitutional embodiment of the extraordinary coupling of Magna Carta to the appealing fiction that "a man's house is his castle." That is, the amendment resulted from embellishments on the insistence, which was rhetorically compelling, though historically without foundation, that government cannot encroach on the private premises of the individual subject. What mattered was not what Magna Carta actually said but what people thought it said or, rather, what it had come to mean. What also mattered was the inspiring imagery that swelled the sense of freedom in the ordinary subject. William Pitt expressed it best in a speech in Parliament in 1763 when he declaimed: "The poorest man may, in his cottage, bid defiance to all the forces of the Crown. It may be frail; its roof may shake; the wind may blow through it; the storm may enter; the rain may enter; but the King of England may not enter; all his force dares not cross the threshold of the ruined tenement." The maxim about a man's home goes back at least to the early sixteenth century, and it was repeated with such frequency that it became a cliché.

The first person to link the privacy of one's home to a right secured by Magna Carta seems to have been Robert Beale, clerk of the Privy Council, in 1589. Beale asked rhetorically what had happened to Chapter 39 of the great charter when agents of a prerogative court, acting under its warrant, could "enter into mens houses, break of their chests and chambers" and carry off as evidence whatever they pleased. That Beale's statement was historically unsound is unimportant compared to the fact that he took a feudal document, which protected the barons, and converted it into a constitution for everyone. Creative glosses like Beale's would make Magna Carta a talismanic symbol of freedom, subjecting all authority, including the royal prerogative, to the rule of law. Construing Chapter 39 to be a ban on general warrants helped make a myth that would transform American thinking about privacy rights against government.

One of the most strategically significant places for the belief that a legal writ authorizing a legitimate search must be specific as to persons and places was Sir Edward Coke's *Institutes of the Laws of England*. From the Puritans of Massachusetts Bay, who studied Coke, to Jefferson, who admiringly said of him that "a sounder Whig never wrote" nor one more learned "in the orthodox doctrines of British liberties," Americans regarded Coke as the foremost authority on English law. Coke's authority legitimated the belief that Magna Carta outlawed general warrants based on mere surmise.

Sir Matthew Hale, another seventeenth-century legal luminary, analyzed the problem of search and seizure more systematically in his book *History of Pleas of the Crown*. Hale criticized warrants that failed to name the persons sought for crime or the places to be searched for evidence of theft. He even laid a basis for the concept of probable cause by maintaining that the person seeking a warrant should be examined judicially under oath so that the magistrate could determine whether he had grounds for his suspicions. Hale also asserted that an officer who made an illegal search and arrest was liable to a civil suit for false arrest.

Beale, Coke, and Hale did not stand alone. They invented a rhetorical tradition against general searches, which Serjeant-at-Law William Hawkins and Sir William Blackstone continued. But the rhetoric was empty; the tradition had almost no practical effect. Beale's views leaked out through officially licensed publications that sought to refute him, but he did not dare publish his manuscript. Coke's own report of Semayne's Case of 1604 refuted the accuracy of the propositions that he advanced in his *Institutes*, for in that case the court had held that although a man's house is his castle, his privacy did not extend to his guests or to "cases where the King is a party." Coke's own experience shows best that the maxim represented only the frailest aspiration, not the law in cases involving the crown. In 1634, when Coke lay dying, the Privy Council's agents searched his home and law chambers for seditious papers and seized not only the manuscripts of his voluminous legal writings but also his valuables, including money, keys, jewelry, his will, and a poem addressed to his children. Hale's book was not even published until sixty years after his death. Pitt spoke in a losing cause; Parliament enacted the excise bill whose passage he so eloquently opposed as dangerous to the liberty of the subject. Blackstone made only a passing remark against general searches; his target, rather, was the general arrest warrant.

In fact, English law was honeycombed with parliamentary enactments that relied on warrantless general searches and on general warrants for their enforcement, including hue and cry methods, sumptuary legislation, and measures aimed at punishing theft, at governing crafts and guilds, bankruptcy, and military recruitment, as well as measures preventing illegal imports, manufactures, poaching, counterfeiting, unlicensed printing, seditious or heretical publications, and nonpayment of taxes. Taxes extended to hearths and stoves, to estates, to intoxicating drinks, to such consumer goods as salt, candles, soap, glass, and papers, and to foreign goods. The king's customs office and his exchequer depended on both the general warrant and warrantless searches as ordinary means of collecting royal revenues, and Parliament passed dozens of pieces of legislation to provide the taxes and authorize general searches. Promiscuously broad warrants allowed officers to search wherever they wanted and to seize whatever they wanted, with few exceptions. An eighteenth-century collection of warrants contains 108 authorized by secretaries of state or by the King's Bench for the period 1700–1763, all but two of them general warrants. The frequency in the use of general warrants increased substantially as time went by.

General searches pervaded colonial law as well as Great Britain's. Colonial legislation on search and seizure either copied Britain's or derived from it; until 1750, all handbooks for justices of the peace, who issued warrants, contained or described only general warrants. William Cuddihy asserts that a "colonial epidemic of general searches" existed—indeed, that until the 1760s, "a man's house was even less of a legal castle in America than in England," because the Americans, when adapting English models, ignored exceptions. As a result, warrants in America tended to give their enforcers every discretion. The Fourth Amendment would not emerge from colonial precedents; rather, it would repudiate them; or, as Cuddihy states, "The ideas comprising the Fourth Amendment reversed rather than formalized colonial precedents. Reasonable search and seizure in colonial America closely approximated whatever the searcher thought reasonable."

Officers or their informants merely reported that an infraction of the law had occurred or that they had a suspicion, not that a particular person was suspected or that a particular place contained evidence of a crime; on the basis of such an assertion, a magistrate issued a warrant. Neither custom, judicial precedent, nor statutory law provided that he should interrogate the seeker of the warrant to determine the credibility of the suspicion or of his informant. The magistrate made no independent determination of his own whether a basis existed for the warrant other than the assertion that a crime had occurred or that a basis existed for some suspicion. Magistrates had an obligation to provide the warrant, rather than deny one or limit one to a particular person or place that was suspected. Probable cause in a modern sense did not exist; not even a reasonable basis for suspicion existed. Although an officer seeking a warrant more than likely would designate a particular person or place if known to him in advance, he need not do so to get a warrant.

Colonial documents contain no suggestion of a right against general warrants. Recommendations for them were common in the manuals that had been published in the colonies before 1763 for the use of justices of the peace. American legal writers even relied on the great authority of Coke and Hale as proof that an officer could forcibly enter a person's house.

In 1756, however, the province of Massachusetts enacted extraordinary legislation that reversed the tide of practice by abandoning general warrants in favor of warrants founded on some elements of particularity. The legislation of 1756 marked a watershed in Massachusetts law, indeed in Anglo-American law. As Cuddihy states, beginning in 1756 "Massachusetts invented the statutory prototypes of the Fourth Amendment." The new legislation resulted mainly from a vehement public clamor against provincial legislation of 1754. The excise act of that year authorized tax collectors to interrogate any subject, under oath, on the amount of rum, wine, and other spirits he had consumed in his private premises in the past year and taxed it by the gallon. Pamphleteers condemned the measure in hyperbolic language. John Lovell, a Boston schoolmaster whose pupils had included John Hancock and Samuel Adams, called it "the most pernicious attack upon *English Liberty* that was ever attempted," and the minister of the Brattle Church imagined that he saw a revival of the Inquisition, requiring people to incriminate themselves. One pamphlet, *The Monster of Monsters* (the excise act), so savagely attacked the legislature that it condemned the tract as seditious libel, and imprisoned its seller and the suspected author. That author warned of the danger of the tax collector having power to break chains, doors, locks, and bolts, and invade bedchambers and winecellars. In the torrent of tracts against excise, it was described as a violation of Magna Carta, of the sanctity of one's home as his castle, and of natural rights.

The provincial impost laws, which employed general warrants for enforcement, provoked such animosity that mobs threatened impost officers who tried to collect duties on uncustomed imports—foreign goods on which the duties had not yet been paid. The hostility for general searches intensified as the result of two other practices. In 1755 the royal governor of Massachusetts issued ex officio writs of assistance, a type of general warrant that became enormously controversial. And, since 1745, British impressment gangs, operating under a general warrant provided by the governor, had been invading private premises as well as taverns and inns, seeking to kidnap able-bodied men for service in the Royal Navy.

Enforcement of the excise and impost acts by general searches, the introduction into the province of writs of assistance, and the general warrants for impressment gangs produced a hullabaloo that the enactments of 1756 sought to allay. The excise and impost acts of that year required an element of probable cause only in the sense that the informant had the obligation to swear on oath that he knew that an infraction of the law had occurred in the place specified. The justices of the peace, who issued the warrants, had no discretion to deny a petition for one; magistrates made no independent judgment whether adequate grounds for the issuance of the warrant existed. The informant, however, had to swear that he had "just cause" for his sworn statement. The officer conducted his search during the daytime, only in the designated location, and could seize only things or objects regulated by the statute that he enforced by his search and seizure. The statutes of 1756 also authorized warrants of arrest for named individuals. "The British, in short," Cuddihy states, "introduced writs of assistance into Massachusetts just as the colony itself was rejecting the legal assumptions on which they were based."

The writ of assistance was a type of general warrant deriving its name from the fact that a crown official possessed the legal authority to command the assistance of a peace officer and the assistance, if necessary, of all nearby subjects, in his execution of the writ. Parliament authorized writs of assistance by an act of 1662 that empowered the Court of Exchequer to issue a writ to a customs official who, with the assistance of a constable, could enter "any

House, shop, Cellar, Warehouse or Room or other Place, and in Case of Resistance to break open Doors, Chests, Trunks and other packages, there to seize" any uncustomed goods. The writ, once issued, lasted for the life of the sovereign, and therefore constituted a long-term hunting license for customs officers on the lookout for smugglers and articles imported in violation of the customs laws. In 1696 Parliament extended the act of 1662 to the colonies, but because the Court of Exchequer did not operate in America, no way existed to enforce it. Massachusetts, however, had extended the jurisdiction of its own high court to include the jurisdiction of the Court of Exchequer, thus opening the possibility of enforcement in that colony and in New Hampshire, which copied Massachusetts.

When George II died, the high court of Massachusetts, presided over by Chief Justice Thomas Hutchinson, heard Paxton's Case, a petition by a customs officer for a new writ of assistance. James Otis, Jr., appeared, he said, on behalf of the inhabitants of Boston to oppose issuance of the writ. Any fastidious legal historian must acknowledge that Otis's argument compounded mistakes and misinterpretations. In effect, he reconstructed the fragmentary evidence buttressing the rhetorical tradition against general searches, and he advocated that any warrant other than a specific one violated the British constitution. That Otis distorted history is pedantic; he was making history. By an old British technique, which Coke himself had practiced, Otis sought the creation of new rights while asserting strenuously that they had existed nearly from time immemorial. His speech electrified young John Adams, who was present in the courtroom and took notes. As an old man, fifty-six years later, he declared, "Otis was a flame of Fire! . . . Then and there was the first scene of the first Act of Opposition to the arbitrary Claims of Great Britain. Then and there the child Independance [sic] was born." On the night before the Declaration of Independence, Adams asserted that he consider "the Argument concerning Writs of Assistance . . . as the Commencement of the Controversy, between Great Britain and America." Adams's reaction to Otis's speech is so important because a straight line of progression runs from Otis's argument in 1761 to Adams's framing of Article XIV of the Massachusetts Declaration of Rights of 1780 to Madison's introduction of the proposal that became the Fourth Amendment.

We have Adams's brief notes of Otis's speech made at the time of the speech and the fuller version made by Adams not long after. The fuller version takes about twenty minutes to be read by comparison with the original, which took Otis four to five hours to deliver. He denounced the writ of assistance as an instrument of "slavery," of "villainy," of "arbitrary power, the most destructive of English liberty and [of] the fundamental principles of the constitution." The writ reminded him of the kind of power that had cost one English king his head and another his throne. The only legal writ, Otis asserted, was a "special warrant directed to specific officers, and to search certain houses, &c. especially set forth in the writ may be granted . . . upon oath made . . . by the person, who asks [for the warrant], that he suspects such goods to be concealed in those very places he desires to search." In the recent past, Otis alleged, only special warrants existed, authorizing search of particularly named houses, and they were issued only after the complainant had taken an oath to support his suspicion; "special warrants only are legal," he concluded. He condemned writs of assistance because they were perpetual, universal (addressed to every officer and subject in the realm), and allowed anyone to conduct a search in violation of the essential principle of English liberty that a peaceable man's house is his castle. A writ that allowed a customs officer to enter private homes when he pleased, on bare suspicion, and even to break locks to enter, was void. An act of Parliament authorizing such writs was void because it violated the British constitution, and courts should not issue an unconstitutional writ.

Otis lost his case. The writs issued, but Americans found a cause and a constitutional argument. In 1762 the Massachusetts legislature passed a bill that would have required all writs to be as specific as the warrants used by provincial officers to enforce the excise and impost acts, but the royal governor vetoed the bill. Thereafter, crowds frequently prevented enforcement or "rescued" goods seized by customs agents. In a 1766 case a Boston merchant, believing that in "Whig Boston Whig furies made Whig law," used force to barricade his home, as a crowd gathered. Officers prudently decided that calling on bystanders to assist as a *posse comitatus* might result in a loss of life—their own—and abandoned efforts to enforce the writ. After a rescue in Falmouth (Portland), Maine, the governor conceded that public opposition had effectively paralyzed the use of writs to conduct searches and seizures. Attorney General William DeGrey of Britain decided that the act of Parliament that authorized the writ allowed them to issue only from the Court of Exchequer, whose writ did not run in America. In London, far more than DeGrey's technical opinion damaged the principle of general warrants.

John Wilkes's studied insults of the king's speech in 1763, in the forty-fifth number of his journal *North Britain*, provoked massive retaliation by the government. One of the secretaries of state issued general search warrants for the arrest of everyone connected with *North Britain*, No. 45. Crown agents enforcing the warrants had unfettered discretion to search, seize, and arrest anyone as they pleased. They ransacked printer's shops and houses, and arrested forty-nine persons, including Wilkes, a member of Parliament, his printer, publisher, and booksellers. The officers seized his private papers for incriminating evidence after a thorough search; thousands of pages and scores of books belonging to persons associated with him were also seized. The House of Commons voted that *North Britain*, No. 45, was a seditious libel and expelled Wilkes, and he was eventually convicted and jailed. The government found, however, that it had mounted a tiger; no one since the time of John Lilburne, more than a century earlier, had proved to be such a resourceful and pugnacious antagonist. Wilkes had quickly filed suits for trespass against everyone, from flunky to minister, connected with the warrant that had resulted in his undoing; others who had suffered searches and arrest filed similar suits. A legal donnybrook ensued. On one hand, the government, based on about two hundred informations, had engaged in mass arrests and searches, and on the other, the victims filed a couple of dozen suits for trespass and false imprisonment. The Wilkes case became the subject of sensational controversies, angry tracts, and confusing trials. Wilkes would emerge from his prosecution a popular idol, the personification of constitutional liberty to Englishmen on both sides of the Atlantic. Although he focused mainly on the dangers of general warrants and the seizures of private papers, some of his supporters also championed freedom of the press and the right against self-incrimination.

In the colonies, "Wilkes and Liberty" became a slogan that patriot leaders exploited in the service of American causes. In New York, for example, Alexander McDougall, a leader of the Sons of Liberty who had censured a bill to provision the king's troops, posed as an American Wilkes and turned his imprisonment into a theatrical triumph, as had Wilkes, while his supporters used the number 45, the seditious issue of *North Britain*, as a symbol of their cause. On the forty-fifth day of the year, for example, forty-five Liberty Boys dined on forty-five pounds of beef from a forty-five-month-old bull, drank forty-five toasts to liberty—liberty of the press, liberty from general warrants, liberty from compulsory self-accusation, liberty from seizure of private papers—and after dinner marched to the jail to salute McDougall with forty-five cheers. On another festive liberty day, forty-five songs were sung to him by forty-five virgins, every one of whom, according to some damned Tory, was forty-five years old. The Fourth Amendment, as well as the First and the Fifth, owes something to the Wilkes cases. Unlike Paxton's Case, the Wilkes cases filled the columns of American newspapers from Boston to Charleston.

The first of these cases, *Huckle v. Money*, established the doctrine, traceable at least to Hale, that crown officers are liable to damage suits for trespass and false imprisonment resulting from unlawful search. Chief Justice Charles Pratt said, when charging the jury, "To enter a man's house by virtue of a nameless warrant, in order to procure evidence, is worse than the Spanish Inquisition, a law under which no Englishman would wish to live an hour." The jury awarded three hundred pounds in damages, an excessive sum for the deprivation of a journeyman printer's liberty for six hours, but on appeal Pratt ruled that the small injury done to one of low rank meant nothing compared to the "great point of the law touching the liberty of the subject" invaded by a magistrate of the king in an exercise of arbitrary power "violating Magna Carta, and attempting to destroy the liberty of the kingdom, by insisting on the legality of this general warrant." In *Wilkes v. Wood* (1763), Pratt presided over a similar trial and engaged in similar rhetoric ("totally subversive of the liberty of the subject"); the jury awarded damages of a thousand pounds to Wilkes, who later got an award of four thousand pounds against the secretary of state who had issued the warrant. In fact, the government paid a total of about one hundred thousand pounds in costs and judgments.

In one of the Wilkes cases, the government appealed to England's highest criminal court, the King's Bench, and Lord Mansfield, the chief justice, agreed that the warrants in the Wilkes cases were illegal. Although the common law, he observed, authorized arrests without warrant and Parliament had often authorized searches and arrests on the basis of general warrants, in this case no circumstance existed justifying warrantless searches or arrests and no act of Parliament was involved. Accordingly, a secretarial warrant, based on executive authority, leaving discretion to the endorsing officer, "is not fit." Mansfield thought that the "magistrate ought to judge; and should give certain directions to the officer"—a foundation for what later emerged as probable cause.

The victories of the Wilkesites encouraged other victims of secretarial warrants in seditious libel cases to bring suits for damages. The most important of those cases, *Entick v. Carrington* (1765), resulted in an opinion by Chief Justice Pratt, now Lord Camden, which the Supreme Court of the United States would describe as "one of the landmarks of English liberty." Victory for the government, Camden declared, would open the secret cabinets of every subject whenever the secretary of state suspected someone of seditious libel. The law required no one to incriminate himself, for that would be "cruel and unjust" to the innocent and guilty alike, "and it should seem, that search for evidence is disallowed upon the same principle." Camden held that neither arrests nor general warrants could issue on executive direction, and he implied that evidence seized on the authority of such a warrant could not be used without violating the right against self-incrimination. Similarly, the Supreme Court in 1886 ruled that the Fourth and Fifth Amendments have an "intimate relation" and "throw great light on each other."

In 1764 and 1765 the House of Commons irresolutely debated whether general warrants should be regarded as illegal, and in 1766 it repeated the debate. The upshot was the passage of three resolutions, not statutes, that revealed a victory for the narrow position of Mansfield rather than the broader one of Camden. The Commons condemned general warrants in all cases involving arrests but condemned paper searches only in cases where the executive branch searched in connection with the crime of seditious libel. Secretarial search warrants in treason cases remained legal. The resolutions of 1766 left in place the elaborate system of warrantless searches when authorized by Parliament and of general searches when undergirded by statutory authority. The House of

Lords rejected a proposal from the Commons that would have restricted general search warrants to cases of treason and felony. Thus, the reforms resulting from the judicial decisions and parliamentary resolves of 1763 to 1766 conformed to the prime directive of English's law of search and seizure: even promiscuously general searches did not violate the liberty of the subject or infringe the maxim about a man's home so long as Parliament had laid down the law.

On the other hand, the Wilkes cases and the parliamentary debates unleashed a lot of rhetoric that went far beyond the reality of actual judicial holdings and legislative resolves. Americans were practiced in making a highly selective use of authorities and other sources that suited their needs. They could even turn Blackstone, that spokesman for parliamentary supremacy, into an advocate of constitutional restraints. In Britain, Englishmen often spoke thunderously but thrashed about with a frail stick; in America they threw the stick away, contenting themselves with the thunder. They found a lot of it in Pitt, Camden, Wilkes, and in "Father of Candor," all of whom they knew well. Father of Candor was the author of a little book of 1764, "on libels, warrants, and the seizure of papers," which had gone through seven editions by 1771. He condemned general warrants as "excruciating torture," and he urged that search warrants should be specific as to persons, places, and things and should be sworn on oath. That was the sort of thing Americans could exploit when confronted by Parliament's determination to impose writs of assistance on the colonies.

Twenty years after the Townshend Acts of 1767, James Madison, speaking in the First Congress on the occasion of recommending the amendments to the Constitution that became the Bill of Rights, recalled that the legislative power constituted a great danger to liberty; in Britain, he noted, "they have gone no farther than to raise a barrier against the power of the Crown; the power of the Legislature is left altogether indefinite." Notwithstanding grandiose rhetoric against general warrants, Parliament in 1767 superseded its act of 1696, which had extended writs of assistance to America without providing a mechanism for granting them under the seal of the Court of Exchequer. The Townshend Acts provided that the highest court in each colony possessed authority to issue writs of assistance to customs officers to search where they pleaded for prohibited or uncustomed goods and to seize them.

The Townshend Acts, therefore, expanded the controversy over writs of assistance to all of the thirteen colonies. What had been a local controversy, centering mainly on Boston, spread continentwide. Only the two colonies, Massachusetts and New Hampshire, that had previously experienced the writs, continued to issue them, although the mobs "liberated" seized goods as often as not. Elsewhere the provincial high courts stalled, compromised, or declined the writ. The New York court issued the writ but deviated from the exact language authorized by Parliament, with the result that the customs officers refused to execute the deviant writ and sought one in the correct form. It was not forthcoming; indeed, applications kept getting lost or mislaid. In 1773, five years after the first application, the New York court held that "it did not appear to them that such Writs according to the form now produced are warranted by law and therefore they could not grant the motion."

Something like that happened in several colonies. In Connecticut, Chief Justice Jonathan Trumbull and Judge Roger Sherman refused to be rushed into making a decision on the application for a writ. Trumbull remarked privately that he and his associates were not clear "the thing was in itself constitutional." Chief Justice William Allen of Pennsylvania was more forthcoming. In 1768 he declared that he had no legal authority to issue the writ. Customs officials sent Allen's statement to Attorney General William De-Grey in London for his opinion. He thought that Allen would see the error of his ways if confronted by a copy of the writ, a copy of the act of Parliament, and a copy of the opinion of England's attorney general. On a new application for the writ backed by English legal artillery, Allen replied that he would grant "particular [not general] writs whenever they are applied for on oath." The customs agent must swear he knew or had reason to believe that prohibited or uncustomed goods were located in a particular place. Allen's groping toward a concept of probable cause as well as specific warrants became clearer as customs officials vainly persisted to engage his cooperation.

In South Carolina a judge, explaining his court's refusal to issue the writ, stated that it "trenched too severely and unnecessarily upon the safety of the subject secured by Magna Charta." After five years of persistence, however, the customs officials got a writ of assistance in South Carolina. In Georgia, where the judges declined to issue the writ, they said they would authorize a search warrant for a specific occasion if supported by an affidavit.

Virginia issued writs of assistance in 1769 but undermined the process by annexing a degree of specificity obnoxious to the customs office. Its agent had to swear an oath in support of his suspicion and could obtain a writ only for a special occasion and for a limited time. The Virginia judges alleged that the writ sought by the customs office under the Townshend Acts was "unconstitutional" because it allowed the officer "to act under it according to his own arbitrary discretion." The customs office appealed to England for support against the Virginia court. Attorney General DeGrey had to acknowledge that he knew of "no direct and effective means" to compel a provincial court to award a writ of assistance. He asserted that judges might be impeached for contumacious refusal to execute an act of Parliament, but he did not know how to proceed in such a case. He preferred to believe that Virginia's judges had acted out of a mistaken understanding of the law. Virginia's court, however, remained contumacious.

Between 1761 and 1776 a glacial drift in American legal opinion can be discerned toward increased reliance on specific warrants. Law books, including manuals of the justices of the peace, began to recommend specific warrants in some cases; most, however, relied on general warrants, as did American judges in actual practice. American rhetoric and reality diverged. John Dickinson's *Letters of a Pennsylvania Farmer*, which circulated in every colony, censured general warrants and repeated the cliché about a man's home being his castle; but Dickinson did not recommend specific warrants in their place or condemn any warrantless searches. Americans never spoke of a right to privacy as such, although they understood the concept and, like their British counterparts, expressed outrage over the possibility that customs agents might "break the rights of domicil," "ransack houses," and "enter private cabinets" or "secret repositories." The best known of such remarks, which received considerable publicity in the colonies, was that of the Boston Town Meeting of 1772, which complained:

> Thus our houses and even our bed chambers, are exposed to be ransacked, our boxes chests & trunks broke open ravaged and plundered by wretches, whom no prudent man would venture to employ even as menial servants; whenever they are pleased to say they suspect there are in the house wares &c for which the dutys have not been paid. Flagrant instances of the wanton exercise of this power, have frequently happened in this and other seaport Towns. By this we are cut off from that domestick security which renders the lives of the most unhappy in some measure agreeable. Those Officers may under colour of law and the cloak of a general warrant break thro' the sacred rights of the Domicil, ransack mens houses, destroy their securities, carry off their property, and with little danger to themselves commit the most horred murders.

In all the American rhetoric, only one writer seems to have urged special warrants in place of warrantless searches and general warrants. Some writers revealed that their objection lay against a parliamentary empowerment rather than one by their own assemblies. General searches continued in the colonies as the prevailing standard, not the specific warrants used in Massachusetts. Nevertheless, some colonies became more familiar with specific warrants and even used them in various kinds of cases. Cuddihy states:

> The failure of colonial legislatures and courts to abandon general searches for domestic consumption locates the "American Revolution Against Writs of Assistance" in clearer perspective. Appeals to Magna Carta notwithstanding, the typical searches actually authorized by judges and legislators in the colonies had remained as general as those in the writs of assistance rejected by local judiciaries and intellectuals. Damning such searches under British auspices was one thing; renouncing them oneself was another matter. In Connecticut, where judicial resistance to those writs was most extreme in 1769, the local code of that year included an impost enforced by search warrants strongly resembling the writs. The same conclusion applied equally to Pennsylvania. Had Allen, Trumbull, or any of the Connecticut newspaper essayists wished to attack general searches on principle alone, they need have looked no further than Pennsylvania and Connecticut, for local session laws and judicial search warrants had read like writs of assistance throughout the histories of those colonies. Only when those searches loomed from a foreign quarter and threatened political autonomy was the civil libertarian threat posed by them announced.

In sum, one need only add that Otis's extraordinary forensic effort of 1761 on behalf of specific warrants, which a Boston newspaper printed in 1773, bore scarce fruit elsewhere, at least not until well after the Revolution.

The Declaration of Independence, however, spurred the definition of American ideals. Although that document, which itemized the king's perfidies, failed to say anything about search and seizure or even about general warrants, it inspired the making of the first state constitutions. In the midst of war, Americans engaged in the most important, creative, and dynamic constitutional achievements in history, among them the first written constitutions and the first bills of rights against all branches of government. Their provisions on search and seizure are significant because they distilled the best American thinking on the subject, constituted benchmarks to show the standard by which practice should be measured, and provided models for the Fourth Amendment.

Virginia, the oldest, largest, and most influential of the new states, anticipated the Declaration of Independence by adopting a Declaration of Rights on June 12, 1776, and completed its constitution before the month ended. Article X of the Declaration of Rights provided: "That general warrants, whereby any officer or messenger may be commanded to search suspected places without evidence of a fact committed, or to seize any person or persons not named, or whose offence is not particularly described and supported by evidence, are grievous and oppressive, and ought not to be granted." Obviously this provision is a substantial step in the direction of specific warrants. Its force is weakened by the wishy-washy climax: certain warrants are grievous, not illegal, and "ought" not be granted, but the language imposes no prohibition against them. The concept of probable cause is stunted with respect to searches but considerably broader with respect to arrests. The search may be conducted, presumably under warrant, if the fact of a crime has been established, though no need exists to show a connection between the crime and the place to be searched, and there is no reference to a need for specificity with respect to the things to be seized. Moreover, the warrant need not be based on a sworn statement. Probable cause must be shown for the criminal involvement of the persons to be arrested; far more than mere suspicion is required for an arrest.

As the first search and seizure provision in any American constitution, Virginia's had egregious deficiencies as well as pioneering attainments. That the attainments might have been better still is evident from the fact that in a committee draft of May 27, the property to be seized had to be "particularly described." We do not know why that clause was omitted in the final draft. We do know that the provision could have been far worse or altogether nonexistent. George Mason, who provided the original draft of the Declaration of Rights, had omitted a search and seizure provision, and Thomas Jefferson's draft of a state constitution omitted one, too. Edmund Randolph may have been right in recalling that his state's search and seizure provision "was dictated by the remembrance of the seizure of Wilkes's paper under a warrant from a Secretary of State," but Virginia went well beyond a condemnation of general warrants issued under executive authority.

In August 1776 Pennsylvania adopted its extraordinary constitution preceded by a Declaration of Rights that was influenced by Virginia yet original in major respects. Its tenth article provided: "That the people have a right to hold themselves, their houses, papers, possession free from search and seizure, and therefore warrants without oaths or affirmations first made, affording a sufficient foundation for them, and whereby any officer or messenger may be commanded or required to search suspected places, or to seize any person or persons, his or their property, not particularly described, are contrary to that right, and ought not to be granted." That provision is memorable because it recognizes a right of the people in affirmative terms rather than merely declaring against general warrants or grievous searches. And the right of the people is broad, promiscuously so; there is no such thing as an absolute right to be free from search and seizure. The provision meant, rather, that searches and seizures made without specific warrants "ought"—that weak word again—not to be granted. Even that proposition had to be subject to exceptions, because no evidence suggests that Pennsylvania intended to depart from common-law exceptions to the need for a warrant if a peace officer was in hot pursuit of a felon or had reason to believe that the felon might escape if the officer called time out to obtain a warrant. Exigent circumstances of various kinds always allowed warrantless arrests and even warrantless searches and seizures of evidence of crime, of weapons, or of contraband. The Pennsylvania provision had the virtue of including a requirement for specificity with respect to the things seized when a warrant was attainable. It was also the first to require that the warrant be available only if the informant swore or affirmed that he had "sufficient foundation" for specific information about the person, place, or things described. Probable cause attested to on oath derives partly from Pennsylvania's contribution to the constitutional law of search and seizure.

Delaware's Declaration of Rights of 1776 derived its search and seizure provision partly from Maryland and partly from Pennsylvania, though the Delaware variant was truncated; it omitted the clause recognizing the right of the people. It also omitted a requirement for specificity respecting the property to be seized under a warrant, yet it deplored as grievous any warrant for the seizure of property not based on a sworn statement. Delaware's contribution consisted, rather, in the fact that its provision was the first to declare "illegal" any warrants not meeting the constitutional requirement of specificity. In this respect, the Delaware provision was based on a draft of the Maryland Declaration of Rights, not yet adopted. The texts of the search and seizure provisions of these two states were nearly the same. As Delaware copied Maryland, North Carolina copied Virginia, and Vermont copied Pennsylvania.

Similarly, New Hampshire in 1784 would copy Massachusetts, which did not adopt its declaration of rights and constitution until 1780. As a source of the Fourth Amendment, the Massachusetts provision on search and seizure was the most important of all the state models, because it was the one that the Fourth Amendment most resembles. The Massachusetts provision was the work of John Adams, the witness to and recorder of Otis's monumental speech in Paxton's Case about twenty years earlier. Through Adams and Article XIV of the Massachusetts Declaration of Rights, Otis's influence at last bore triumphant fruits. Article XIV declared:

Every subject has a right to be secure from all unreasonable searches, and seizures of his person, his houses, his papers, and all his possessions. All warrants, therefore, are contrary to this right, if the cause or foundation of them be not previously supported by oath or affirmation; and if the order in the warrant to the civil officer, to make search in suspected places, to arrest one or more suspected persons, or to seize their property, be not accompanied with a special designation of the persons or objects of search, arrest, or seizure: and no warrant ought to be issued but in cases and with the formalities, prescribed by the laws.

The detail of the provision is striking. No other right received such particularity in the Massachusetts constitution, and like the provision of Pennsylvania, which Adams borrowed, it is a "right" that is protected. The right is to be secure against "unreasonable searches, and seizures," the first use of the phrase that would become the prime principle of the Fourth Amendment. The warrant must be based on sworn statement providing "cause or foundation" for the warrant, but the provision omits, amazingly, a requirement that the search, arrest, or seizure occur within specifically designated premises.

The war years were the worst possible for testing whether American practices matched American ideals or constitutional provisions. Search and seizure was a method of fighting the enemy and those suspected of adhering to that cause. Perhaps the grossest violation of a constitutional provision occurred in Pennsylvania in 1777. Three years earlier Congress had complained about customs officials breaking and entering without authority. In 1777, though, Congress urged Pennsylvania's executive council to search the homes of Philadelphians, mostly Quakers, whose loyalty to the American cause was suspect. Congress wanted to disarm such persons and to seize their political papers. Pennsylvania's executive council authorized a search of the homes of anyone who had not taken an oath of allegiance to the United States. The searches of at least six Quaker homes were conducted cruelly and violently, and all sorts of books, papers, and records were confiscated; more than forty people were arrested and deported without trial, let alone conviction, to Virginia, where they were detained until the next year. Nothing that the British had done equaled the violation of privacy rights inflicted by Pennsylvania on its "Virginia Exiles," in defiance of the state constitution and a writ of habeas corpus by the state chief justice, but with the support of Congress.

American adherence to professed principles stands up far better and is more fairly tested after the shooting stopped. Between 1782 and the ratification of the Constitution, five states—Maryland, New York, North and South Carolina, and Georgia—employed general searches. The southern states conventionally employed warrantless searches without restriction against slaves, especially to detect vagrants and fugitives. But all five states used general warrants to enforce their impost laws. Although Maryland's constitution banned general warrants, Maryland used them to enforce excise laws and laws regulating bakers. Such laws, however, derived from past experience. Most significant, perhaps, is the fact that the laws of Massachusetts kept faith with its commitment to specific warrants. Moreover, Rhode Island, which had no constitution, and New Jersey, which had one but did not include a search and seizure clause, enacted legislation that required the use of specific warrants. In the remaining states, general warrants continued to be used, but specific warrants were becoming more common, especially in cases of theft. In Virginia, the trend toward specificity was pronounced, if belated.

In Connecticut, which, like Rhode Island, had no constitution, the state supreme court delivered an opinion of major consequence, in *Frisbie v. Butler* (1787), that voided a general warrant directed against every person and place suspected by the victim of a theft. The state chief justice ruled that a justice of peace, in granting a warrant, had an obligation "to limit the search to such particular place or places, as he, from the circumstances, shall judge there is reason to suspect," and he must limit the arrests under the warrant to those persons found with stolen goods. The warrant before the court, the chief justice concluded, "is clearly illegal," because not specific. *Frisbie v. Butler* shows that probable cause as determined independently by a magistrate was not an unknown concept.

The failure of the Framers to include in the Constitution a bill of rights exposed it to the withering criticism of those who opposed ratification for any reason. Ten days after the Convention adjourned, Richard Henry Lee of Virginia, a member of Congress, sought to wreck the ratification process by moving that Congress adopt a bill of rights. Acting out of a genuine fear of the proposed national government, Lee had troubled to frame his own bill of rights rather than simply urging the famous one of his own state. He omitted numerous liberties of importance but included a search and seizure clause of significance: "the Citizens shall not be exposed to unreasonable searches, seizures of their papers, houses, persons, or property." Lee had constructed the clause from the Massachusetts Constitution of 1780. It was the broadest on the subject.

Lee's colleague from Virginia James Madison led the fight against Lee's motion. Madison observed that the Articles of Confederation required that all thirteen state legislatures would have to approve the Lee proposals if endorsed by Congress. That would cause confusion because of the Convention's rule that ratification by nine state conventions would put the Constitution into operation. Lee's motion lost, but he did not quit. He wrote his *Federal Farmer* letters, the best of the Anti-Federalist tracts.

In an early letter, Lee discoursed on the rights omitted from the proposed Constitution. The second one he mentioned was the right against unreasonable warrants, those not founded on oath or on cause for searching and seizing papers, property, and persons.

In another letter he included the term *effects,* which would become part of the Fourth Amendment. In his final word on the subject, he urged a constitutional provision "that all persons shall have a right to be secure from all unreasonable searches and seizures of their persons, houses, papers, or possessions; and that all warrants shall be deemed contrary to this right, if the foundation of them be not previously supported by oath, and there be not in them a special designation of persons or objects of search, arrest, or seizure."

Other Anti-Federalists also popularized the demand for a provision on searches and seizures, and some used significant language. "Centinel" employed an extract from the Pennsylvania constitution. The "Dissent" of the Pennsylvania convention's Anti-Federalists, which also circulated throughout the country in newspapers and pamphlet form, used a truncated form of the same provision. "Brutus," another whose writings were reprinted almost everywhere, used his own formulation against warrants that were not specific. Anti-Federalists who addressed the issue usually opposed general warrants in purple language, either reflecting fear or calculated to inspire it. Newspapers in the four largest states reprinted the rant of "A Son of Liberty," who depicted federal officers dragging people off to prison after brutal searches and confiscations that shocked "the most delicate part of our families." No one could compete with the florid fears expressed by that first-rate demagogue Patrick Henry.

Virginia's convention ratified the Constitution with recommendations for amendments to be considered by the First Congress. Among them was a detailed provision on the right of every free person "to be secure from all unreasonable searches and seizures"; the provision also required sworn warrants to be based on "legal and sufficient cause." The Virginia recommendation of 1788, of unknown authorship, was moved by George Wythe on behalf of a powerful bipartisan committee that included James Madison. The committee blended the precedents of the Pennsyl-

vania and Massachusetts state constitutions and the recommendations of Richard Henry Lee. Virginia was the first state to ratify
with a search and seizure recommendation. North Carolina copied
it in its recommended amendments; New York and Rhode Island
did so also, with slight changes.

Without a single supporter when he began his fight in the
House for amendments safeguarding personal liberties, Madison
struggled to overcome apathy and opposition from members of his
own party as well as the Anti-Federalists. He meant to win over the
great body of people who withheld their support of the new government in the sincere belief that the Constitution should secure
them against the abuse of powers by the United States. And he
meant to isolate the leaders of the opposition by depriving them of
their supporters. But Madison could have achieved his goals and
redeemed his campaign pledge by taking the least troublesome
route. On the issue of search and seizure, for example, he might
have shown up the Anti-Federalists by proposing that the United
States would not enforce its laws by searches and seizures that
violated the laws of the states, most of which still allowed general
warrants. That would have put the burden on the states to bring
about reforms securing the rights of citizens against unreasonable
searches and seizures. Or Madison might have simply proposed
that the United States would not employ general warrants. Or he
might have recommended the weak formulation of his own state's
constitution, with its omission of specificity for the things to be
seized, its failure to require a sworn statement, and its flabby
assertion that "grievous" warrants "ought" not to be granted.
Even Virginia's excellent 1788 recommendation for a search and
seizure provision to be added to the federal Constitution employed
the same "ought."

If Madison had chosen a formulation narrower than the one he
offered, only the citizens of Massachusetts could consistently have
criticized him. Facing a variety of minimal options, any of which

would have been politically adequate, Madison chose the maximum protection conceivable at the time. He recommended: "The rights of the people to be secured in their persons, their houses, and their other property, from all unreasonable searches and seizures, shall not be violated by warrants issued without probable cause, supported by oath or affirmation, or not particularly describing the places to be searched, or the persons or things to be seized." No one previously had proposed the imperative voice, "shall not be violated," rather than the wishful "ought not," which allowed for exceptions. "Probable cause" was also a significant contribution, or became so; it required more than mere suspicion or even reasonable suspicion, as had its antecedents such as "just cause" and "sufficient foundation." Above all, Madison used the positive assertion drawn from Pennsylvania and Massachusetts that the people have rights against "unreasonable searches and seizures"— John Adams's formulation for the Massachusetts constitution.

A House Committee of Eleven, composed of one member from each state, deleted the crucial phrase that establishes the general principle of the Fourth: no "unreasonable searches and seizures." Specificity in warrants is the lesser half of the amendment, because it provides the standard of reasonableness only when a search or seizure is conducted with a warrant. But the standard of reasonableness must also apply to warrantless searches according to the Fourth Amendment. The committee version initially declared that the "rights of the people to be secured in their persons, houses, papers, and effects, shall not be violated by warrants issuing without probable cause, supported by oath or affirmation, and not particularly describing the places to be searched, and the persons or things to be seized." During the debate by the House acting as the Committee of the Whole, Elbridge Gerry of Massachusetts moved the restoration of "unreasonable seizures and searches." Oddly, he said he did so on the presumption that a "mistake" had been made in the wording of the clause, which he corrected by changing "rights" to "right" and "secured" to "secure." The effect was to provide security or, as we might say, privacy to the people; Gerry's motion changed the meaning from a protection of the right to a protection of individuals in their persons, homes, papers, and effects. The Committee of the Whole adopted his motion but defeated others that were also important. According to the House Journal, the defeated motions of August 17 were reported as agreed upon by the Committee of the Whole. Thus, the provision recommended to the House, in the articles arranged by a special committee of three read: "The right of the people to be secure in their persons, houses, papers, and effects, against unreasonable searches and seizures, shall not be violated; and no warrants shall issue, but upon probable cause, supported by oath or affirmation, and particularly describing the place to be searched, and the persons or things to be seized." The changes that seem to have been sneaked in did more than eliminate a double negative. The entire provision was split into two parts separated by a semicolon. The first part fixed the right of the people and laid down the standard against unreasonable searches and seizures. The second part required probable cause for the issue of a specific warrant. No other changes were made except in the number of the article. Its text remained the same as adopted by the House and accepted by the Senate. Thus, Otis and Adams finally had a belated but cardinal impact on the making of the Fourth Amendment, even though Madison was immediately influenced by Lee and Virginia's recommendation. Lee, whom Virginia's legislature had elected to the United States Senate instead of Madison, bitterly complained to Patrick Henry that the idea of recommending amendments to the Constitution turned out to be political suicide; the Bill of Rights made impossible the amendments most desired by the Anti-Federalists limiting national powers concerning taxes, treaties, and commerce.

When Madison had first recommended to the House that it

consider amendments to the Constitution, some Anti-Federalists thought the House should not neglect the more important business of passing a law for the collection of duties. That law, which passed seven weeks before the amendments were adopted for state consideration, contained a clause on search and seizure. It allowed collectors and naval officers to enter and search any ships suspected of having uncustomed goods and to seize such goods. That is, Congress authorized general searches for the search and seizure of ships—warrantless, general searches. By contrast, if an officer suspected the concealment of uncustomed goods in a building on land, he must apply for a specific warrant before a magistrate and under oath state the cause of his suspicion, and he "shall . . . be entitled to a warrant to enter such house, store, or any place [in the day time only]" and to conduct the search for and seizure of uncustomed goods. Thus, the statute enacted before the framing of the Fourth Amendment required magistrates to issue the warrant on the basis of the officer's suspicion, not on the magistrate's independent judgment of the question of whether probable cause existed.

Allowing the officer who executed a warrant to determine its specificity put the fox in charge of the chicken coop. The magistrate in effect accepted the officer's sworn statement that he was acting in good faith. That is difficult to reconcile with the fact that the good faith execution of a general warrant by a customs officer in the years before the Revolution did not, to American whigs, validate the warrant or the seizures under it.

The adoption of the Fourth Amendment changed the situation drastically. In March 1791, before the amendment had been formally ratified but after approval by nine state legislatures, Congress enacted a tax on liquor, whether imported or distilled in the United States. The statute reflected the meaning of the Fourth Amendment. Unlike the collections act of 1789, the act of 1791 explicitly empowered magistrates to decide for themselves whether an officer had probable cause. Any judge with jurisdiction might issue a "special warrant" for the detection of fraudulently concealed spirits, but the warrant was lawful only "upon reasonable cause of suspicion, to be made out to the satisfaction of such judge or justice of the peace" and sworn under oath. That became the basis in federal law for the determination of probable cause.

The amendment constituted a swift liberalization of the law of search and seizure. Its language was the broadest known at the time. It provided no remedy, however, for an illegal search or seizure or for the introduction in evidence of illegally seized items. It contained principles that were as vague as they might be comprehensive; "probable" and "unreasonable," even if judicially determined, remained uncertain in meaning, and Congress made no provision for the liability, civil or criminal, of federal officers who violated the amendment. Moreover, no exclusionary rule existed. Consequently, the right of privacy created by the amendment, though better secured by the fundamental law in comparison to previous practices and standards, depended on congressional and judicial adherence to the spirit of the amendment. In effect, the meaning of the right to privacy depended then, as now, upon the interpretation of the "probable cause" that justified a specific warrant and, above all, on the reasonableness of searches and seizures.

CHAPTER EIGHT

The Fifth Amendment:
The Right Against Self-Incrimination

S ORIGINALLY proposed by James Madison, when he introduced the recommendations that became the Bill of Rights, the Fifth Amendment's self-incrimination clause was part of a miscellaneous article that read: "No person shall be subject, except in cases of impeachment, to more than one punishment or trial for the same offense; nor shall be compelled to be a witness against himself; nor be deprived of life, liberty, or property, without due process of law; nor be obliged to relinquish his property, where it may be necessary for public use, without a just compensation." That hodge-podge reflects the industriousness and creativity of Madison's work. He stated that he merely sought to satisfy a widespread conviction that the United States should be restrained from violating personal rights. But no state, either in its own constitution or in its recommended amendments, had a self-incrimination clause phrased as generously as that introduced by Madison: "no person . . . shall be compelled to be a witness against himself."

Not only was Madison's phrasing original; his placement of the clause was also unusual. In the widely imitated model of his own state, the clause appeared in the midst of an enumeration of the procedural rights of the criminally accused at his trial. Only Delaware and Maryland had departed from this precedent by giving the clause independent status and applicability in all courts, thereby extending it to witnesses as well as parties and to civil as well as criminal proceedings. In presenting his amendment, Madison said nothing whatever that explained his intentions concerning the self-incrimination clause. Nor do his papers or correspondence illuminate his meaning. We have only the language of his proposal, and that revealed an intent to incorporate into the Constitution the whole scope of the common-law right.

Madison's proposal certainly applied to civil as well as criminal proceedings and in principle to any stage of a legal inquiry, including the initial interrogation in a criminal case and the swearing of a deposition in a civil one. It extended to any kind of governmental inquiry, judicial or otherwise. Moreover, the unique phrasing, that no one could be compelled to be a witness against himself, was far more comprehensive than a prohibition against self-incrimination. But the conventional phrasing, that no one should be compelled to accuse oneself or furnish evidence against oneself, also comprehended more than self-incrimination. By its terms the clause could also apply to any testimony that fell short of making one vulnerable to criminal jeopardy or civil penalty or forfeiture but that nevertheless exposed one to public disgrace or obloquy, or other injury to name and reputation. Finally, Madison's phrasing protected third parties, those who were merely witnesses called to give testimony for one side or the other, whether in civil, criminal, or equity proceedings. According to customary procedure, witnesses, unlike parties, could in fact be compelled to give evidence, under oath, although they were safeguarded against the necessity of testifying against themselves in any manner that might open them to prosecution for a criminal offense or subject them to a forfeiture or civil penalties. By contrast, neither the criminal defendant nor the parties to a civil suit could be compelled to give testimony. They could furnish evidence neither for nor against themselves. The law did require mere witnesses to give evidence for or against the parties but not against themselves. Madison, going beyond the recommendations of the states and the constitution of his own state, phrased his own proposal to make it coextensive with the broadest practice.

Comparing his proposal with its precedents is revealing. To George Mason of Virginia belongs the credit for initiating the constitutionalization of the old English rule of evidence that a person, in Mason's words, "cannot be compelled to give evidence against himself." That was the language adopted by Virginia in section 8 of its Declaration of Rights of 1776, prefacing its first state constitution. But the guarantee appeared in the context of an enumeration of the rights of the criminally accused. Therefore, Virginia's constitutional right against self-incrimination did not extend to anyone but the accused, nor did it apply to any proceedings other than a criminal prosecution. As a matter of actual practice, however, Virginia's courts allowed a right against self-incrimination in all stages of equity and common-law proceedings and also allowed witnesses as well as defendants to invoke the right. Indeed, it could be claimed by a criminal suspect at a preliminary examination before a justice of the peace; by a person testifying at a grand jury investigation into crime; by anyone giving evidence in a suit between private parties; and, above all perhaps, by the subject of an inquisitorial proceeding before any governmental or nonjudicial tribunal, such as a legislative committee or the governor and council, seeking to discover criminal culpability. If one's disclosures could make him vulnerable to legal peril, he could invoke his right to silence. He might even do so if his answers revealed infamy or disgrace yet could not be used against him in a subsequent prosecution. The law of Virginia at this time, as in England, shielded witnesses against mere exposure to public obloquy. The right against self-incrimination incorporated a protection against self-infamy and was broad as the jeopardy against which it sought to guard. Yet the Virginia Declaration of Rights, though vesting a testimonial rule with the impregnability of constitutional guarantee, provided only a stunted version of the common law.

Read literally and in context, the right seemed to apply only to a criminal defendant at trial. If that was its meaning, it was a superfluous guarantee, because the defendant at trial was not even permitted to testify. If he had not confessed, the prosecution had to prove its case against him by the testimony of witnesses and other evidence; the prisoner, in turn, made his defense by witnesses, if he had them, by cross-examining the prosecution's witnesses and by commenting on the evidence against him. If he could afford counsel, he need never open his mouth during the trial. With or without counsel, he could neither be placed on the stand by the prosecution nor take the stand if he wished. Consequently, neither George Mason nor his colleagues in the legislature, who were acting as a constitutional convention, could have meant what they said. More likely, they failed to say what they meant. The provision against self-incrimination was the product of bad drafting, which the Virginia convention failed to remedy. But no evidence exists to show that it was taken literally or regarded as anything but a sonorous declamation of the common-law right of long standing. Other common-law rights that had been entirely overlooked by Virginia's constitution makers, including such vital rights as habeas corpus, grand jury indictment, and representation by counsel, continued to be observed in daily practice. Thus the great Declaration of Rights did not alter Virginia's system of criminal procedure nor express the totality of rights that actually flourished. The practice of the courts was simply unaffected by the restrictions inadvertently or unknowingly inserted into section 8. Thus, the language of a constitutional text does not necessarily reveal original intent or contemporaneous practice.

Section 8, nevertheless, became a model for other states and for the United States Bill of Rights. Indeed, the Virginia Declaration of Rights became one of the most influential constitutional documents in American history. The committee draft was reprinted in the Philadelphia newspapers even before Independence, making it available to the delegates from all the states assembled in the Second Continental Congress. That committee draft was republished all over America, and even in England and on the Continent, in time to be a shaping force in the framing of other state constitutions. Except for the corporate colonies of Rhode Island and Connecticut, which stood pat with their old colonial charters, the other states followed Virginia's example of framing a state constitution. Eight states, including Vermont, which was technically an independent republic from 1776 until admitted to the Union in 1791, annexed separate bills of rights to their constitutions.

Every one of the eight states protected the right against self-incrimination, and every one in essentially the language of Virginia's section 8, because each followed the basic formulation that no man can be "compelled to give evidence against himself." In 1776, Pennsylvania adopted section 8 in entirety, adding only the right to be represented by counsel and retaining the self-incrimination clause verbatim. In 1776 Delaware introduced a subtle but crucial change by making that clause an independent section instead of inserting it among the enumerated rights of the criminally accused. Moreover, Delaware's guarantee, "That no Man in the Courts of common Law ought to be compelled to give evidence against himself," extended the right against self-incrimination to witnesses as well as parties, in civil and as well as criminal cases. Maryland in the same year also placed the self-incrimination clause in a section by itself and broadened it, as did Delaware, extending it not only to "a common court of law" but also to "any other court," meaning courts of equity. But Maryland simultaneously qualified the right by providing for exceptions to it "in such cases as have been usually practised in this State, or may hereafter be directed by the Legislature." That qualification, in effect, required a man to give evidence against himself if a pardon or a grant of immunity against prosecution exempted him from the penal consequences of his disclosures. North Carolina in 1776 followed Virginia's section 8, as did Vermont in 1777. In 1780 Massachusetts slightly modified the Virginia phraseology. Referring to a criminal defendant, Massachusetts provided that he should not be compelled "to accuse, or furnish"—instead of "give"—evidence against himself. In 1784 New Hampshire followed suit. George Mason's observation that his Declaration of Rights was "closely imitated" was certainly accurate with respect to the self-incrimination clause.

Of the four states—New Jersey, New York, Georgia, and South Carolina—that did not preface their constitutions with a separate bill of rights, none secured the right against self-incrimination. All, however, guaranteed some rights, even if only a few, at various points in their constitutions. New Jersey, for example, had an omnibus clause that kept the common law of England in force, thereby protecting the right against self-incrimination. Superfluously, New Jersey specifically protected the right to counsel and trial by jury. New York also provided that the common law should continue as the law of the state, yet the right to indictment and trial by jury, which were expressly mentioned in New York's constitution, were secured by the common law. Why those two were singled out above all other common-law rights is inexplicable, especially because the courts were enjoined to "proceed according to the course of the common law," and citizens were additionally protected by the standard "law of the land" clause, the equivalent of a due process of law clause. The constitution also protected the right to vote, the free exercise of religion, representation by counsel, and a qualified freedom from bills of attainder. Perhaps these rights were singled out because they were either unprotected or, at best, inadequately protected by the common law. Yet, other rights in the same category were ignored, while trial by jury was super-fluously secured. The whole process of selection in New York was baffling. No reasoned explanation nor any drawn from the evidence is available.

Although the right against self-incrimination was not mentioned in New York's constitution, neither were the rights to freedom of speech and press—shade of Zenger!—nor the writ of habeas corpus. New York also ignored protections against unreasonable searches and seizures, ex post facto laws, and double jeopardy. The absence of express guarantees simply cannot be construed to indicate that these rights were not present in practice. One could no more reasonably argue that the omission of a ban against compulsory self-incrimination proved that it did not exist or was regarded without respect than he could argue that the right to the writ of habeas corpus was illusory because it, too, was not constitutionally protected. In its enumeration of rights, New York's constitution was framed in an incredibly haphazard fashion, like New Jersey's, with no discernible principle of selection. The same observation applied to the constitutions of South Carolina and Georgia, neither of which protected the right against self-incrimination.

The history of the writing of the first American bills of rights and constitutions simply does not bear out the presupposition that the process was a diligent or systematic one. Those documents, which we uncritically exalt, were imitative, deficient, and irrationally selective. In the glorious act of framing a social compact expressive of the supreme law, Americans tended simply to draw up a random catalog of rights that seemed to satisfy their urge for a statement of first principles—or for some of them. That task was executed in a disordered fashion that verged on ineptness. Original intent as the basis for constitutional jurisprudence seems, therefore, equally disordered or irrational, for its premises are based on illusions. At any rate, the inclusion or exclusion of any particular right neither proved nor disproved its existence in a state's colonial history.

In the First Congress, there was no debate on the self-incrimination clause. Only one speaker, John Laurence, a Federalist lawyer of New York, addressed himself to what he called the proposal that "a person shall not be compelled to give evidence against himself." Interestingly, he restated Madison's phrasing in the language of the more familiar clause deriving from section 8 of the Virginia Declaration of Rights, as if they were the same. Calling it "a general declaration in some degree contrary to laws passed," Laurence thought that it should "be confined to criminal cases," and he moved an amendment for that purpose. The House adopted Laurence's motion for an amendment without discussion; the clause as amended was adopted unanimously. The speed with which the House seems to have acted, without the record showing any controversy over the significant restriction of the scope of the clause, is bewildering. Simple respect for the House's own distinguished select committee, a nonpartisan group that included one member from each state, five of whom had been delegates to the Philadelphia Constitutional Convention of 1787, ought to have required some explanation. The select committee, following Madison, had intended what Laurence rightly called "a general declaration." Taken literally, the amended clause, "No personal shall . . . be compelled in any criminal case, to be a witness against himself," excluded from its protection parties and witnesses in civil and equity suits as well as witnesses before nonjudicial governmental proceedings such as legislative investigations. As amended it applied only to parties and witnesses in criminal cases, presumably to all stages of proceedings from arrest and examination to indictment and trial.

Laurence's passing remark that the committee proposal was "in some degree contrary to laws passed" was inaccurate yet illuminated the purpose of his motion to amend. Exactly a month earlier, on July 17, the Senate had passed and sent to the House the bill that became the Judiciary Act of 1789. Thanks to Madison's efforts, the House tabled the judiciary bill while it attended to the matter of amending the Constitution. Not until the House approved of the proposed amendments and sent them to the Senate on August 24 did the Committee of the Whole take up the judiciary bill. Its provisions contained a section to which Laurence may have alluded when referring to "laws passed." Section 15 in the original Senate draft empowered the federal courts to compel civil parties to produce their books or papers containing relevant evidence. It also provided that a plaintiff might require a defendant, on proving to the satisfaction of a court that the defendant had deprived him of evidence to support his cause, "to disclose on oath his or her knowledge in the cause in cases under circumstances where a respondent might be compelled to make such a disclosure on oath by aforesaid rules of chancery." Opponents of that final clause described it as an authorization for "inquisitorial powers." Senator William Maclay of Pennsylvania argued that "extorting evidence from any person was a species of torture. . . . [H]ere was an attempt to exercise a tyranny of the same kind over the mind. The conscience was to be put on the rack; that forcing oaths or evidence from men, I consider equally tyrannical as extorting evidence by torture." The clause, he concluded, would offend his constituents, whose state bill of rights provided that no person could be compelled to give evidence against himself. As a result of such opposition the oath provision was stricken from the bill as adopted by the Senate. Nevertheless, it retained the clause forcing the production of books or papers that contained pertinent evidence in civil cases "under circumstances where they might be compelled to produce the same by the ordinary rules of proceeding in Chancery," that is, in courts of equity.

According to an early federal court ruling, this provision was intended to prevent the necessity of instituting equity suits to obtain from an adverse party the production of documents related to a litigated issue. The provision did not suspend or supersede the right against self-incrimination, but it did limit the reach of the general principle that no one could be compelled to be a witness against himself. The documents in question could be against the party without incriminating him. He might, for example, be forced to produce a deed proving plaintiff's ownership, thereby exposing himself to a civil, but not a criminal, liability. Thus Laurence, with this pending legislation in mind, may have moved the insertion of the words "in any criminal case" in order to retain the customary equity rule that compelled evidence of civil liability. To compel a civil defendant to produce records or papers "against himself," harming his case, in no way infringed his traditional right not to produce them if they could harm him criminally. The House, incidentally, passed the judiciary bill with section 15 unchanged.

In the Senate, the House's proposed amendments to the Constitution underwent further change. However, the Senate accepted the self-incrimination clause without change. The double jeopardy clause in the same article was rephrased and a clause on the grand jury, which the House had coupled with guarantees relating to the trial of crimes, was transferred to the beginning of what became the Fifth Amendment. In what was to be the Sixth Amendment the Senate clustered the procedural rights of the criminally accused after indictment. That the self-incrimination clause did not fall into the Sixth Amendment indicated that the Senate, like the House, did not intend to follow the implication of Virginia's section 8, the original model, that the right not to give evidence against oneself applied merely to the defendant on trial. The Sixth Amendment, referring explicitly to the accused, protected him alone. Indeed, the Sixth Amendment, with the right of counsel added, was the equivalent of Virginia's section 8 and included all of its rights except that against self-incrimination. Thus, the location of the self-incrimination clause in the Fifth

Amendment rather than the Sixth proves that the Senate, like the House, did not intend to restrict that clause only to the criminal defendant nor only to his trial. The Fifth Amendment, even with the self-incrimination clause restricted to criminal cases, still expressed its principle broadly enough to apply to witnesses and to any phase of the proceedings.

The clause also protected against more than just "self-incrimination," a phrase that had never been used in the long history of its origins and development. The "right against self-incrimination" is a shorthand gloss of modern origin that implies a restriction not in the constitutional clause. The right not to be a witness against oneself imports a principle of wider reach, applicable, at least in criminal cases, to the self-production of any adverse evidence, including evidence that made one the herald of one's own infamy, thereby publicly disgracing the person. The clause extended, in other words, to all the injurious as well as incriminating consequences of disclosure by witness or party. Clearly, to speak merely of a right against self-incrimination stunts the wider right not to give evidence against oneself, as the Virginia model put it, or not to be a witness against oneself, as the Fifth Amendment stated. The previous history of the right, both in England and in America, proves that it was not bound by rigid definition. After the adoption of the Fifth Amendment, the earliest state and federal cases were in accord with that previous history, which suggests that whatever the wording of the constitutional formulation, it did not supersede or even limit the common-law right.

Pennsylvania's experience is to the point. The state constitution of 1776 had followed the Virginia model by placing in the context of criminal prosecutions the principle that "no man" should be compelled to give evidence against himself. In 1790 Pennsylvania, in a new constitution, replaced the "no man" formulation with a specific reference to "the accused." Nevertheless, in the first Pennsylvania case involving this clause, the state supreme court ignored the restriction introduced in 1790 or, rather, interpreted it as expressing the historic maxim that no person is obliged to accuse himself. The case involved a prosecution for violating an election law that required answers on oath to questions concerning loyalty during the American Revolution. Counsel for defense argued that the constitutional clause of 1790 protected against questions the answers to which might tend to result in a prosecution or bring the party into disgrace or infamy. Chief Justice Edward Shippen, who had studied at Middle Temple and had begun his legal practice in Pennsylvania way back in 1750, believed the following opinion:

> It has been objected that the questions propounded to the electors contravene an established principle of law. The maxim is, "Nemo tenetur seipsum accusare (sen prodere)." It is founded on the best policy, and runs throughout our whole system of jurisprudence. It is the uniform practice of courts of justice as to witnesses and jurors. It is considered cruel and unjust to propose questions which may tend to criminate the party. And so jealous have the legislatures of this commonwealth been of this mode of discovery of facts that they have refused their assent to a bill brought in to compel persons to disclose on oath papers as well as facts relating to questions of mere property. And may we not justly suppose that they would not be less jealous of securing our citizens against this mode of self-accusation? The words "accusare" and "prodere" are general terms, and their sense is not confined to cases where the answers to the questions proposed would induce to the punishment of the party. If they would involve him in shame or reproach, he is under no obligation to answer them.

The same court applied a similar rule in a purely civil case, holding that no one could be forced to take the oath of a witness if his testimony "tends to accuse himself of an immoral act."

The state courts of the Framers' generation endorsed the extension of the right to cover self-infamy as well as self-incrimination, although the self-infamy rule eventually fell into disuse. Both federal and state courts followed in all other respects Shippen's far-reaching interpretation of what on its face and in context was a narrow clause. In the earliest federal case on the right against self-incrimination, Justice James Iredell of the Supreme Court, in circuit duty, ruled that a witness was not bound to answer a question that might tend to "implicate" or criminate himself. In one of the most famous cases in American constitutional history, *Marbury v. Madison,* Attorney General Levi Lincoln balked at a question relating to his conduct as acting secretary of state when Jefferson became president. Marbury's commission as a justice of the peace for the District of Columbia had been signed by the outgoing president and affixed with the seal of the United States by the then secretary of state, John Marshall, who had had no time to deliver it. What, asked Chief Justice Marshall, had Lincoln done with that commission? Lincoln, who probably had burned it, replied that he did not think that he was bound to disclose his official transactions while acting as secretary of state, nor should he "be compelled to answer any thing which might tend to criminate himself." Marbury's counsel, Charles Lee, who was himself a former attorney general of the United States, and Chief Justice Marshall were in agreement: Lincoln, who was in the peculiar position of being both a witness and a counsel for the government in a civil suit, was not obliged to disclose anything that might incriminate him. In Aaron Burr's trial, Chief Justice Marshall, without referring to the constitutional clause, again sustained the right of a witness to refuse answer to an incriminating question. The courts have always assumed that the meaning of the constitutional clause is determined by the common law.

Whether the Framers of the Fifth Amendment intended it to be fully coextensive with the common law cannot be proved—or disproved. The language of the clause and its Framers' understanding of it may not have been synonymous. The difficulty is that its Framers, from Mason to Madison and Laurence, left too few clues. Slight explication emerged during the process of state ratification of the Bill of Rights from 1789 through 1791. Indeed, in legislative and convention proceedings, in letters, newspapers, and tracts, in judicial opinions, and law books, the whole period from 1776 to 1791 reveals neither sufficient explanation of the scope of such a clause nor the reasons for it. That it was a ban on torture and a security for the criminally accused were the most important of its functions, but these were not all of its functions. Still, nothing can be found of a theoretical nature expressing a rationale or underlying policy for the right in question or its reach.

The probable reason is that by 1776 the right against self-incrimination was simply taken for granted and was so deeply accepted that its constitutional expression had the mechanical quality of a ritualistic gesture in favor of a self-evident truth needing no explanation. The clause itself, whether in Virginia's section 8 or the Fifth Amendment, might have been so imprecisely stated, or misstated, as to raise vital questions of intent, meaning, and purpose. But constitution makers, in that day at least, did not explain themselves and did not regard themselves as framers of detailed codes. To them the statement of a bare principle was sufficient, and they were content to put it spaciously, if ambiguously, in order to allow for its expansion as the need might arise and in order to avoid the controversy that detail or explanation might provoke.

By stating the principle in the Bill of Rights, which was also a bill of restraints upon government, the Framers were once again sounding the tocsin against the dangers of government oppression of the individual; they were also voicing their conviction that the right against self-incrimination was a legitimate defense possessed by every individual against government. Tough-minded revolutionists, the equal of any in history in the art of self-government, they were willing to risk lives and fortunes in support of their beliefs that government is but an instrument of the people, its sovereignty held in subordination to their rights. They cannot justly be accused of having been naive or disregardful of the claims of law and order. They were mindful, nevertheless, that the enduring interests of the community required justice to be done as fairly as possible. The Constitution with its amendments was an embodiment of their political morality, an ever-present reminder of their view that the citizen is the master of the government, not its subject. As Justice Abe Fortas observed, "The principle that a man is not obliged to furnish the state with ammunition to use against him is basic to this conception." The state, he acknowledged, must defend itself and, "within the limits of accepted procedure," punish lawbreakers. "But it has no right to compel the sovereign individual to surrender or impair his right of self-defense." The fundamental value reflected by the Fifth Amendment "is tangible, it is true; but so is liberty, and so is man's immortal soul. A man may be punished, even put to death, by the state; but . . . he should not be made to prostrate himself before its majesty. Mea culpa belongs to a man and his God. It is a plea that cannot be exacted from free men by human authority. To require it is to insist that the state is the superior of the individuals who compose it, instead of their instrument."

The same point underlay the statements of another distinguished federal judge, Calvert Magruder who observed, "Our forefathers, when they wrote this provision into the Fifth Amendment of the constitution, had in mind a lot of history which has been largely forgotten today." The remark applies with equal force, of course, to the right of representation by counsel, trial by jury, or any of the other, related procedural rights that are constitutionally sanctified. With good reason the Bill of Rights showed a preoccupation with the subject of criminal justice. The Framers understood that without fair and regularized procedures to protect the criminally accused, liberty could not exist. They knew that from time immemorial, the tyrant's first step was to use the criminal law to crush his opposition. Vicious and ad hoc procedures had always been used to victimize nonconformists and minorities of differing religious, racial, or political persuasions. The Fifth Amendment was part and parcel of the procedures that were so crucial, in the minds of the Framers, to the survival of the most treasured rights. One's home could not be his "castle," his property be his own, his right to express his opinions or to worship his God be secure, if he could be searched, arrested, tried, or imprisoned in some arbitrary or ignoble manner.

The Framers of the Bill of Rights saw their injunction, that no man should be a witness against himself in a criminal case, as a central feature of the accusatory system of criminal justice. While deeply committed to perpetuating a system that minimized the possibilities of convicting the innocent, they were no less concerned about the humanity that the fundamental law should show even to the offender. Above all, the Fifth Amendment reflected their judgment that in a free society, based on respect for the individual, the determination of guilt or innocence by just procedures, in which the accused made no unwilling contribution to this conviction, was more important than punishing the guilty.

As Justice Felix Frankfurter declared, "The privilege against self-incrimination is a specific provision of which it is peculiarly true that 'a page of history is worth a volume of logic.'" That page of history begins with the origins of the right against self-incrimination. Frederic William Maitland's epigram that the "seamless web" of history is torn by telling a piece of it is borne out by any effort to explain the origins of that right. The American origins derive largely from the inherited English common-law system of criminal justice. But the English origins, so much more complex, spill over legal boundaries and reflect the many-sided religious, political, and constitutional issues that racked England during the sixteenth and seventeenth centuries: the struggles between Anglicanism and Puritanism, between Parliament and king, between limited government and arbitrary rule, and between freedom of conscience and suppression of heresy and sedition. Even within the more immediate confines of law, the history of the right against self-incrimination is enmeshed in broad issues: the contests for supremacy between the accusatory and the inquisitional systems of procedure, between the common law and the royal prerogative, and between the common law and its canon and civil law rivals. Against this broad background the origins of the concept that "no man is bound to accuse himself" (*nemo tenetur seipsum prodere*) must be understood and the concept's legal development traced.

The right against self-incrimination originated as an indirect product of the common law's accusatory system and of its opposition to rival systems that employed inquisitorial procedures. Toward the close of the sixteenth century, just before the concept first appeared in England on a sustained basis, all courts of criminal jurisdiction habitually sought to exact self-incriminatory admission from persons suspected of or charged with crime. Although defendants in crown cases suffered from this and many other harsh procedures, even in common-law courts, the accusatory system afforded a degree of fair play not available under the inquisitional system. Moreover, torture was never sanctioned by the common law, although it was employed as an instrument of royal prerogative until 1641.

By contrast, torture for the purpose of detecting crime and inducing confession was regularly authorized by the Roman codes of the canon and civil law. "Abandon all hope, ye who enter here" well describes the chances of an accused person under inquisitorial procedures characterized by presentment based on mere rumor or suspicion, indefiniteness of accusation, the oath ex officio, secrecy, lack of confrontation, coerced confessions, and magistrates acting as accusers and prosecutors as well as "judges." This system of procedures, by which heresy was most efficiently combated, was introduced into England by ecclesiastical courts.

The use of the oath ex officio by prerogative courts, particularly by the ecclesiastical Court of High Commission, which

Elizabeth I reconstituted, resulted in the defensive claim that "no man is bound to accuse himself." The High Commission, an instrument of the crown for maintaining religious uniformity under the Anglican establishment, used the canon law inquisitorial process, but made the oath ex officio, rather than torture, the crux of its procedure. Persons suspected of "heretical opinions," "seditious books," or "conspiracies" were summoned before the High Commission without being informed of the accusation against them or the identity of their accusers. Denied due process of law by common-law standards, suspects were required to take an oath to answer truthfully to interrogatories that sought to establish guilt for crimes neither charged nor disclosed.

Nonconformist victims of the High Commission found themselves thrust between hammer and anvil: refusal to take the oath, or having taken it, refusal to answer the interrogatories, meant a sentence for contempt and invited Star Chamber proceedings; to take the oath and respond truthfully to questioning often meant to convict oneself of religious or political crimes and, moreover, to supply evidence against nonconformist accomplices; to take the oath and then lie meant to sin against the Scriptures and risk conviction for perjury. Common lawyers of the Puritan party developed the daring argument that the oath, although sanctioned by the crown, was unconstitutional because it violated Magna Carta, which limited even the royal prerogative.

The argument had myth-making qualities, for it was one of the earliest to exalt Magna Carta as the symbol and source of English constitutional liberty. As yet there was no contention that one need not answer incriminating questions after accusation by due process according to the common law. But a later generation would use substantially the same argument—"that by the Statutes of the Magna Carta . . . for a man to accuse himself was and is utterlie inhibited"—on behalf of the contention that one need not involuntarily answer questions even after one had been properly accused.

Under Chief Justice Edward Coke the common-law courts,

with the sympathy of the House of Commons, vindicated the Puritan tactic of litigious opposition of the High Commission. The deep hostility between the canon and common-law systems expressed itself in a series of writs of prohibition issued by Coke and his colleagues, staying the commission's proceedings. Coke, adept at creating legal fictions that he clothed with the authority of resurrected "precedents" and inferences from Magna Carta, grounded twenty of these prohibitions on the allegedly ancient common-law rule that no man is bound to accuse himself criminally.

In the 1630s the High Commission and the Star Chamber, which employed similar procedures, reached the zenith of their powers. But in 1637 a flinty Puritan agitator, John Lilburne, refused the oath. His well-publicized opposition to incriminatory questioning focused England's attention upon the injustice and illegality of such practices. In 1641 the Long Parliament, dominated by Puritans and common lawyers, condemned the sentences against Lilburne and others, abolished the Star Chamber and the High Commission and prohibited ecclesiastical authorities from administering any oath obliging one "to confess or to accuse himself or herself of any crime."

Common-law courts, however, continued to ask incriminating questions and to bully witnesses into answering them. The rudimentary idea of a right against self-incrimination was nevertheless lodged in the imperishable opinions of Coke, publicized by Lilburne and the Levellers, and firmly associated with Magna Carta. The idea was beginning to take hold of men's minds. Lilburne was again the catalytic agent. At his various trials for his life, in his testimony before investigating committees of Parliament, and in his ceaseless tracts, he dramatically popularized the demand that a right against self-incrimination be accorded general legal recognition. His career illustrates how the right against self-incrimination developed not only in conjunction with a whole gamut of fair procedures associated with "due process of law" but also with demands for freedom of conscience and expression. After Lilburne's time the right became entrenched in English jurisprudence, even under the judicial tyrants of the Restoration. As the state became more secure and as fairer treatment of the criminally accused became possible, the old practice of bullying the prisoner for answers gradually died out. By the early eighteenth century the accused was no longer put on the stand at all; he could not give evidence in his own behalf even if he wished to, although he was permitted to tell his story, unsworn. The prisoner was regarded as incompetent to be a witness for himself.

After the first quarter of the eighteenth century, the English history of the right centered primarily upon the preliminary examination of the suspect and the legality of placing in evidence various types of involuntary confessions. Incriminating statements made by suspects at the preliminary examination could be used against them at their trials; a confession, even though not made under oath, sufficed to convict. Yet suspects could not be interrogated under oath. One might be ensnared into a confession by the sharp and intimidating tactics of the examining magistrate; but there was no legal obligation to answer an incriminating question—nor, until 1848, to notify the suspect or prisoner of his right to refuse answer. One's answers, given in ignorance of his right, might be used against him. However, the courts excluded confessions that had been made under duress. Only involuntary confessions were seen as a violation of the right. Lord Chief Baron Geoffrey Gilbert in his *Law of Evidence* (1756) declared that although a confession was the best evidence of guilt, "this Confession must be voluntary and without compulsion; for our Law . . . will not force any Man to accuse himself; and in this we do certainly follow that Law of Nature," which commands self-preservation.

Thus, opposition to the oath ex officio ended in the common-law right to refuse to furnish incriminating evidence against one-self even when all formalities of common-law accusation had first been fulfilled. The prisoner demanded that the state prove its case against him, and he confronted the witnesses who testified against him. The Levellers, led by Lilburne, even claimed a right not to answer any questions concerning themselves, if life, liberty, or property might be jeopardized, regardless of the tribunal or government agency directing the examination, be it judicial, legislative, or executive. The Leveller claim to a right against self-incrimination raised the generic problem of the nature of sovereignty in England and spurred the transmutation of Magna Carta from a feudal relic of baronial reaction into a modern bulwark of the rule of law and regularized restraints upon government power.

The claim to this right also emerged in the context of a cluster of criminal procedures whose object was to ensure fair play for the criminally accused. It harmonized with the principles that the accused was innocent until proven guilty and that the burden of proof was on the prosecution. It was related to the idea that a man's home should not be promiscuously broken into and rifled for evidence of his reading and writing. It was intimately connected to the belief that torture or any cruelty in forcing a man to expose his guilt was unfair and illegal. It was indirectly associated with the right to counsel and the right to have witnesses on behalf of the defendant, so that his lips could remain sealed against the government's questions or accusations. It was at first a privilege of the guilty, given the nature of the substantive law of religious and political crimes. But the right became neither a privilege of the guilty nor a protection of the innocent. It became merely one of the ways of fairly determining guilt or innocence, like trial by jury itself; it became part of due process of the law, a fundamental principle of the accusatorial system. It reflected the view that society benefited by seeking the defendant's conviction without the aid of his involuntary admissions. Forcing self-incrimination was thought to brutalize the system of criminal justice and to produce untrustworthy evidence.

Above all, the right was closely linked to freedom of speech and religious liberty. It was, in its origins, unquestionably an invention of those who were guilty of religious crimes like heresy, schism, and nonconformity and, later, of political crimes like treason, seditious libel, and breach of parliamentary privilege. More often than not, the offense was merely criticism of the government, its policies, or its officers. The right was associated, then, with guilt for crimes of conscience, of belief, and of association. In the broadest sense it was not so much a protection of the guilty, or even the innocent, but a protection of freedom of expression, of political liberty, and of the right to worship as one pleased. The symbolic importance and practical function of the right was certainly a settled matter, taken for granted, in the eighteenth century. And it was part of the heritage of liberty which the common law bequeathed to the English settlers in America.

Yet, the right had to be won in every colony, invariably under conditions similar to those that generated it in England. The first glimmer of the right in America was evident in the heresy case of John Wheelwright, tried in 1637 in Massachusetts. In colony after colony people exposed to the inquisitorial tactics of the prerogative court of the governor and council refused to answer to incriminating interrogatories in cases heavy with political implications. By the end of the seventeenth century the right was unevenly recognized in the colonies.

As the English common law increasingly became American law and the legal profession grew in size, competence, and influence, Americans developed a greater familiarity with the right. English law books and English criminal procedure provided a model. From Edmond Wingate's *Maxims of Reason* (1658), which included the earliest discussion of the maxim "nemo tenetur accusare seipsum," to Gilbert's *Evidence*, law books praised the right. It so grew in popularity that in 1735 Benjamin Franklin, hearing that a church wanted to examine the sermons of an unorthodox minister, could declare: "It was contrary to the common Rights of Mankind, no Man being obliged to furnish Matter of Accusation against himself." In 1754 a witness parried a Massachusetts legislative investigation into seditious libel by quoting the well-known Latin maxim, which he freely translated as "A Right of Silence as the Priviledge of every Englishman." In 1770 the attorney general of Pennsylvania ruled that an admiralty court could not oblige people to answer interrogatories "which may have a tendency to criminate themselves, or subject them to a penalty, it being contrary to any principle of Reason and the Laws of England." When a right becomes so profoundly accepted that it has been hallowed by its association with Magna Carta and has been ranked as one of the common rights of man deriving from the law of nature, it receives genuflection and praise, not critical analysis; and it gets exalted as a fundamental liberty that receives constitutional expression.

CHAPTER NINE

Double Jeopardy

THE LEGAL PRINCIPLE that a person should not be tried more than once for the same offense is very old and widespread. Variants of it, usually in rudimentary form, can be found in early legal systems, including Roman, Talmudic, and canon law. In the Emperor Justinian's *Digest* of the sixth century, government was commanded not to permit "the same person to be again accused of crime of which he had been acquitted." In English law, glimmerings can be found in the English Yearbooks of the later fifteenth century. The King James Version of the Bible succinctly stipulates that "affliction shall not rise up a second time." Sir Edward Coke affirmed a stunted form of the principle against double jeopardy when he endorsed the general notion that a previous attainder could bar a subsequent prosecution; he also believed that a previous acquittal based on a plea of self-defense in a homicide case protected the individual against being tried again. But there are mutterings in Coke to the effect that a former acquittal does not always prohibit subsequent prosecution in nonhomicide cases.

Since the time of Coke, the concept of double jeopardy has been associated in England primarily if not exclusively with criminal cases, and it took the form of allowing a defendant to plead that because he had been tried previously for some offense, he could not be tried for it again. It did not matter whether he pleaded *auterfois acquit* (acquitted previously) or *auterfois convict* (convicted previously) because in either case, retrial was illegal. The King's Bench, England's highest criminal court, endorsed a spacious concept of double jeopardy in a case of 1696. After defendants were acquitted on a charge of breaking and entering, they were accused again for the same conduct but on the charge of larceny, a different crime. Nevertheless, their previous acquittal formed the basis for the court's ruling that they could not be indicted for larceny or on any charge "for the same fact" or deed.

Sir William Blackstone in his *Commentaries* summed up the English law of the matter when he declared that the plea of a former acquittal was "grounded on this universal maxim of the common law of England, that no man is to be brought into jeopardy of his life, more than once, for the same offence." In Coke and Blackstone the ban on double jeopardy applied as a protection only in felony cases, although a maxim that became popular protected the right far more broadly: "It is a rule of law that a man shall not be twice vexed for one and the same cause."

English courts did not expatiate on the reasons for the rule against double jeopardy beyond the principle that a person should not be vexed again for the same cause. No doubt the courts sought to make the most economic use of their time by refusing to rehear a case that had previously been decided. Any alternative course would have produced onerous multiple actions, exposed the innocent to egregious harassment, and put the public and accused persons to the cost of litigation and the stigma of persistent prosecutions.

In the American colonies the principle against double jeopardy was well known, and the fact that it was not restricted to jeopardy of life or even to felony cases allowed its application in broader form. In Massachusetts Bay, the ban even affected non-criminal trespasses. The Body of Liberties of 1641 generously affirmed, "No man shall be twice sentenced by civil justice for one and the same crime, offense, or trespass." But when Massachusetts codified its laws in 1648, it restricted the ban against double jeopardy to criminal cases by providing that every action in "criminal causes" shall be entered into record and "not afterwards brought again to the vexation of any man." This formulation was the model for similar ones in other New England colonies and in the middle colonies as well.

In the South, too, the law was similar. Maryland was the first state, in 1639, to declare that all its free people possessed the rights of Englishmen as if they still resided in the mother country. Declarations of that sort were common among the colonies, and the English common law, of course, guaranteed protection against double jeopardy. As a reflection of that fact, in 1669, when John Locke, the great philosopher, framed a constitution for the Carolinas that never went into effect, one section affirmed, "No cause shall be twice tried in any one court, upon any reason or pretence whatsoever." Virginia allowed a criminal defendant to plead that he had been tried for an offense previously, whether acquitted, convicted, or pardoned for it; however, if an indictment was dismissed as defective, the individual could be indicted and tried for the offense, because the dismissal of the defective indictment signified that he had not previously been in jeopardy.

In New York City, several men were charged with violation of the laws governing bread-making, and when the same men were subsequently accused of the same offense, in 1700, they were "discharged from the presentment of the Grand Jurors, having been fined before for the same fact." In an Albany case of 1758, the court discharged a prisoner on learning that he had been fined and had paid the fine for virtually the same offense. In another case of about the same time, when Britain and France were at war, a man named Cunningham was accused of trading with the enemy and supplying privateers. Although he had committed more than one crime by the same act, he pleaded that he was being exposed to double jeopardy, which was "oppressive, contrary to the spirit of government and the dictates of law and reason." The outcome of the case is unclear.

In 1770 Alexander McDougall, a popular leader of the patriot party during the years of controversy with Great Britain, was summoned before the bar of the New York Assembly to answer for a tract lambasting its weak policies toward Britain. McDougall, already under arrest for seditious libel and pending trial in court, refused to answer any questions, not only because he might tend to incriminate himself but also because the legislature, having found the tract to be criminal, exposed him to double jeopardy. Despite his argument he was imprisoned for the remainder of the assembly's term, but his case popularized the rights he claimed against compulsory self-incrimination and double jeopardy. The historians of law enforcement in colonial New York say that there were not many double jeopardy cases because royal officials were solicitous that "there be no double prosecutions." Yet, the cases were sufficiently numerous to show that subjecting a person to double jeopardy allowed him to make effective a claim that his rights had been breached, even though none of the great English liberty documents (Magna Carta, Petition of Right, Bill of Rights) sanctioned his claim.

In several other states, courts prohibited double jeopardy and disallowed the second trial of an individual who showed a previous acquittal. In 1784 New Hampshire became the first state to provide constitutional protection against double jeopardy by banning a subsequent trial for anyone previously held not guilty of a particular offense. In 1788 the Pennsylvania high court stated: "By the law it is declared that no man shall be twice put in jeopardy for the same offense; and yet, it is certain that the enquiry, now

proposed by the Grand Jury, would necessarily introduce the oppression of a double trial. Nor is it merely upon the maxims of
law, but I think, likewise, upon principles of humanity, that this
innovation should be opposed." In the same year Maryland was
the first state to recommend that the new federal Constitution
should be amended to include a provision banning a "second trial
after acquittal."

When the First Congress met, James Madison, introducing the
amendments that became the Bill of Rights, proposed: "No person
shall be subject, except in case of impeachment, to more than one
trial or one punishment for the same offence . . ." In view of
the fact that only two states had recommended such a provision,
which had no precedent in the Articles of Confederation, Madison's proposal shows how conscientiously he undertook the task of
framing amendments in the nature of a bill of rights. He did far
more than was necessary merely to satisfy a public alarm that
insufficient checks existed on the new government.

During the short debate on Madison's proposal, Egbert Benson of New York claimed that its meaning was "doubtful," and so
opposed it. According to Benson, it seemed contrary to the very
right it sought to protect, for it did not even allow a convicted
defendant to appeal. The purpose of protecting against double
jeopardy, he argued, was "humane," because its objective was "to
prevent more than one punishment" for a single offense. Accordingly, Benson moved to amend Madison's motion by striking out
the words "one trial or." Roger Sherman of Connecticut agreed,
saying that as the clause was proposed by Madison, a person found
guilty could not get an arrest of judgment against himself in order
to obtain a second trial. Although a person acquitted at trial could
never be tried a second time, if he was convicted he should be
entitled to a second trial, said Sherman, if "anything should appear to set the judgment aside." Madison's proposal deprived him
of that opportunity. Samuel Livermore of New Hampshire also

opposed exposing a person to the danger of more than one trial for the same offense, even if he was guilty but evidence failed to prove it. Nevertheless, Benson's motion lost by a large majority. So did a motion to insert "by any law of the United States" after "same offence." The House then adopted Madison's proposal.

The Senate struck the last half of it, substituting in its place "be twice put in jeopardy of life and limb in any public prosecution." When the proposal emerged from a joint conference committee, the words "in any public prosecution" had also been struck. There being no record of the debate, we cannot be sure whether a predominate meaning of the double jeopardy provision existed in the minds of Congress. In all likelihood, the clause was meant to apply to all crimes, even though the phrase "life or limb" would have limited it only to felony cases. The Framers of the Bill of Rights were rarely exact with respect to their intentions and as often as not failed to say what they contemplated or mean what they said.

The double jeopardy clause, for example, is inappropriately specific. Its Framers did not mean "limb" when they referred to "life and limb," unless they contemplated the highly unlikely possibility that Americans might one day authorize tearing people apart as a punishment for crime or chopping off arms and legs. The constitutional phrase should be "life or liberty" rather than "life or limb." The reference to jeopardy of limb is misleading or superfluous. The infliction of a punishment that results in loss of limb would surely constitute a violation of the Eighth Amendment's guarantee against "cruel and unusual" punishment. Yet, that very phrase, "cruel and unusual punishment," cannot mean what it says either, because punishment need not be unusual as well as cruel; any punishment that is cruel would meet the constitutional ban whether or not it is also unusual; unusual punishment by itself, such as the electric chair when first invented, is not unconstitutional.

No claim against the constitutionality of the death penalty makes constitutional sense in view of the Fifth Amendment's due process clause. Life can be taken if one received due process of law and is not exposed to double jeopardy. Yet limb cannot be taken, despite the language of the Fifth Amendment. If limb cannot be taken yet life can be, the reason is that the Fifth Amendment also provides for indictment by grand jury if a person is accused of a "capital" crime. The language is that no one should be "held to answer for a capital, or otherwise infamous crime." The text of the Fifth Amendment, even when seemingly explicit, is simply not clear. The text aside, overwhelming evidence shows that the Framers and ratifiers approved of the death penalty for certain offenses. Similarly, the double jeopardy clause seriously lacks clarity.

CHAPTER TEN

The Double Jury System:
Grand and Petty

KING HENRY II, who governed England from 1154 to 1189, was a man of powerful will and reforming spirit. Reformation of the machinery of justice at the expense of trial by battle was one of his foremost achievements. He tremendously increased both the civil and criminal jurisdiction of his royal courts in order to enhance his revenues and his authority. Henry regarded crimes against persons and property as offenses against the peace of his royal realm that were to be tried in his courts. Before his time, crimes were tried in the courts of the lords in whose immediate jurisdiction they had occurred.

The inquest, a device once used by the crown only for administrative and financial inquiries, became a means of obtaining verdicts or truthful answers to questions of ownership and of guilt or innocence. Henry II relied on the inquest to accomplish his ends. He made it available to litigants as an alternative and more equitable form of proceedings than any form of ordeal. From the inquest developed our double jury system: the grand jury of accusation and the petty jury of trial. Trial by jury was a form of trial available only in the king's courts and eventually triumphed over other forms of trial because it was the only one that offered a decision based on facts rather than on divine miracles, as in the instance of trial by water or fire or any other ordeal.

Under an ordinance of 1164 known as the Constitutions of Clarendon, the sheriff, acting at the instigation of the bishop, could swear twelve men of the countryside to give a verdict—that is, to speak the truth on issues involving property rights. The twelve presumably knew the facts of the case, so the sheriff put them under oath, and then, in the presence of the litigants, royal judges required the twelve to decide whether a tenant had been dispossessed. No one could be evicted or dispossessed of his land without the prior approval of a jury verdict. A verdict in his favor restored him to possession of the land. Thus trial by jury emerged as the legal remedy for a person who had faced dispossession.

According to an ordinance of 1179 any person challenged to trial by battle in a case involving a proprietary right might, for a price payable to the crown, obtain a writ transferring jurisdiction to a royal court; he thereby consented to having the question settled by a jury that was carefully chosen to ensure disinterestedness. The sheriff selected four knights, who in turn chose twelve others from the neighborhood where the disputed property was located, and those twelve, mainly from their own knowledge, declared which party had the better right to it. If the jury sustained the applicant's plea, the appeal that could lead to trial by battle was quashed. What in essence was a jury's verdict was therefore substituted in some instances for ordeals.

Before the emergence of the jury that tried criminal cases, the grand jury developed as the institution that made accusations. The assize (ordinance) of Clarendon, which Henry promulgated in 1166, provided a foundation for the grand jury and prompted a variety of significant procedural reforms. The king instructed the royal judges on circuit, or eyre, to take jurisdiction over certain serious crimes presented to them by sworn inquests, which were representative juries of various localities. Under an ordinance of 1176 twelve men from each hundred of the county and four from each township or vill of the hundred were to be summoned by the sheriff to attend the public eyre. The sixteen, which eventually became the grand jury, were enjoined to inquire into all crimes committed since the beginning of the king's reign and to report under oath all persons accused or suspected by the vicinage. In some cases mere presentment was tantamount to a verdict of banishment, but generally it was no more than an accusation, which was tried at first by ordeal, later by jury. Trial by jury in civil cases developed first, providing a model that could be copied later in criminal cases.

By the time of Magna Carta the inquest in civil cases was becoming fairly well established as the trial jury, although not in criminal cases. Civil disputes of virtually any description, not just those involving property, might be referred to the verdict of local jurors if both parties to a dispute consented to the procedure. The grand inquest that had been provided in 1166 by the assize of Clarendon presented criminal accusations; they were tried by ordeal, but a provision of Magna Carta ensured that no one could be put to an ordeal unless formally accused by the jury of presentment before the royal judges on circuit. The celebrated chapter 29 of Magna Carta did not guarantee trial by jury; its use in criminal cases was still unknown in 1215. At best chapter 29 ensured that indictment and trial by whatever was the appropriate test, whether battle or ordeal, must precede sentence.

When the Fourth Lateran Council in 1215 forbade the participation of the clergy in the administration of ordeals, it divested that mode of proof of its rationale as a judgment of God. Consequently, the ordeal died as a form of trial in western Europe, and some other procedure was needed to take its place. Unlike Continental nations and the Church, which turned to the Inquisition, England found in its own form of the inquest a device at hand that would fill the gap left by ordeals. The absence of heresy in England and therefore the absence of a papal inquisition allowed the inquest to evolve into a means of bringing accusations and judging them.

When a grand jury made an accusation, ascertaining its truth was a necessity, and the royal judges on circuit duty turned for help to the inquest, whose members were sworn to tell the truth. The circuit, or eyre, was a great event, a sort of county parliament, because all the parties were present—the local nobles and bishops, the knights and freeholders, and numerous juries. As in the ordinance of 1176, from every hundred of the county a jury of twelve was present and from every township four representatives. Surrounded by the various juries, the judge in a criminal case could take the obvious course of seeking the sense of the community. The original jurors of presentment were already sworn, presumably knew most about the facts, and were a representative group. Their indictment of a prisoner had not necessarily voiced their belief in his guilt; it affirmed the fact that he was commonly suspected. Although practice varied considerably at first, the judges began to ask the jury of presentment to render a verdict of guilty or not guilty on its accusation. The jury of presentment was more likely than not to sustain its indictment, even though it had sworn only that the accused was suspected and not that he was guilty. The judges usually swore in the representatives of the surrounding townships and asked whether they concurred. The jury of another hundred might be conscripted to corroborate the verdict. In effect a body of the countryside gave the verdict. The practice of enlarging the original jury of presentment or seeking a series of verdicts from different juries was common in the thirteenth century. What became the petty jury was thus initially larger than the grand jury but was too cumbersome. Twelve was the number of the presenting jury and twelve the jury in many civil cases; gradually only twelve jurors were chosen to try the indictment, and they always included within their number some of the original jury of presentment. The unfairness inherent in that practice and the theory that the accused must consent to his jury eventually led to a separation of the grand jury and the petty or trial jury.

The trial jury developed in criminal cases as a result of permitting the prisoner to challenge members of the presenting or grand jury who were impaneled to serve on his trial jury. Henry de Bracton, writing about 1258, noted that the defendant might object to the inclusion of false and malicious accusers, and Britton, near the end of the thirteenth century, said that the defendant might object if the jurors included enemies who sought his destruction or had been suborned by the lord who sought his land "through greediness of the escheat." In 1305 Prince Edward, later Edward II, acting on behalf of a friend who had been indicted for murder, requested the judge to provide a jury that excluded all members of the accusing jury. With increasing frequency, defendants challenged petty jurors who had first served as their indictors; judges resisted the challenges, because indictors were more likely to convict. For that very reason in the 1340s the Commons twice protested against the inclusion of indictors, but not until 1352 did the king agree to a statute that gave the accused a right to challenge members of the petty jury who had participated in the indictment.

As a result of the statute of 1352, the two juries became differentiated in composition and function. From about 1376 the custom of requiring a unanimous verdict from twelve petty jurors developed. By then the size of the grand jury had been fixed at twenty-three, a majority of whom decided whether accusations should be proferred. There is no adequate explanation for the reason that twelve rather than some other number originated as the size of the trial jury. A jury of more than twelve might have seemed cumbersome and a smaller one unrepresentative. Moreover, twelve was a hallowed number because of the twelve tribes of

Israel and the twelve apostles of Christ. Somehow twelve men constituted most early juries and the number stuck.

By the middle of the fifteenth century twelve-member juries were beginning to hear evidence that was gathered in court, although the jurors still continued to obtain facts from their own knowledge or inquiry. As late as the 1450s it was still common for the jurors to visit witnesses at their homes in the country to take their testimony, but jurors were also beginning to pass judgment on the evidence given in their presence in court. More important, the fiction developed that they were objective triers of fact whose verdict was based on the truth as best they could determine. Even so, juries were costly and time-consuming. In cases of petty crime, they thwarted society's interest in swift and cheap justice, with the result that by the end of the fifteenth century Parliament authorized magistrates to decide any case not involving a felony or major crime. Magistrates therefore developed summary powers of judgment when the offenses before them were petty, and Parliament began to exempt most new crimes, if not very serious, from the ambit of juries, allowing magistrates to decide misdemeanor cases without juries.

A substantial number of cases were tried summarily before magistrates. At the time of Blackstone, the number of petty offenses approximated one hundred and constituted most cases. Blackstone mentioned only a few by name and referred readers to books on justices of the peace for "a vast variety of others." One of the most widely used manuals was *Justice of the Peace* by Richard Burn, first published 1755. Almost two thousand pages dealt with the law of summary jurisdiction by magistrates.

Judges governed trials but not verdicts of guilt except in cases of petty offenses. A judge could dismiss charges or direct a verdict of not guilty, but only juries, which did not have to provide reasons, could convict if a case involved life or limb. Judges were moderators, ideally nonpartisan, and had an obligation to maintain decorum in the courtroom while jurors heard and decided cases. Judges might address the jury, advise it on the law, even comment on the evidence, explaining it and focusing a jury's attention on certain facts. But in felony cases judges could not intrude on the jury's task of determining which facts should influence its verdict, and judges could not direct the jury to return a guilty verdict; jurors, for the most part, determined the nature of punishment for guilt.

Defendants could challenge without cause as many as thirty-five potential jurors to help ensure fairness. Witnesses for the crown (the accused was not yet allowed any witnesses) gave evidence in "open court," wrote Sir John Fortescue in the mid-fifteenth century, "in the presence and hearing of a jury, of twelve men, persons of good character, neighbours where the fact was committed, apprised on the circumstances in question, and well acquainted with the lives and conversations of the witnesses, especially as they be near neighbours, and cannot but know whether they be worthy of credit, or not."

Juries were supposedly representative of the community, not that twelve men could possibly include members of every sect, class, or group; yet the theory was that they were a cross-section of the public rather than an organ of any part of it, and no one could be excluded from the panels from which jurors were selected because of membership in some particular group. Jury service was a function of citizenship, a privilege as well as a duty.

The rule that a jury's verdict of guilt must be unanimous supposedly reflected the notion that the jury spoke for the community. The rule itself derived from a case of 1367 in which a court ruled that a verdict agreed to by eleven of twelve jurors was unacceptable. Possibly the rule of unanimity originated and prevailed because it was consistent with the obligation of the prosecution to prove guilt beyond a reasonable doubt. The need for unanimity also encouraged jury deliberation: the majority has to convince dissenters in order to be able to render a verdict. Failure to do so results in a hung jury.

Of course, trial by the local community could be trial by local prejudice; moreover, juries could be improperly influenced in a variety of ways. Some early juries reached results not in accord with the facts, probably because of prejudiced direction from the bench or threats from partisans of one of the parties. A wrong verdict could result in the punishment of jurors. They could be fined, imprisoned, and subjected to forfeiture of property for verdicts proved to be wrong. They could also be punished when judges, appointees of the crown and still its lackies, disagreed with a verdict that conflicted with the crown's wishes.

Punishing jurors for their verdict died out after Bushell's case of 1670. The case developed out of the prosecution of William Penn and other Quakers for the crime of disturbing the peace. A generation earlier, the first Quakers did in fact disturb the peace and the quiet worship of other Christians whom the early Quakers regarded as anti-Christs. But by 1670 the Quakers were becoming law-abiding quietists who wanted only to be let alone and no longer disrupted the religious services of others. But Anglicans, who returned to power as the established church after the demise of the Cromwells, remembered Quakers with considerable hostility. Parliamentary legislation, dictated by Anglican hostility, inflicted fines and imprisonment on the supposedly dangerous opinions and practices of Quakers. Only Anglican worship was lawful until the Toleration Act of 1689. Before that act, the mere assembly of any dissenters for the purposes of worship not authorized by law constituted a crime. Accordingly when Penn and the others, who had been dispossessed from their meetinghouses, congregated in public places to conduct peaceable worship, they were apprehended, jailed, and prosecuted.

The court of ten judges that tried Penn and his fellow Quakers verbally harassed the defendants and demanded a verdict of guilty from the jury if the jury concluded that the Quakers had met at all, as in fact they had. But the jurors, while acknowledging that the Quakers had met, refused to obey; their verdict, as delivered by their foreman, was "Guilty of speaking in Grace Church Street." The presiding judge, the recorder of London, ridiculed that verdict as equivalent to saying nothing at all, and the judges sought to persuade the jury to return a verdict of "guilty" but the jury was recalcitrant. Despite being told that its verdict was useless, the jury persistently repeated itself even against efforts by the court to bully the jurors. The court threatened that the jury would not be dismissed "till you bring in a verdict which the court will accept. You shall be locked up, without meat, drink, fire and tobacco. You shall not think thus to abuse the court. We will have a verdict by the help of God or you shall starve for it." Nevertheless, the jurors persisted even after two days and nights without heat, food, or drink. Because the jury would not change its verdict, the court fined all the jurors and jailed them until they paid their fines.

One member of the jury, Edward Bushell, sued for a writ of habeas corpus from the Court of Common Pleas and won the freedom of the jurors. Chief Justice Sir John Vaughan, speaking for the court, upheld Bushell and his fellow jurors. The judgment, in a technical sense, was reversed, because the matter was criminal and Vaughan's court, which was the high court in civil matters, lacked jurisdiction to decide it. But the principle decided by the case prevailed: the jury's verdict was final and jurors could not be challenged or punished for it. Thereafter, juries were able to decide cases as their convictions dictated, without being subject to attaint. In John Peter Zenger's case, tried in New York in 1735, his counsel referred to Bushell's case by name when advising the jury to find a verdict agreeable to their consciences rather than in accord with the law as laid down by the presiding judge.

Regardless of the faults of the criminal justice system, the prisoner in a criminal case knew the charges against him, confronted his accusers, and had freedom to give to the jury his own explanations; furthermore, he could question and argue with the prosecution's witnesses in the presence of the jury sitting in judgment. Criminal defendants suffered from many disadvantages—lack of counsel, lack of witnesses on their own behalf, lack of time to prepare their defense—yet the public trial before a jury was supremely fair, judged by any standard known in the world of that day. Sir William Blackstone summed up when he wrote:

> But in settling and adjusting a question of fact, when entrusted to any single magistrate, partiality and injustice had an ample field to range in; either by asserting that to be proved which is not so, or by more artfully suppressing some circumstances, stretching and varying others, and distinguishing away the remainder. Here, therefore, a competent number of sensible and upright jurymen, chosen by lot from among those of the middle rank, will be found the best investigators of truth, and the surest guardians of public justice. For the most powerful individuals in the state will be cautious of committing any flagrant invasion of another's right, when he knows that the fact of his oppression may be examined and decided by twelve indifferent men, not appointed until the hour of trial; and that, when once the fact is ascertained, the law must of course redress it. This, therefore, preserves in the hands of the people that share which they ought to have in the administration of general justice, and prevents the encroachments of the more powerful and wealthy citizens.

The grand jury, like the trial jury, evolved into a bastion of popular rights rather than a crown agent. By refusing to indict, grand juries protected individuals whom prosecutors would have liked to put to trial without a well-founded accusation. Eventually the theory developed that no one should be indicted without a prima facie case of guilt—enough proof of guilt to convict if standing by itself, unrebutted. Sir John Hawles, in his tract *The Englishman's Rights* (1680), championed grand juries as defenders of individual freedom because they protected against unfounded or spiteful prosecution. Further, Hawles argued that no courts or government agencies could punish grand juries by fines or imprisonment. The refusal of a grand jury of 1681 to indict Lord Shaftesbury for treason despite the urgings of Charles II enhanced Englishmen's respect for the grand jury as an institution that shielded from vindictive or malicious motives of the state; however, Shaftesbury fled the country to avoid an indictment by a more compliant grand jury in another county.

Lord chancellor of England Sir John Somers declared in his aptly entitled tract of 1682, *The Security of Englishmen's Lives:* "Grand juries are our only security, in as much as our lives cannot be drawn into jeopardy by all the malicious crafts of the devil, unless such a number of our honest countrymen shall be satisfied in the truth of the accusations." Henry Care's *English Liberties, or, The Free-Born Subject's Inheritance* (1698) vigorously repeated the same point. Grand jurors did more than stand between the king's prosecutor and the trial jury; they also acted as representatives of their locality by denouncing governmental abuses, recommending new laws, and even administering statutory law. Blackstone's *Commentaries* explained that grand juries stood between the liberties of the people and the prerogative of the crown, thus permitting the grand jury to thwart executive impulses to imprison or exile politically obnoxious men.

In the American colonies, where grand juries were chosen by such law-enforcement officers as sheriffs or constables or by county court judges, the jurors were usually large freeholders or prosperous townfolk. In most of the colonies, prosecutors tried criminal cases that had first involved an accusation by a grand jury. Hawles's *Englishman's Rights*, Somers's *Security of Englishmen's Lives*, and Care's *English Liberties* were reprinted at least twice each in America and circulated throughout the colonies, serving as manuals on the functions and authority of grand juries. Had a grand jury been able to prevail in New York, Zenger would never have been tried for seditiously libeling the provincial governor. Two grand juries refused to indict him, forcing the crown prosecutor to proceed by independently filing in court the accusation against him known as an "information." The prosecutor filed an information by himself—that is, he made the decision without grand jury endorsement to prosecute.

The earliest American grand juries met in the towns of Massachusetts in accordance with an act of the provincial legislature ordering town meetings to select grand jurors. These early grand juries presented scores and scores of suspected offenders, including even some of the magistrates of Massachusetts. Town meetings elected the jurors, who after 1641 were obligated to serve for one year. They were free to investigate any abuses of governmental power and laxity in town governance. Thus, grand jurors reproved towns for failing to repair bridges and roads, for questionable land sales, and for other failures to serve the public properly. Additionally, grand juries presented individuals for their abuse or neglect, such as giving short weight when selling commodities, not properly grinding grain, violating the Sabbath, getting intoxicated in public, or using foul language.

Connecticut was responsible for an innovation that became influential. Instead of leaving presentments to town meetings, Connecticut relied on local prosecutors to file an "information," which was a sworn, written accusation before a court. In most colonies county courts, rather than town meetings, selected the grand jurors who brought the accusation in most serious cases; in some colonies, sheriffs selected panels of prosperous freeholders; in still other colonies, justices of the peace named the grand jurors. Usually grand juries attended county courts, but their functions remained diverse. They not only brought accusations of crime; they also undertook a variety of investigations on behalf of county courts and even administered various laws. Practice varied, of course, in each colony. In New Jersey, grand juries assisted county courts in levying county taxes. In Pennsylvania grand juries inspected public works such as court houses, jails, and roads, in order to determine whether any officials had been neglectful. In Georgia grand juries reflected a variety of complaints on behalf of the public against the government.

Grand juries also became a favorite instrument for Americans to express their protests against British colonial policies. Grand jurors were able to protect Americans in some colonies because of provincial statutes that banned prosecutions except upon a presentment originating with a grand jury or except upon an accusation by a prosecutor who had the endorsement of a grand jury. Previously, crown prosecutors had been able to decide, by themselves, who should be put to trial by merely filing an information. Americans would not have been able to challenge royal powers as effectively as they did if grand juries had not stood between royal prosecutors and trial by jury. American grand jurors, for example, would not indict rioters who in 1765 destroyed the stamps in Boston and three years later refused to indict the newspaper editors who libeled the royal governor of Massachusetts. Indeed, for fear of retaliation, no one would testify before a grand jury in cases involving recent British policies affecting the American colonies. As a result, those policies failed at the enforcement level, leaving crown officials impotent.

In Massachusetts grand juries were a patriotic American instrument for harassing tactics that aimed to stymie British policies. Consequently, Britain sought to evade grand juries. Lord North, the British leader, persuaded the House of Commons to change the charter of Massachusetts by preventing town meetings except when called by the royal governor. Moreover, the Commons authorized Massachusetts sheriffs to appoint all jurors. Previously the people in their town meetings had elected grand jurors whenever they were needed. Lord North censured grand juries for opposing British measures. In turn, the people of Massachusetts vehemently denounced Britain and in circular letters to other colonies declared that the appointment of grand jurors by sheriffs constituted tyranny. Throughout Massachusetts, town meetings, which repudiated the new system as subversive of justice, encouraged law enforcement officers to ignore the new law. The towns persisted in holding their meetings at which those in attendance elected grand jurors. Sheriffs who complied with the law were coerced into reconsidering their fealty to British policy.

Grand jurors in most colonies defied royally appointed judges who had encouraged them to indict their neighbors for having illegally opposed Britain. In several colonies, grand juries issued public statements intended as propaganda for the patriot cause, and some patriot judges indulged in equally offensive charges to grand and petty juries alike. In Philadelphia, a grand jury denounced the payments and salaries of royal officials from revenues collected from the tea tax, and the grand jury even advocated a boycott against English products. Grand juries commonly advocated intercolonial actions to redress grievances against Britain. Like trial juries, the grand juries of the prerevolutionary era, claiming the rights of Englishmen, curbed the enforcement of objectionable acts by government officials. Grand juries promoted American resistance and generally served as popular spokesmen. Even during the War for Independence, grand juries continued their multiple civic functions. They governed their localities as well as indicted offenders. They investigated not only law enforcement but also the physical conditions of roads, bridges, and ferries; they supervised the prices of commodities; and they fixed the rates of taxes, audited public records, and generally compelled local governing bodies to be more responsive to public needs and to meet regularly.

From the earliest possible date, English colonists in the American wilderness enjoyed trial by jury in criminal cases. Royal instructions of 1606 for the governance of Virginia provided that offenders be tried by jury before the governor and council. Moreover, the Virginia charter of 1606 contained a provision that was repeated in later charters of Virginia and in the charters of virtually all other colonies, guaranteeing colonists the rights of Englishmen as if they still resided in the mother country. In Massachusetts, for example, as soon as courts began to operate, they worked with trial juries. The right to trial by jury received formal recognition in 1641 in the Massachusetts Body of Liberties, which authorized parties in civil suits, as well as persons accused of crime, to choose whether to be tried by judges or by a jury, and also authorized challenges to potential jurors for cause. If a jury could not reach a verdict, its members were free to consult with any person for advice. In some sparsely settled areas, six member juries tried cases involving minor infractions, such as trespass or drunkenness, or involving small amounts, usually less than ten pounds. But virtually all colonial charters possessed a clause similar to that in the charter of West New Jersey, which specified that unless convicted by a jury consisting of twelve men of the neighborhood, no one could lose life, limb, liberty, or property in a civil or criminal case.

In the most celebrated case of colonial history, the trial of John Peter Zenger in New York for the offense of seditious libel, in 1735, his counsel successfully challenged the partiality of jurors whom Governor Cosby, the target of Zenger's newspaper, initially selected. Knowing that the law was against his client, Zenger's counsel played to the jury above the head of the court, urging the jury to acquit. The trial judge had accurately instructed the jurors that they should apply the law as defined by the court and merely return a verdict based on their judgment whether the defendant had in fact used the words attributed to him; the court would then decide as a matter of law whether defendant's language constituted the crime charged. But Zenger's counsel boldly informed the jury that they, not the court, were the judges of the law as well as the facts, and if they did not understand Zenger's words to be false, his publications were not criminal. If, that is, contrary to the court's instructions, the jury believed that Zenger had published the truth, they should return a general verdict in his favor by deciding on the law as well as the facts. Thus, counsel used the jury as a court of public opinion. But if Zenger had attacked the provincial assembly instead of a despised royal governor, he would have been summarily convicted before the bar of the house for breach of parliamentary privilege, with the result that he would have been imprisoned and forgotten by posterity. Instead, he was tried by a jury that acquitted because he symbolized a popular cause. Zenger's counsel did not have to worry that one man's truth is another's falsehood or that political opinions are not necessarily susceptible to proof as truth or falsehood. Moreover, a jury in a case of seditious libel is a court of public opinion, often synonymous with public prejudice, and is hardly an adequate instrument for measuring the truth of an accusation against the government, its officials, or its policies.

When judges were dependent tools of the government, a jury of one's peers or neighbors might seem to be a promising bulwark against the tyrannous prosecution of free expression. But juries, with the power of ruling on the guilt or innocence of alleged criminal libels, could be as influenced by prevailing passions as judges when deciding the fate of defendants who had voiced unpopular views. In England, where the power of juries in libel cases was secured by Fox's Libel Act of 1792, the most repressive prosecutions, with few exceptions, were successful. In America only one verdict of "not guilty" was returned in the numerous prosecutions under the Sedition Act of 1798, which entrusted criminality to the jury and admitted truth as a defense. Thus, Zengerian principles scarcely protected freedom of the press so long as the law cosseted the concept of seditious libel. The power of juries to decide the whole issue, the law as well as the facts, by returning a general verdict did not expand the bounds of freedom. Moreover, the power of legislatures to punish alleged breaches of parliamentary privilege, which included unwanted criticism, restricted those bounds.

By the era of the American Revolution trial by jury was probably the most common right in all the colonies. When Parliament imposed the Stamp Act of 1765, authorizing admiralty courts to enforce its provisions, John Adams voiced the American reaction: "But the most grievous innovation of all, is the alarming extension of the power of courts of admiralty. In these courts, one judge presides alone! No juries have any concern there! The law and the fact are both to be decided by the same single judge." Thus, the Stamp Act Congress protested the denial of one of "the most essential rights and liberties of the colonists," and the Boston town meeting of 1772, which framed "A List of Infringements and Violations of Rights," included trial by jury, which it hailed as "the grand bulwark and security of English property." Colonists vehemently denounced admiralty courts because they worked without juries. Selectively quoting from Blackstone's *Commentaries*, the colonists praised his remarks to the effect that trial by jury was the "sacred palladium" of English liberties that might be undermined by new or different methods of trial.

Americans formally claimed trial by a jury of the vicinage as a right of Englishmen whenever they apprehended that Britain threatened that right, as when a provision of the Coercive Acts of 1774 authorized the trial in England of certain persons who violated the acts. The first Continental Congress in 1774 approved of an intercolonial "Declaration of Rights" based on natural law, the English Constitution, and the provincial charters. The Declaration of Rights included "the great and inestimable privilege of being tried by their peers of the vicinage" according to the common law. And when Congress sought to enlist Canadian support for its cause, its letter to the inhabitants of Quebec, in 1774, specified trial by jury as the preserver of life, liberty, and property against arbitrary and capricious men. In the 1775 Declaration of the Causes and Necessity of Taking Up Arms, Congress censured Britain for having passed statutes "extending the jurisdiction of courts of admiralty and vice-admiralty beyond their ancient limits; for depriving us of the accustomed and inestimable privilege of trial by jury, in cases affecting both life and property." In the Declaration of Independence, Congress criticized George III for "depriving us, in many cases, of the benefit of trial by jury."

When Virginia framed its constitution in 1776, the first state to do so, it declared that in all criminal prosecutions the defendant had a right to a "speedy trial by an impartial jury of his vicinage," language echoed by Pennsylvania. Delaware's constitution described juries as the triers of facts and added that no person accused of crime should be found guilty unless he had received a "speedy trial" by an impartial jury. Maryland copied that phrasing and North Carolina used similar language. Vermont guaranteed a speedy trial by "an impartial jury of the country," and Massachusetts framed a provision that influenced the writing of the Bill of Rights, saying that the legislature should not subject any person to a capital or infamous punishment without trial by jury. New Hampshire adopted the same language. Every state that framed a constitution secured trial by jury. No other personal right received protection from the constitutions of so many states. The Northwest Ordinance of 1787, that measure of genius which thwarted the development of colonial problems on the American continent by guaranteeing statehood to territories, also guaranteed trial by jury.

At the Philadelphia Constitutional Convention of 1787 the first right recognized was trial by jury. The convention did not frame a bill of rights but included several rights within the body of the Constitution. The Committee of Detail, thanks to the recommendation of John Rutledge of South Carolina, proposed trial by jury in criminal cases in the state that was the locale of the offense. James Wilson of Pennsylvania and Charles Pinckney of South Carolina lent their support to such a provision, which eventually became lodged in Article III, section 2. The right to trial by jury in civil cases received belated recognition when Elbridge Gerry of Massachusetts claimed that civil juries guarded against "corrupt" judges. Pinckney cooperated with Gerry in urging a provision, for Article III, that would secure trial by jury "as usual in civil cases," but the Convention let the recommendation die when others observed that jury practices throughout the nation were not uniform so that no one could be sure of the meaning of the phrase "as usual." Gerry, who refused to sign the Constitution, inaccurately declared that it established a "tribunal without juries, which will be a Star-chamber as to Civil cases." George Mason of Virginia, who belatedly lamented the omission of a bill of rights, offered a few specific recommendations, including trial by jury in civil cases.

During the controversy over the ratification of the Constitution, Richard Henry Lee of Virginia was one of the first of several Anti-Federalists to declare misleadingly that the Constitution, if ratified, would abolish trial by jury in civil cases. That was one of the most frequently trumpeted Anti-Federalist charges. Lee invoked Sir Edward Coke, Sir Matthew Hale, Sir John Holt, and Blackstone "and almost every other legal or political writer" to prove that trial by jury in civil cases was an essential right necessary to maintain freedom and to keep courts from becoming arbitrary. Patrick Henry promiscuously alleged that the Constitution jeopardized trial by jury, and the influential minority report of the Anti-Federalists in Pennsylvania declared that trial by jury in civil cases ought not be abolished. An essay by an anonymous writer in a Philadelphia newspaper grieved for the death of "that sacred bulwark of liberty," trial by jury in civil cases, and so it went routinely in Anti-Federalist speeches and publications. "Centinel," a prolific Philadelphia newspaper essayist, predicted that the federal courts would "supersede the state courts" because of the Constitution's failure to provide for civil jury trials. The minority in Maryland, with greater restraint and good sense, urged a provision that "there shall be a trial by jury in all criminal cases according to the course of proceeding in the state where the offence is committed." That recommendation did not distort the Constitution's provision for trial by jury, as most Anti-Federalists did. "Aristocrotis," the author of a pamphlet published in Pennsylvania, distorted facts for the sake of irony. Predicting that Congress would deprive the people of trial by jury, because it was so absurd a right, he claimed that it allowed twelve ignorant and probably illiterate plebians to be judges of law, which had the authority of lawyers who sat in legislatures and courts. A "Columbian Patriot," who was probably Mercy Otis Warren, writing in a Boston newspaper, insinuated that an "inquisition" would be the result of abolishing trial by jury in civil cases. The fullest and best repudiation of such Anti-Federalist hysteria was Alexander Hamilton's long essay in *The Federalist*, No. 83. He discoursed on the differences in state practices and on the power of Congress to establish courts and therefore trial by jury.

Some of the hysteria regarding trial by jury may be explained by the Anti-Federalists' reaction to attempted subversions of trial by jury in several states. In *Respublica v. Doan*, the defendant was legislatively convicted for a felony and outlawed; when he was captured in 1784, the state ordered his execution, but he demanded a trial by jury, as guaranteed by the state constitution. The state judges, however, ruled that Doan had in effect rejected trial by jury when he fled from custody and became a fugitive. He was hanged without having had a trial by jury. In *Trevett v. Weeden*, a Rhode Island case of 1786, at issue was a state act that compelled the observance of a state paper-money act that made anyone refusing to accept paper money at par with specie triable without a jury. Weeden refused acceptance but demanded trial by jury. The court declined to decide the issue by ruling that it lacked jurisdiction, but some of the judges censured the statute because it failed to provide for trial by jury. In *Bayard v. Singleton,* decided in North Carolina in 1787, the high court of that state supported trial by jury against a legislative attempt to undermine it in a case involving property rights. The legislature summoned the judges before it to determine whether they had committed a malpractice by refusing to give effect to a statute that subverted trial by jury, and the court boldly held void the measure that adversely affected the right to trial by jury on behalf of one of the parties.

In the First Congress, Representative James Madison recommended amendments to the Constitution that became the Bill of Rights. One of his proposals, which he conceived to be "the most valuable amendment in the whole list," would have prohibited the states from infringing on various rights, including trial by jury in criminal cases. That one passed the House but the Senate rejected it for unknown reasons. Among the proposals that received congressional and state endorsement was one that became the Sixth Amendment, guaranteeing a speedy and public trial by an impartial jury of the vicinage, and another that became the Seventh Amendment, guaranteeing trial by jury in civil suits.

CHAPTER ELEVEN

The Eighth Amendment

T HE EIGHTH AMENDMENT provides: "Excessive bail shall not be required, nor excessive fines imposed, nor cruel and unusual punishments inflicted." The amendment duplicates a provision in the English Bill of Rights of 1689. Its clause banning excessive bail was intended to prevent the once-frequent judicial practice of devising methods for keeping victims imprisoned indefinitely without trial. Judges used to fix bail at impossibly high rates, far in excess of a prisoner's capacity to raise. Parliament, in effect, reformed that situation when it enacted that punishment should approximate the severity of the crime.

The notion that punishment should not be barbarous or unduly severe but, rather, should be proportioned to the offense goes back to the Old Testament. Leviticus 24:19–20 says, "If a man injures his neighbor, what he has done must be done to him: broken limb for broken limb, eye for eye, tooth for tooth. As the injury inflicted, so must be the injury suffered." This rule of *lex talionis* found expression in Magna Carta. Section 20 (later renumbered section 14) stipulated that "a freeman shall be amerced for a small offence only according to the degree of the offence; and for a grave offence he shall be amerced according to the gravity of the offence." A document of the thirteenth century required that amercements or fines should be "according to their offences" and not "exceed the just penalty of the offence." A fourteenth-century document, purportedly copying the laws of Edward the Confessor of the eleventh century, made the policy on amercements applicable to physical punishments; it provided that punishment should be imposed "according to the nature and extent of the offence." In the mid-sixteenth century Parliament acknowledged that the kingdom would be more secure if the subjects loved their king and if laws did not inflict great penalties for disobedience; nevertheless, Parliament directed that murderers should be dissected and gibbeted. Only a small number of offenses were capital, yet in the time of Henry VIII the death sentence was inflicted on about seventy-two thousand people. As time passed, the number of capital felonies increased until they reached about two hundred offenses. Death was actually inflicted in only a small proportion of the cases, however, because the sentences were usually mitigated by transportation either to America or, later, Australia. The law on the books was savage, in practice far more moderate.

In a book of 1583 Robert Beale, the clerk of the Privy Council, condemned "the racking of grievous offenders, as being cruel, barbarous, contrary to law, and unto the liberty of English subjects." Beale was the first person to object to torture even when authorized by the crown and one of the few Englishmen ever to object to "cruel" punishments. The conventional English objection was aimed at excessive, not cruel, punishments. In 1615 the Court of King's Bench, England's highest criminal court, censured as unlawful or extreme the punishment of a man who, for having criticized an officer of the crown, had been thrown into a dungeon with no bed or food. Imprisonment, the court said, "ought always to be according to the quality of the offence," a point buttressed by a quotation from Magna Carta. Thus, England had long prohibited excessive or extreme punishments but never actually outlawed "cruel" punishments. A punishment could be extreme without being cruel, as in the instance of a very long imprisonment for some trifling offense.

If an offense was criminal, a man could not suffer loss of life, limb, or property unless he had first been convicted by a jury, but he could not be tried without his consent. The court always asked an accused person whether he would "put himself on the country"—that is, agree to be tried by a jury. If he refused to plead, because he feared the consequences of conviction, his consent was extorted by "punishment strong and hard," or *peine forte et dure*. He was stripped, put in irons on the ground in the worst part of the prison, and fed only coarse bread one day and water the next. Then the refinement of "punishment" was added: he was slowly pressed, spread-eagled on the ground, with as much iron placed on his body as he could bear "and then more." The punishment by pressing, exposure, and slow starvation continued until the prisoner agreed to be tried or died.

The purpose of peine forte et dure was not to extort a confession or force a person to incriminate himself or others; the purpose, rather, was simply to extort a plea. The law did not care whether the individual pleaded guilty or not guilty, only that he pleaded. In 1772 a statute provided that a prisoner standing mute to the indictment of felony should be treated as if he had been convicted by a verdict or by a confession, thus ending peine forte et dure. But the law permitted a prisoner's thumbs to be painfully tied together. Not until 1827 was the rule altered to direct the court to enter a plea of not guilty for a prisoner who stood mute or refused to plead.

Sir William Blackstone in his *Commentaries on the Law of England* proudly declared that the "humanity of the English nation has authorized, by tacit consent, an almost general mitigation of . . . torture or cruelty." English history, he said, showed "very few instances" of anyone being disemboweled or burned alive unless first deprived of sensation by strangling. Physical punishments usually consisted of exile, banishment, transportation, or loss of liberty by imprisonment. England confiscated property, personal and real, and imposed disabilities on holding office, employment, or inheritance, and it sometimes mutilated or dismembered an offender by cutting off a hand or foot. Blackstone added that England also stigmatized people by slitting nostrils or by branding, and it also punished by imprisonment at hard labor, by using the pillory, the stocks, or ducking stool, but England never broke anyone's back on the wheel, or tied people to wild horses which pulled them apart, or buried them alive. Even so, in Blackstone's time, capital punishment was still the penalty for more than 160 offenses. Blackstone believed that the severe punishments imposed in the time of James II by the Court of King's Bench accounted for the provision in the English Bill of Rights that the Eighth Amendment copied. He had in mind the fact that Lord Chief Justice George Jeffreys sent 292 prisoners to their deaths and brutally punished hundreds of others. He sentenced 841 prisoners to be sent to the West Indies as slaves for not less than ten years. In one case a young boy named Tutchin who had criticized the government was convicted of seditious libel; he was sentenced to be imprisoned for seven years and to be flogged through every market town in his shire during each of those years, which meant every other week for seven years. The punishment was later mitigated.

Though English common-law courts did not sentence anyone to be tortured, the monarch could authorize the rack by special royal warrant. The rack in the Tower of London was frequently used, especially during the time of the Tudors. Moreover, English law had permitted such grisly punishments as "pulling out the tongue," slicing off the nose, cutting off the genitals, and, for capital crimes, boiling to death. Torture was thought to mean only the infliction of cruel punishment for the purpose of coercing a suspect to confess a crime. English judges tended to be harsh and sometimes abused defendants in court by overawing and threatening them, but judges also boasted that torture was illegal at common law and that they preferred guilty parties to escape punishment rather than convict innocent ones. When Sir Thomas Smith, writing about 1565, declared that torture "to put a malefactor to excessive paine, to make him confesse of himselfe, or of his fellowes or complices, is not used in England," he meant that common-law courts never employed it. But prerogative courts did. The monarch and the Privy Council or its judicial arm, the Court of Star Chamber, could and did authorize torture. The penalty for high treason was particularly gruesome, though it did not come within the ambit of the common law's understanding of torture. The victim, if male, was hanged but cut down while still alive; his genitals were cut off and burned before him; he was disemboweled, still alive, and then he was cut into four parts and beheaded. That penalty was last inflicted in 1817, though beheading and quartering were not prohibited until 1870. Women convicted of treason were sentenced to being burned alive, although they were usually first strangled until unconscious. The burning of women ended in 1790, and whipping them ended in 1841.

Branding and nose slitting as well as flogging were inflicted as punishments for lesser crimes. In 1630 Alexander Leighton, a Puritan clergyman who had libeled the Anglican bishops, was fined the staggering amount of ten thousand pounds, defrocked by the highest ecclesiastical court, unmercifully whipped until almost dead, pilloried, one ear nailed to the pillory and then cut off, his cheek branded, and his nose slit; a week later he suffered the same mutilations on the other side of his face, and he was imprisoned for the rest of his life. William Prynne, another Puritan martyr, maligned theater productions that included women, though the queen occasionally acted on the stage. Prynne was mistreated in the pillory, branded on the forehead, and suffered the cutting off of his ears; he was also heavily fined and sentenced to prison for life. Others suffered similar punishments. The Long Parliament freed Leighton, Prynne, and others in 1640. Although the Star Chamber was also abolished, England did not by law then or later prevent excessively severe punishments.

In 1685, after the abortive rebellion of the duke of Monmouth, Chief Justice George Jeffreys of the King's Bench conducted his "Bloody Assize" against captured rebels, for which James II awarded him the lord chancellorship. But the provision of the Bill of Rights of 1689 against "cruel and unusual punishments" had nothing to do with a hostile parliamentary reaction to Jeffreys's conduct. The chief prosecutor during the Bloody Assize was Sir Henry Pollfexen, a close friend and supporter of Jeffreys who did not view the Bloody Assize as illegal; Pollfexen was one of the chief backers of the Bill of Rights. Its provision against cruel and unusual punishments derived mainly from the reaction to the case of Titus Oates.

Oates underwent punishments that even then seemed excessive or unduly severe, although he was not mutilated as Leighton and Prynne had been. A cleric of the Church of England, Oates was the author of the infamous Popish Plot hoax, an accusation that English Catholics, led by Jesuit priests, intended to assassinate Charles II. In the national hysteria that followed Oates's sensational accusations, fifteen people, including the leader of the Jesuit order in England, were disemboweled, quartered, and beheaded for high treason. When evidence of Oates's hoax was revealed in 1685, he was indicted for perjury. Two of his four judges, Francis Withens and George Jeffreys, expressed regret that the law did not permit Oates to be hanged for perjuries that had resulted in the deaths of so many innocent people. The court sentenced Oates to be defrocked, to pay a fine of two thousand marks (approximately ten thousand dollars), to be whipped from Aldgate to Newgate, a distance of about a mile and a half, and, after a day's intermission, to be whipped from Newgate to Tyburn, another two miles, and then to be imprisoned for life as well as be pilloried four times annually. Oates's case is the only one in which contemporaries described his punishment as "cruel" as well as extreme or excessive, even though severe floggings and sentences of life imprisonment were not unusual.

Following the Revolution of 1689, Oates was released, and he petitioned Parliament for redress. His judges initially contended that his sentence was deserved because his perjuries had resulted in innocent deaths. A majority of the House of Lords agreed, but several dissenting lords argued that the judgment against Oates had been erroneous, that the secular court could not defrock a clergyman, and that the severe whippings and the sentence of imprisonment for life in a case of perjury were "barbarous," "inhuman," "unchristian," and "unjust." With Oates in mind, the majority of the House of Lords, including the common-law judges who had sentenced him, declared that "excessive bail ought not to be required nor excessive fines imposed, nor cruel nor unusual punishments inflicted." Despite Oates's whippings, he had not undergone any physically brutal treatment as Leighton had, and whipping was not cruel as a matter of law. Indeed, whipping continued as a punishment in England well into the twentieth century. However, the House of Commons agreed with the dissenters in the House of Lords, and as a result the English Bill of Rights of 1689 outlawed cruel and unusual punishments.

In America, colonial Virginia in 1610 sentenced a soldier to lose rank, have his sword broken, stand in the pillory with both his ears nailed, and pay a fine of one hundred pounds sterling—a huge amount—or suffer having both ears cut off. Section 46 of the Massachusetts Body of Liberties of 1641, drafted by Nathanael Ward of Ipswich, declared that "for bodilie punishments we allow amongst us none that are inhumane Barbarous or cruell." This was the first American ban on cruel punishments. Nevertheless, Massachusetts required robbers, especially highwaymen, to be burned on the forehead and in some cases suffer life imprisonment. Horse thieves as well as other thieves were branded and flogged. Generally speaking, punishments in America were probably more lenient than in England. Mutilations were rare, and women were hanged, not burned, for the crime of witchcraft. Whipping was the most common punishment, though humiliating penalties like the ducking stool, the pillory, and a variety of public penances such as the scarlet letter were also common.

On the other hand, the provision of the 1689 Bill of Rights on excessive bail and fines and cruel and unusual punishments was widely copied in America. Several states, including Virginia and Pennsylvania, added that punishments ought to be moderate. Maryland stipulated that sanguinary laws ought to be avoided consistent with the safety of the state and made the ban on cruel and unusual punishments apply to legislative enactments as well as judicial sentences. South Carolina required punishments to be proportionate to crimes. Six of the first thirteen states constitutionally prohibited cruel and unusual punishments, and a seventh did so by statute.

New Hampshire most fully provided a constitutional section on punishment: "All penalties ought to be proportioned to the nature of the offence. No wise legislature will affix the same punishment to the crimes of theft, forgery and the like, which they do to those of murder and treason; where the same undistinguishing severity is exerted against all offences; the people are led to forget the real distinction in the crimes themselves; and to commit the most flagrant with as little compunction as they do those of the lightest dye. For the same reason a multitude of sanguinary laws is both impolitic and unjust. The true design of all punishments being to reform; not to exterminate, mankind." And in another section of its constitution, New Hampshire banned magistrates and courts from demanding excessive bail or sureties, imposing excessive fines, or inflicting cruel and unusual punishments.

In the Northwest Ordinance of 1787, the Congress of the Confederation provided a bill of rights with a clause saying, "All fines shall be moderate, and no cruel or unusual punishments shall be inflicted." That same Congress, however, rejected a variety of proposals by Richard Henry Lee of Virginia to frame a bill of rights for the nation as well as for the northwest territories. One of Lee's proposals would have prohibited "cruel and unusual punishments." During the controversy over the ratification of the Constitution, a Massachusetts delegate objected to the Constitution because it did not prohibit Congress from inflicting cruel and unusual punishments. "Racks and gibbets," he predicted, "may be amongst the most mild instruments of their description." In Virginia, Patrick Henry and other Anti-Federalists claimed that Congress would prescribe "tortures" and "barbarous punishments" as well as excessive fines. The Pennsylvania minority, also expecting the worst, proposed a bill of rights whose provisions outlawed infliction of cruel and unusual punishments. North Carolina, New York, and Rhode Island also ratified the Constitution with recommendations for amendments, among them one that would ban cruel and unusual punishments.

When the Eighth Amendment was being framed in the First Congress, one member, Samuel Livermore of New Hampshire, argued that death by hanging was sometimes necessary, moreover that some offenders deserved to be whipped and even have their ears cut off. He hoped those punishments would still be possible and not come within the prohibition of cruel and unusual punishments. Representative James Madison, when introducing the proposals that became the Bill of Rights, offered one that became the Eighth Amendment. It said that excessive fines and cruel and unusual punishments "shall" not be inflicted. Madison was personally responsible for the imperative verb "shall," using it in place of its universal flabby predecessor, "ought." The Senate accepted Madison's proposal verbatim.

Cruel and unusual punishment referred to methods of punishment as well as their severity; they had to be as swift and painless as possible and in no circumstances involve a lingering death or any form of torture. Death itself was an acceptable punishment. Life can be extinguished by the state if it provides due process of law to convict an offender. Unusual punishment must always be cruel to come under the constitutional ban. An unusual or novel punishment that is administered speedily and humanely passes constitutional muster. But punishment must also be proportioned to the offense. A conventional punishment, such as whipping, could not be so excessive as to become a form of cruelty. Imprisonment for many years would be excessive punishment for a petty crime.

CHAPTER TWELVE

The Ninth Amendment: Unenumerated Rights

FOR 175 years, from 1791 to 1965, the Ninth Amendment lay dormant, a constitutional curiosity comparable in vitality to the Third Amendment (no quartering of troops in private homes) or to the privileges and immunities clause of the Fourteenth Amendment after the Supreme Court had "interpreted" the meaning out of it in the Slaughterhouse Cases of 1873. The Court held that almost all rights depended on state, rather than federal, protection. Obscurity shrouded the meaning of the Ninth Amendment. One member of the Supreme Court, Robert H. Jackson, in a speech made after some reflection, acknowledged that the rights secured by the Ninth Amendment were "still a mystery."

The year 1965 marks the beginning of Ninth Amendment jurisprudence. For the first time the Court mentioned the amendment, at least in part, as a basis for holding a government measure unconstitutional. Justice William O. Douglas for the Court confronted a state act that made the use of contraceptives criminal, even when counseled by a physician treating a married couple. From the First, Third, Fourth, and Fifth Amendments and in part from the Ninth Amendment, Douglas derived a "right of privacy older than the Bill of Rights" with respect to the "sacred precincts of marital bedrooms," and three justices believed that the Ninth Amendment, unfortified by the "penumbras" and "emanations" of other provisions of the Bill of Rights, supported the voiding of the offensive state act. Justice Arthur Goldberg for the three wrote a concurring opinion based on the Ninth Amendment, buttressed by the "liberty" guaranteed by the Fourteenth Amendment.

Within fifteen years the Ninth Amendment, once the subject of only incidental references, was invoked in more than twelve hundred state and federal cases in the most astonishing variety of matters. After the Court had resuscitated the amendment, litigants found its charms compelling precisely because of its utter lack of specificity with respect to the rights that it protects. It says: "The enumeration in the Constitution, of certain rights, shall not be construed to deny or disparage others retained by the people." Those who have relied on this amendment for constitutional armament include schoolboys and police officers seeking relief from regulations that govern the length of their hair, citizens eager to preserve the purity of water and air against environmental polluters, and homosexuals claiming a right to be married. The question whether the Ninth Amendment was intended to be a cornucopia of unenumerated rights produces as many answers as there are points of view.

Oddly enough, those who advocate a constitutional "jurisprudence of original intention" and assert that the Constitution "said what it meant and meant what it said," are the ones who most vigorously deny content to the Ninth Amendment and to the concept of a "living Constitution." Presumably they would not swear fealty to a dead Constitution, not even to a static one of the sort endorsed by Chief Justice Roger Taney in the Dred Scott case. Nevertheless they reject as absurd the idea that the Ninth Amendment could have been intended as a repository for newly discovered rights that activist judges embrace.

The fact that the Framers did not intend most, if any, of the rights that litigants read into the Ninth and would have found bizarre the notion that the Constitution protects any of those rights is really of no significance. We must remember, after all, that the Framers would have found absurd and bizarre most features of our constitutional law as well as of our politics, cities, industries, and society. Justice Hugo L. Black, in the very case of 1965 that breathed life into the Ninth Amendment, could not find much justification for the discovery of a right to privacy anywhere in the Constitution, let alone in the Ninth Amendment. The judicial reading of rights into it or out of it, he cautioned, "would make of this Court's members a day-to-day constitutional convention." Figuratively, however, that is what the Supreme Court is—a continuous constitutional convention. The Court has functioned as if it were that since John Marshall's time, if not earlier, and few justices in the history of the Court have contributed so much to the Court's effectiveness as a constitutional convention as Justice Black, especially in his First and Fifth Amendment opinions.

To say that the Framers did not intend the Court to act as a constitutional convention or to shape public policies by interpreting the Constitution is, again, to assert historical truth. However, that truth does not invalidate judicial decisions that the Framers failed to foresee; it reveals, rather, their human incapacity to predict how the system that they designed would work. They did not expect the development of a judicial power that influenced public policies. They did not expect judicial activism whether conservative or liberal. Nor did they foresee political parties, administrative agencies, overwhelming executive domination of foreign policy, national governance of the economy, foreign policy made without knowledge of any elected members of the government, or management of fiscal policies by the Federal Reserve Board. The argument for or against some judicial interpretation of the constitution progresses not at all by the allegation, even if verifiable, that the Framers would have been shocked or surprised by such an interpretation.

The starting points for interpreting the Ninth Amendment are the text itself and the rule of construction which holds that if a plain meaning exists, it should be followed. As Justice Joseph Story said, "The first and fundamental rule in the interpretation of all instruments is, to construe them according to the sense of the terms, and the intention of the parties." If a plain meaning does not exist, the language of the text must be construed so as not to contradict the document at any point, and meaning must be sought in its purposes or in the principles that it embodies as understood from "its nature and objects, its scope and design." We know enough about the making of the Ninth Amendment and about its historical context to apply these rules with considerable confidence, wherever they might lead. They lead first to the indisputable fact that the amendment by force of its terms protects unenumerated rights of the people. That opens the question, What are those rights? The answer depends on a preliminary question: Why would the Framers have included an amendment that acknowledges the existence of unenumerated rights that are no more subject to abridgment than the rights that are specified in the first eight amendments?

We must remember, by way of an answer, that ratificationists, including the most sophisticated of Framers, had made the enormously unpopular and weak argument that a bill of rights was superfluous in the United States because government derived from the people and had only delegated powers. Alexander Hamilton, James Wilson, Oliver Ellsworth, and James Madison, among others, also argued that no need for a bill of rights existed because the government could not use its limited powers to encroach on reserved rights; no powers extended, for example, to religion or the press. That argument shriveled against contentions that Congress might exercise its delegated powers in such a way that abridged unprotected rights. The power to tax, implemented by the ominous necessary and proper clause, could be used to destroy a critical press and might be enforced by general warrants enabling the government to ransack homes and businesses for evidence of criminal evasion of the revenue laws or for evidence of seditious publications.

The Federalist, No. 84, argued that particularizing rights was "not only unnecessary in the proposed Constitution but would even be dangerous. They would contain various exceptions to powers which are not granted; and, in this very account, would afford a colorable pretext to claim more than were granted." If no power had been granted to restrict the press, Hamilton reasoned, no need existed to declare that the liberty of the press ought not be restricted. To make such a declaration furnished "a plausible pretense for claiming that power" to violate the press. A provision "against restraining the liberty of the press afforded a clear implication that a power to prescribe proper regulations concerning it was intended to be vested in the national government." Ratificationists had also argued unconvincingly that a bill of rights would be "dangerous" because any right omitted from it might be presumed to be lost.

This argument proved far too much. First, it proved that the particular rights that the Constitution already protected—no religious test, no bills of attainder, trials by jury in criminal cases, among others—stood in grave jeopardy: specifying a right implied a power to violate it. Second, the inclusion of some rights in the original text of the constitution implied that all unenumerated ones were relinquished.

James Wilson, in the course of arguing that a bill of rights was not only unsuitable for the United States but dangerous as well, made another well-publicized statement of the ratificationist position: "A bill of rights annexed to a constitution is an enumeration of the powers reserved. If we attempt an enumeration, everything that is not enumerated is presumed to be given. The consequence is, that an imperfect enumeration would throw all implied powers into the scale of government; and the rights of the people would be rendered incomplete." Oliver Ellsworth advocated the same position. Madison more carefully declared in his state's ratifying convention, "If an enumeration be made of all our rights, will it not be implied that everything omitted is given to the general government?" He, too, thought that "an imperfect enumeration"—that is, an incomplete one—"is dangerous."

Madison switched to the cause of adding amendments to the Constitution that would protect individual liberties and allay the fears of people who would likely support the Constitution, if given a sense of security about their rights. When he proposed his amendments to the House, he was mindful that proponents of ratification had warned that a bill of rights might be dangerous because the government could violate any right omitted. During the course of his great speech of June 8, 1789, Madison repeatedly reminded Congress of the need to satisfy the legitimate fears of "the great number of our constituents who are dissatisfied" with the Constitution because it seemed to put their rights in jeopardy. We must, he added, "expressly declare the great rights of mankind secured under this constitution." The "great object in view," Madison declared, "is to limit and qualify the powers of Government, by excepting out of the grant of power those cases in which the government ought not act, or to act only in a particular mode. They [state recommendations] point these exceptions sometimes against the abuse of the executive power, sometimes against the legislative, and in some cases, against the community itself; or, in other words, against the majority in favor of the minority." Clearly, Madison was referring to constitutional prohibitions upon government to protect not only the rights of the people but even unpopular rights, such as those exercised by a minority that needed protection.

Defending his recommendation that became the Ninth Amendment, Madison acknowledged that a major objection against a bill of rights consisted of the argument that "by enumerating particular exceptions to the grant of power, it would disparage those rights which were not placed in that enumeration; and it might follow, by implication, that those rights which were not singled out, were intended to be assigned into the hands of the General Government, and were consequently insecure." He called that "one of the most plausible arguments" he had ever heard against the inclusion of a bill of rights. It was an argument that he himself had made, and it had become a Federalist cliché, although it self-destructed by virtue of the fact that the Constitution explicitly protected several rights, exposing all those omitted—including, by Madison's description, "the great rights of mankind"—to governmental violation. He was, therefore, answering his own previous objection, not one that had been advanced by Anti-Federalists, when he devised the simple proposal that became the Ninth Amendment. It was, he said, meant to guard against the possibility that unenumerated rights might be imperiled by the enumeration of particular rights. By excepting many rights from the grant of powers, no implication was intended, and no inference should be drawn, that rights not excepted from the grant of powers fell within those powers. As Madison phrased his proposal, it declared: "The exceptions [to power] here or elsewhere in the constitution made in favor of particular rights, shall not be so construed as to diminish the just importance of other rights retained by the people, or as to enlarge the powers delegated by the constitution; but either as actual limitations on such powers, or as inserted merely for greater caution." Madison improvised that proposal. No precise precedent for it existed. It was one of several proposals by Madison that stamped the Bill of Rights with his creativity. Changing the flaccid verb "ought" to "shall" fell into the same category. So did his selection of particular rights for inclusion. No state, for example, had a due process of law clause in its own constitution, and only New York had recommended such a clause in place of the more familiar "law of the land" clause. Either phrasing carried the majesty and prestige of Magna Carta. Sir Edward Coke had taught, and Americans believed, that due process of law meant accordance with regularized common-law procedures, especially grand jury accusation and trial by jury, both of which Madison provided for. Madison also provided the basis for a radical alteration of the law of search and seizure by his choice of the broadest possible language available at the time. Madison enumerated several rights whose constitutional protection was uncommon. Only New Hampshire by its state constitution provided against double jeopardy, and only Massachusetts and Vermont had constitutionally guaranteed just compensation when private property is taken for a public use. Madison's personal choice of the phrasing of several provisions of the Bill of Rights also became significant. Instead of saying that a person could not be compelled to give evidence against himself, Madison preferred to say that he could not be compelled to be a witness against himself, thereby laying the basis for a future distinction between testimonial and nontestimonial compulsion. Notwithstanding the personal touch Madison imposed on his proposed amendments, he claimed that he had recommended only the familiar and avoided the controversial. He warned against enumerating anything except "simple, acknowledged principles," saying that amendments of a "doubtful nature" might damage the constitutional system.

The House did not take the time or trouble to review his recommended amendments with the attention they deserved. In committee or as a result of debate, the House added only one important right to Madison's list, freedom of speech, which Pennsylvania had constitutionally protected. Some major principles, which appropriately prefaced a bill of rights, were deleted, despite their commonplaceness. Madison, for example, had urged a statement that power derives from and rests with the people, that government should be exercised for their benefit, and that they have a right to change that government when inadequate to its purposes. He had lifted his statement of those purposes from his own state's 1776 constitution and from its 1788 recommendations for inclusion in a national bill of rights. Those purposes expressed the idea that governments are instituted to secure the people, said Madison, "in the enjoyment of life and liberty, with the right of acquiring and using property, and generally of pursuing and obtaining happiness and safety." The Declaration of Independence had made the points more concisely and felicitously, but not with such generosity. The Virginia version proposed by Madison (and adopted in numerous state constitutions) spoke not only about the pursuit of happiness but of obtaining it. Conceivably, the committee that eliminated Madison's prefatory principles believed them to be implicit in its streamlined version of what became the Ninth Amendment: "The enumeration in this Constitution of certain rights shall not be construed to deny or disparage others retained by the people." Both houses approved.

The Ninth Amendment was a definitive solution to the ratificationists' problem of how to enumerate the rights of the people without endangering those that might be omitted. The amendment was also a device for Congress to avoid making a systematic enumeration when framing the Bill of Rights. Framing it was not high on Congress's agenda and, except for Madison's nagging insistence, might not have been attempted at all or, perhaps, would have been disposed of in an even more perfunctory fashion. The Ninth Amendment functioned as a sweep-it-under-the-rug means of disposing as swiftly as possible of a task embarrassing to both parties and delaying the organization of the government and providing for its revenues. And the Ninth Amendment could also serve to draw the sting from any criticism that the catalog of personal freedoms was incomplete. Another conclusion one must draw from the text of the amendment is that the enumeration of rights in the preceding text was not meant to be exhaustive.

What rights did the Ninth Amendment protect? They had to be either "natural rights" or "positive rights," to use the terms Madison employed in the notes for the great speech of June 8 advocating amendments. In that speech he distinguished "the pre-existent rights of nature" from those "resulting from a social compact." In his notes, he mentioned freedom of "speach" as a natural right, yet he failed to provide for it in his recommended amendments. That is an example of Madison having acknowledged the existence of important rights that he had not enumerated or believed to be included within the unenumerated category. Freedom of speech was a right that preexisted government; it was inherent in human nature and did not depend for its existence on organized society. In 1775 Alexander Hamilton wrote that "the sacred rights of mankind are not to be rummaged for among old parchments or musty records. They are written, as with a sunbeam, in the whole volume of human nature, by the hand of the divinity itself, and can never be erased or obscured by mortal power." Another tough-minded American materialist had led the way to such thinking. John Dickinson, speaking of "the rights essential to happiness," rhapsodized: "We claim them from a higher source—from the King of kings, and Lord of all the earth. They are not annexed to us by parchments and seals. They are created in us by the decrees of Providence, which establish the laws of our nature. They are born with us; exist with us; and cannot be taken from us by any human power without taking our lives. In short, they are founded on the immutable maxims of reason and justice." Such opinions were commonplace.

So, too, the directly related views expressed by Jefferson in the preamble of the Declaration of Independence reflected commonly held principles. In 1822 John Adams, who had been a member of the committee of Congress that Jefferson had chaired in 1776, observed that there was "not an idea in it [the Declaration] but what had been hackneyed." Jefferson asserted that "all American whigs thought alike" on those matters. The purpose of the Declaration, he wrote, was not "to find out new principles, or new arguments . . . but to place before mankind the common sense of the subject." These views are central to the meaning of the Ninth Amendment. Contrary to cynical legal scholars of today, the ideas of the preamble to the Declaration did not go out of fashion in a decade and a half; and those ideas were as appropriate for writing a frame of government as for writing a "brief."

The proof derives from both text and context. The text of the Ninth Amendment does protect the unenumerated rights of the people, and no reason exists to believe that it does not mean what it says. The context consists of Madison's remarks about natural rights during the legislative history of the amendment and also the references to natural rights in the opinions of the time, or what Madison called "contemporaneous interpretations." The last of the state constitutions that came out of the Revolution, that of New Hampshire, began with a bill of rights of 1783 whose language Madison might have used in his first proposed amendment, the one that included the pursuit and obtaining of happiness. Virginia's 1788 recommendations for amendments to the Constitution began similarly, as had New York's and North Carolina's. At the Pennsylvania ratifying convention, James Wilson, who had been second only to Madison as an architect of the Constitution, quoted the preamble of the Declaration of Independence, and he added: "This is the broad basis on which our independence was placed; on the same certain and solid foundation this system [the Constitution] is erected."

The pursuit of happiness, a phrase used by Locke for a concept that underlay his political ethics, subsumed the great rights of liberty and property, which were inextricably related. Lockean thought, to which the Framers subscribed, included within the pursuit of happiness that which delighted and contented the mind and a belief that indispensable to it were good health, reputation, and knowledge. There was nothing radical in the idea of the right to the pursuit of happiness. The anti-American Tory Dr. Samuel Johnson had used the phrase, and Sir William Blackstone, also a Tory, employed a close equivalent in his *Commentaries* in 1765 when remarking "that man should pursue his own happiness. This is the foundation of what we call ethics, or natural law."

In the eighteenth century property did not mean merely the ownership of material things. Locke himself had not used the word to denote merely a right to things; he meant a right to rights. In his *Second Treatise on Government,* he remarked that people "united for the general preservation of their lives, liberties, and estates, which I call by the general name—property." And, he added, "by property I must be understood here as in other places to mean that property which men have in their persons as well as goods." At least four times in his *Second Treatise,* Locke used the word *property* to mean all that belongs to a person, especially the rights he wished to preserve. Americans of the founding generation understood property in this general Lockean sense, which we have lost.

This view of property as a human right is the theme of a 1792 essay by Madison on property. He described what he called the "larger and juster meaning" of the term *property.* It "embraces," he said, "every thing to which a man may attach a value and have a right." In the narrow sense it meant one's land, merchandise, or money; in the broader sense, it meant that "a man has property in his opinions and the free communication of them. He has a property of peculiar value in his religious opinions, and in the profession and practices dictated by them. He has property very dear to him in the safety and liberty of his person. He has an equal property in the free use of his faculties and free choice of the objects on which to employ them. In a word, as a man is said to have a right to his property, he may be equally said to have a property in his rights." If the Fifth Amendment incorporated this broad meaning of "property" in the due process clause (no person shall be deprived of life, liberty, or property without due process of law), then "Property" had a dual meaning in that clause, but only the narrower, materialistic meaning in the eminent domain or takings clause (private property shall not be taken for a public use except at a just compensation) survived. This inconsistency in the different uses of the same word in the same amendment seems baffling. But, no matter how defined, property rights nourished individual autonomy.

Not only were liberty, property, and the pursuit of happiness deeply linked in the thought of the Framers, but they also believed in the principle that all people had a right to equal justice and to equality of rights. When Lincoln at Gettysburg described the creation of a new nation "conceived in liberty and dedicated to the proposition that all men are created equal," he reminded the nation that it could not achieve freedom without equal rights for all nor could it maintain equality without keeping society free. Liberty and equality constituted the master principles of the founding, which the Framers perpetuated as constitutional ideals, even if slyly. In a society that inherited a system of human slavery, the Framers compromised by accepting political reality; they could not abolish slavery and still form a strong Union, but they did what was feasible. Nowhere in the Constitution is any person described in derogatory terms. Nowhere is slavery even acknowledged as a human condition. The Framers in effect spoke to the future by using circumlocutions that acknowledged only the status of "persons held to service"—a term that could be applied to white indentured servants. Race was not mentioned in the Constitution, not until the Fifteenth Amendment. The three-fifths rule, which applied both to direct taxation and to representation, was a device by which the Convention tied southern voting strength in Congress to southern liability for direct taxes on land and people. The Framers did not intentionally insult the humanity of blacks held to service. The same Constitution authorized Congress to extinguish the slave trade in twenty years, and thus prevented untold tens of thousands of people from being enslaved, but the authorization refers only to the "importation of such persons" as some states had thought proper to admit. The point is that the Constitution as amended by the Ninth Amendment provided a subsequent foundation for equal justice to all persons, regardless of race, sex, or religion. The Reconstruction amendments did not require the deletion or alteration of any part of the Constitution.

The Ninth Amendment is the repository for natural rights, including the right to pursue happiness and the right to equality of treatment before the law. Madison, presenting his proposed amendments, spoke of "the perfect equality of mankind." Other natural rights come within the protection of the amendment as well, among them the right, then important, to hunt and fish, the right to travel, and very likely the right to intimate association or privacy in matters concerning family and sex, at least within the bounds of marriage. Such rights were fundamental to the pursuit of happiness. But no evidence exists to prove that the Framers intended the Ninth Amendment to protect any particular natural rights. The text expressly protects unenumerated rights, but we can only guess what the Framers had in mind. On the basis of tantalizing hints and a general philosophy of natural rights, which then prevailed, conclusions emerge that bear slight relation to the racial, sexual, or political realities of that generation.

In addition to natural rights, the unenumerated rights of the people included positive rights, those deriving from the social compact that creates government. What positive rights were familiar, when the Ninth became part of the Constitution, yet were not enumerated in the original text or the first eight amendments? The right to vote and hold office, the right to free elections, the right not to be taxed except by consent through representatives of one's choice, the right to be free from monopolies, the right to be free from standing armies in time of peace, the right to refuse military service on grounds of religious conscience, the right to bail, the right of an accused person to be presumed innocent, and the person's right to have the prosecution shoulder the responsibility of proving guilt beyond a reasonable doubt—all these were among existing positive rights protected by various state laws, state constitutions, and the common law. Any of these, among others, could legitimately be regarded as rights of the people before which the power of government must be exercised in subordination.

In addition to rights then known, the Ninth Amendment might have had the purpose of providing the basis for rights then unknown, which time alone might disclose. Nothing in the thought of the Framers foreclosed the possibility that new rights might claim the loyalties of succeeding generations. As the chief justice of Virginia's highest court mused when the Bill of Rights was being framed, "May we not in the progress of things, discover some great and important [right], which we don't now think of?"

To argue that the Framers had used natural rights as a means of escaping obligations of obedience to the king but did not use natural rights "as a source for rules of decision" is hogwash. One has only to read the state recommendations for a bill of rights to know that the natural rights philosophy seized the minds of the Framers as it had the minds of the rebellious patriots of 1776. One can also read natural rights opinions by members of the early Supreme Court to arrive at the same conclusion. Without doubt, natural rights, if read into the Ninth Amendment, "do not lend themselves to principled judicial enforcement," but neither do positive rights. That is, the enumerated rights, such as freedom of speech and the right to due process of law, have resulted in some of the most subjective result-oriented jurisprudence in our history. That judicial decisions can be unprincipled does not detract from the principle expressed in a right, whether or not enumerated. If the Ninth Amendment instructs us to look beyond its four corners for unenumerated rights of the people, as it does, it must have some content, contrary to its detractors. Some cannot stomach the thought of such indefiniteness, and they disapprove of a license for judicial subjectivity; so they draw conclusions that violate the commonsensical premises with which they begin. John Hart Ely, for example, initially suggests that the amendment should be read for what it says and that it is the provision of the Constitution that applies the principle of equal protection against the federal government. "In fact," he wrote, "the conclusion that the Ninth Amendment was intended to signal the existence of federal constitutional rights beyond those specifically enumerated in the Constitution is the only conclusion its language seems comfortably able to support." Yet Ely ridicules natural rights theory and believes that it swiftly became passé. He ends by leaving the amendment an empty provision, significant only as a lure to judicial activism.

Raoul Berger is an even more hostile critic of the amendment, but he is so eager to keep it the feckless provision that was a mystery to Justice Robert S. Jackson that he confuses the Ninth and Tenth Amendments. For example, he speaks of "the ninth's retention of rights by the states or the people," when in fact it is the Tenth Amendment, not its predecessor, that speaks of states' rights, that is, of powers retained by the states or the people. "The ninth amendment," added Berger, ". . . was merely declaratory of a basic supposition: all powers not 'positively' granted are reserved to the people." It added no unspecified rights to the Bill of Rights. But an explicit declaration of the existence of unenumerated rights is an addition of unspecified rights to the Bill of Rights, whose Tenth Amendment, not Ninth, reserved powers not granted.

Confusion between the Ninth and Tenth Amendments seems to originate with two amendments proposed by Virginia in 1788. One in modified terms was modeled after Article II of the Articles of Confederation, retaining to each state every power not delegated to the United States. The other amendment concerned clauses in the Constitution declaring that Congress shall not exercise certain powers (for example, no bills of attainder). That amendment proposed that such clauses should not be construed to extend the powers of Congress; rather, they should be construed "as making exceptions to the specified powers where this shall be the case, or otherwise, as inserted merely for greater caution." Neither proposal addressed the issue of reserving to the people unenumerated rights. Yet the Virginia Assembly, in 1789, when debating whether to ratify the amendments proposed by Congress, initially rejected what became the Ninth and Tenth Amendments. The Assembly preferred instead its two proposals of 1788. The reasoning behind the Assembly's action was confused and gave rise to the confusion between the Ninth and Tenth Amendments.

According to Hardin Burnley, a member of the Assembly who kept Madison informed about the progress of his amendments in the state legislature, Edmund Randolph, who led the opposition to the Ninth Amendment (then the eleventh), objected to the word *retained* because it was too indefinite. Randolph had argued that the rights declared in the preceding amendments (our First through Eighth) "were not all that a free people would require the exercise of; and that there was no criterion by which it could not be determined whether any other particular right was retained or not." Thus Randolph argued that the Ninth was not sufficiently comprehensive and explicit. From that point he concluded, illogically, that the course of safety lay, not in retaining unenumerated rights, but in providing against an extension of the powers of Congress. Randolph believed that the Ninth Amendment did not reduce rights to a "definitive certainty."

Madison soon after sent to George Washington Burnley's information (and language) as if his own. The letter, as construed by those who find the Ninth Amendment an empty vehicle, became a means of putting Madison's authority behind the proposition that the Ninth Amendment means no more than the Tenth. Plagiarizing Burnley, Madison informed Washington that he found Randolph's distinction to be without force, because "by protecting the rights of the people & of the States, an improper extension of power will be prevented & safety made equally certain." Madison did not challenge Randolph's assertion that the amendments preceding the Ninth and Tenth did not exhaust the rights of the people that needed protection against government. Nor did he challenge the assertion that the Ninth was too vague. Rather, Madison disagreed that adoption of the Virginia proposals of 1788 more effectively secured the rights deserving of protection.

In the only part of his letter that did not repeat Burnley's, Madison expressed regret that the confusion had come from Randolph, "a friend to the Constitution," and he added: "It is a still greater cause of regret, if the distinction [made by Randolph] be, as it appears to me, altogether fanciful. If a line can be drawn between the powers granted and the rights retained, it would seem to be the same thing, whether the latter be secured, by declaring that they shall not be abridged, or that the former shall not be extended. If no line can be drawn, a declaration in either form would amount to nothing." The reference to "whether the latter be secured" meant the retention of a specific right. In effect, Madison argued that the line between a power granted and a right retained amounted to the same thing if a right were named. Thus, to say that the government *may* not abridge the freedom of the press is the equivalent of saying that the government *shall* not abridge the freedom of the press. If, as Madison said, a line cannot be drawn between rights retained and powers denied, retaining unenumerated rights would be useless against a power of government to violate them. Whether the formulation of the First Amendment is used—"Congress shall make no law"—or whether that of the Fourth Amendment is used—"The right of the people to be secure . . . against unreasonable searches and seizures, shall not be violated"—the effect is the same. In the case of unenumerated rights, however, one can only argue that no affirmative power has been granted to regulate.

Randolph had identified a problem that remains without a solution. Madison's response was by no means a satisfactory one in all respects. Although both houses of Virginia's legislature finally ratified the Bill of Rights, the Ninth Amendment continues to bedevil its interpreters. Courts keep discovering rights that have no literal textual existence, that is, rights not enumerated, only to meet howls of denunciation from those who deplore the result—whether the right of a woman to an abortion, a right of privacy against electronic eavesdropping, or a right to engage in nude dancing. Opponents have another string to their bow, which they find in a declaration by Madison in the First Congress, when he proposed his amendments. Adding a bill of rights to the Constitution, he argued, would enable courts to become "the guardians of those rights; they will be an impenetrable bulwark against every assumption of power in the legislative or executive; they will be naturally led to resist every encroachment upon rights expressly stipulated for in the constitution by the declaration of rights." "Expressly stipulated" can be read to mean that Madison either opposed or failed to predict judicial review in cases involving unenumerated rights. And, without doubt he was not referring to the desirability of giving courts what Raoul Berger calls "a roving commission to enforce a catalog of unenumerated rights against the will of the states."

Madison might well, however, have approved of courts' enforcing against the states the amendment that he thought "the most valuable amendment in the whole list"—one that prohibited the states from infringing upon the equal rights of conscience, the freedom of speech or press, and the right to trial by jury in criminal cases. The House passed but the Senate defeated that proposal, making enforcement by the federal courts against the states impossible. The incorporation doctrine, drawn from the Fourteenth Amendment, superseded whatever limitations the Framers of the Bill of Rights had in mind concerning judicial review over state acts.

So long as we continue to believe that government is instituted for the sake of securing the rights of the people and must exercise powers in subordination to those rights, the Ninth Amendment should have the vitality intended for it. The problem is not whether the rights it guarantees are as worthy of enforcement as the enumerated rights; the problem, rather, is whether our courts should read out of the amendment rights worthy of our respect, which the Framers might conceivably have meant to safeguard, at least in principle.

Appendix: Key Documents

ONE

====

Table for Sources of the
Provisions of the
Bill of Rights

The following table facilitates convenient reference to the sources for any particular provision of the Bill of Rights. Topics in capital letters were ultimately included in the ten amendments ratified. The first thirty-three topics were included in Madison's proposals to Congress. The other topics in the table were proposed by one or more states but not considered in Congress.

Figures in the first column refer to the substantive items in Madison's proposals as discussed in my text; those in the second column to his proposals as numbered when offered in Congress. The next five columns refer to the Select Committee's report (as numbered in the *Annals of Congress*), the seventeen articles adopted by the House, the twelve articles adopted by the Senate, the twelve articles agreed to after conference, and the ten amendments ratified, respectively. Then follow references to the English Bill of Rights, the Virginia Bill of Rights, and the proposals of the eight states which formulated amendments. The last column shows the number of states favoring a particular proposal.

Sources of the Provisions of the Bill of Rights

Number	Subject	Madison Item	Madison Numbers	Select Committee	House	Senate	Conference	Ratified	English Bill of Rights	Virginia Bill of Rights	Va. Convention Bill of Rights	Va. Convention Amendments	Pennsylvania	Massachusetts	Maryland Majority	Maryland Minority	So. Carolina	New Hampshire	New York Bill of Rights	New York Amendments	No. Carolina Bill of Rights	No. Carolina Amendments	Number of States Favoring
1	Power from people	1	1(1)	1	d	d				2	2								1	1	2		3
2	Government for people	1	1(2)	1	d	d				3	3								1		3		3
3	Right to change govt.	1	1(3)	1						3	3								3		3		2
4	Representation	2	2	2	1	1	1a	NR				2		2					3	1		2	6
5	Compensation	3	3	3	2	2	2	NR				18								13		19	5
6	RELIGIOUS FREEDOM	4	4(1)	4(1)	3	3	3a	1		16	20		1		12	15		11	4		20		6
7	SPEECH & PRESS	5	4(2)	4(2)	4	3	3	1		12	16				12				16†		16		5
8	ASSEMBLY & PETITION	6	4(3)	4(3)	4	4	4	1	5		15				14				16		15		4
9	BEAR ARMS	7	4(4)	4(4)	5	4	4	2	7	13	17,19							12			17,19		5
10	QUARTERING SOLDIERS	8	4(5)	4(5)	6	5	5	3	pr. 5		18				10			10	8		18		5

† Press only.

Explanation of Symbols

a = amended in conference
d = defeated in House or Senate
M = from Magna Carta
pr. = preliminary recital in English Bill of Rights
NR = not ratified by three-fourths of the States
e = eliminated by the method adopted of adding amendments as supplementary articles

Sources of the Provisions of the Bill of Rights

Number	Subject	Madison Item	Madison Numbers	Select Committee	House	Senate	Conference	Ratified	English Bill of Rights	Virginia Bill of Rights	Va. Convention Bill of Rights	Va. Convention Amendments	Pennsylvania	Massachusetts	Maryland Majority	Maryland Minority	So. Carolina	New Hampshire	New York Bill of Rights	New York Amendments	No. Carolina Bill of Rights	No. Carolina Amendments	Number of States Favoring
11	DOUBLE JEOPARDY	9	4(6)	4(5)	8	7	7	5	5										10				2
12	SELF INCRIMINATION	9	4(6)	4(5)	8	7	7	5	5	8	8										8		3
13	DUE PROCESS	9	4(6)	4(5)	8	7	7	5	M	8	9		3	3				9			9		4
14	JUST COMPENSATION	9	4(6)	4(5)	8	7	7	5															0
15	EXCESSIVE BAIL	10	4(7)	4(6)	13	10	10	8	8	9	13		4	4					12		13		4
16	SEARCHES & SEIZURES	11	4(8)	4(7)	7	6	6	4	10	10	14		5	5	8				15		14		5
17	SPEEDY & PUBLIC TRIAL	12	4(9)	7(1)	9	8	8	6		8	8		3						13		8		4
18	CAUSE & NATURE	12	4(9)	7(1)	9	8	8	6	8	8	8		3								8		3
19	CONFRONTATION	12	4(9)	7(1)	9	8	8	6	8	8	8		3								8		3
20	WITNESSES	12	4(9)	7(1)	9	8	8	6	8	8	8		3								8		3
21	COUNSEL	12	4(9)	7(1)	9	8	8	6		8	8										8		3
22	RETAINED RIGHTS	13	4(10)	4(8)	15	11	11	9				17							3			18	3
23	State violations	14	5	5	14	d																	0
24	Minimum value	15	6(1)	6(1)	11	d									7			7					3
25	RE-EXAMINATION OF FACTS	15	6(2)	6(2)	11	9	9	7				14		7	3,4			7	20			15	4
26	JURY OF VICINAGE	16	7(1)	6(2)	10	d	8a	6		8	15	15	3		3,5				13		8		5
27	GRAND JURY	16	7(2)	7(2)	10	7	7	5	11	8	8			6	2			6	13		8		3
28	Place of trial	16	7(3)	7(2)	10	d												13					1

The following is a cross-reference concordance table. Column header identifiers (upper left):

16	7(4)	7(2)	d
17	7(5)	7(3)	12
18	8(1)	8	16
19	8(2)	9	17
	9	10	e

Provision	Cross-references (as printed)
29 Outside county	1 … 13 … 1
30 JURY TRIAL (CIVIL)	8 14 … 2 8 3,5 … 11 11 … 5 … 7
31 Separation of powers	12 … 5 … 3
32 RESERVATION OF POWERS =	1 … 2 1 15 1 1 … 10 … 1 8
33 Renumber Article VII	e
34 Regulation of elections	16 10 3 … 9 7 … 2 1 3 … 4 … 17 8
35 Curb taxing power	3 9 4 … 3,9 … 3 4 … 2,3,15 … 3 8
36 No monopolies	5 … 5 … 6 … 22 4
37 No titles of nobility	9 … 9 … 30 … 3
38 No other religious test	4 … 1
39 No standing army	6 13 17 … 9 7 … 4 … 10 7 17 9 6
40 Ineligibility to office	4 … 8 … 17 … 4 4
41 Publish journals	5 … 14 … 5 3
42 Publish accounts	6 … 6 2
43 Commercial treaties	7 … 7 2
44 Navigation laws	8 … 7 … 8 3
45 Time of enlistment	10 … 9 … 10 3
46 Control of militia	11 11 … 13 1 … 6 29 … 11 5
47 Government of district	12 … 13 2
48 Term of president	13 … 17 … 14 3
49 Judicial power	14 14 … 22 24,28 … 15 4
50 Challenging jury	15 … 16 2
51 Impeachment of senators	19 … 20 2
52 Salaries of judges	20 … 21 2
53 Natural rights	1 … 2 … 1 3

Sources of the Provisions of the Bill of Rights

Number	Subject	Madison Item	Madison Numbers	Select Committee	House	Senate	Conference	Ratified	English Bill of Rights	Virginia Bill of Rights	Va. Convention Bill of Rights	Va. Convention Amendments	Pennsylvania Amendments	Massachusetts	Maryland Majority	Maryland Minority	So. Carolina	New Hampshire	New York Bill of Rights	New York Amendments	N.C. Bill Rights	N.C. Amendts.	Number of States Favoring
54	No hereditary office											4										4	2
55	Frequent elections									8	6	6										6	2
56	Suspension of laws									1	7	7										7	2
57	Habeas corpus											10							11			10	3
58	Right to remedy											12										12	2
59	Right to hunt and fish												8										1
60	Executive council												12			11							2
61	Collusive jurisdiction														6				23				2
62	Mutiny bill														11								1
63	Tax credit to States															13							1
64	State districts																		18				1
65	Ex post facto laws																		19				1
66	Appeals and error																		20				1
67	Suits against States																		21				1
68	Effect of treaties												13			6			24			23	4
69	Disabilities of foreign born																			5			1
70	Borrowing money																			8			1
71	Declaring war																			9			1

English Bill of Rights
December 16, 1689

Whereas the late King *James* the Second, by the assistance of divers evil counsellors, judges, and ministers employed by him, did endeavour to subvert and extirpate the protestant religion, and the laws and liberties of this kingdom.

1. By assuming and exercising a power of dispensing with and suspending of laws, and the execution of laws, without consent of parliament.

2. By committing and prosecuting divers worthy prelates, for humbly petitioning to be excused from concurring to the said assumed power.

3. By issuing and causing to be executed a commission under the great seal for erecting a court called, *The court of commissioners for ecclesiastical causes.*

4. By levying money for and to the use of the crown, by pretence of prerogative, for other time, and in other manner, than the same was granted by parliament.

5. By raising and keeping a standing army within this kingdom in time of peace, without consent of parliament, and quartering soldiers contrary to law.

6. By causing several good subjects, being protestants, to be disarmed, at the same time when papists were both armed and employed, contrary to law.

7. By violating the freedom of election of members to serve in parliament.

8. By prosecutions in the court of King's bench, for matters and causes cognizable only in parliament; and by divers other arbitrary and illegal courses.

9. And whereas of late years, partial, corrupt, and unqualified persons have been returned and served on juries in trials, and particularly divers jurors in trials for high treason, which were not freeholders.

10. And excessive bail hath been required of persons committed in criminal cases, to elude the benefit of the laws made for the liberty of the subjects.

11. And excessive fines have been imposed; and illegal and cruel punishments have been inflicted.

12. And several grants and promises made of fines and forfeitures, before any conviction or judgment against the persons, upon whom the same were to be levied.

All which are utterly and directly contrary to the known laws and statutes, and freedom of this realm.

And whereas the said late king *James* the Second having abdicated the government, and the throne being thereby vacant . . . the said lords spiritual and temporal, and commons . . . do in the first place (as their ancestors in like case have usually done) for the vindicating and asserting their ancient rights and liberties, declare;

1. That the pretended power of suspending of laws, or the execution of laws, by regal authority, without consent of parliament, is illegal.

2. That the pretended power of dispensing with laws, or the execution of laws, by regal authority, as it hath been assumed and exercised of late, is illegal.

3. That the commission for erecting the late court of commissioners for ecclesiastical causes, and all other commissions and courts of like nature are illegal and pernicious.

4. That levying money for or to the use of the crown, by pretence of prerogative, without grant of parliament, for longer time, or in other manner than the same is or shall be granted, is illegal.

5. That it is the right of the subjects to petition the King, and all committments [sic] and prosecutions for such petitioning are illegal.

6. That the raising or keeping a standing army within the kingdom in time of peace, unless it be with consent of parliament, is against law.

7. That the subjects which are protestants, may have arms for their defence suitable to their conditions, and as allowed by law.

8. That election of members of parliament ought to be free.

9. That the freedom of speech, and debates or proceedings in parliament, ought not to be impeached or questioned in any court or place out of parliament.

10. That excessive bail ought not to be required, nor excessive fines imposed; nor cruel and unusual punishments inflicted.

11. That jurors ought to be duly impanelled and returned, and jurors which pass upon men in trials for high treason ought to be freeholders.

12. That all grants and promises of fines and forfeitures of particular persons before conviction, are illegal and void.

13. And that for redress of all grievances, and for the amending, strengthening, and preserving of the laws, parliaments ought to be held frequently.

And they do claim, demand, and insist upon all and singular the premisses, as their undoubted rights and liberties; and that no declarations, judgments, doings or proceedings, to the prejudice of the people in any of the said premisses, ought in any wise to be drawn hereafter into consequence or example.

. . .

VI. Now in pursuance of the premisses, the said lords spiritual and temporal, and commons, in parliament assembled, for the ratifying, confirming and establishing the said declaration, and the articles, clauses, matters, and things therein contained, by the force of a law made in due form by authority of parliament, do pray that it may be declared and enacted, That all and singular the rights and liberties asserted and claimed in the said declaration, are the true, ancient, and indubitable rights and liberties of the people of this kingdom, and so shall be esteemed, allowed, adjudged, deemed, and taken to be, and that all and every the particulars aforesaid shall be firmly and strictly holden and observed, as they are expressed in the said declaration; and all officers and ministers whatsoever shall serve their Majesties and their successors according to the same in all times to come.

. . .

XI. All which their Majesties are contented and pleased shall be declared, enacted, and established by authority of this present parliament, and shall stand, remain, and be the law of this realm for ever; and the same are by their said Majesties, by and with the advice and consent of the lords spiritual and temporal, and commons, in parliament assembled, and by the authority of the same, declared, enacted, and established accordingly.

THREE

Virginia Bill of Rights
June 12, 1776

A DECLARATION OF RIGHTS *made by the representatives of the good people of Virginia, assembled in full and free Convention; which rights do pertain to them, and their posterity, as the basis and foundation of government.*

1. That all men are by nature equally free and independent, and have certain inherent rights, of which, when they enter into a state of society, they cannot, by any compact, deprive or divest their posterity; namely, the enjoyment of life and liberty, with the means of acquiring and possessing property, and pursuing and obtaining happiness and safety.

2. That all power is vested in, and consequently derived from, the people; that magistrates are their trustees and servants, and at all times amenable to them.

3. That government is, or ought to be, instituted for the common benefit, protection, and security, of the people, nation, or community; of all the various modes and forms of government that is best, which is capable of producing the greatest degree of happiness and safety, and is most effectually secured against the danger of maladministration; and that whenever any government shall be found inadequate or contrary to these purposes, a majority of the community hath an indubitable, unalienable, and indefeasible right, to reform, alter, or abolish it, in such manner as shall be judged most conducive to the publick weal.

4. That no man, or set of men, are entitled to exclusive or separate emoluments or privileges from the community, but in consideration of publick services; which, not being descendible, neither ought the offices of magistrate, legislator, or judge, to be hereditary.

5. That the legislative and executive powers of the state should be separate and distinct from the judicative; and that the members of the two first may be restrained from oppression, by feeling and participating the burthens of the people, they should, at fixed periods, be reduced to a private station, return into that body from which they were originally taken, and the vacancies be supplied by frequent, certain, and regular elections, in which all, or any part of the former members, to be again eligible, or ineligible, as the laws shall direct.

6. That elections of members to serve as representatives of the people, in assembly, ought to be free; and that all men, having sufficient evidence of permanent common interest with, and attachment to, the community, have the right of suffrage, and cannot be taxed or deprived of their property for publick uses without their own consent, or that of their representatives so elected, nor bound by any law to which they have not, in like manner, assented, for the publick good.

7. That all power of suspending laws, or the execution of laws, by any authority without consent of the representatives of the people, is injurious to their rights, and ought not to be exercised.

8. That in all capital or criminal prosecutions a man hath a right to demand the cause and nature of his accusation, to be confronted with the accusers and witnesses, to call for evidence in his favour, and to a speedy trial by an impartial jury of his vicinage, without whose unanimous consent he cannot be found guilty, nor can he be compelled to give evidence against himself; that no man be deprived of his liberty except by the law of the land, or the judgment of his peers.

9. That excessive bail ought not to be required, nor excessive fines imposed, nor cruel and unusual punishments inflicted.

10. That general warrants, whereby any officer or messenger may be commanded to search suspected places without evidence of a fact committed, or to seize any person or persons not named, or whose offence is not particularly described and supported by evidence, are grievous and oppressive, and ought not to be granted.

11. That in controversies respecting property, and in suits between man and man, the ancient trial by jury is preferable to any other, and ought to be held sacred.

12. That the freedom of the press is one of the great bulwarks of liberty, and can never be restrained but by despotick governments.

13. That a well regulated militia, composed of the body of the people, trained to arms, is the proper, natural, and safe defence of a free state; that standing armies, in time of peace, should be avoided, as dangerous to liberty; and that, in all cases, the military should be under strict subordination to, and governed by, the civil power.

14. That the people have a right to uniform government; and therefore, that no government separate from, or independent of, the government of *Virginia*, ought to be erected or established within the limits thereof.

15. That no free government, or the blessing of liberty, can be preserved to any people but by a firm adherence to justice, moderation, temperance, frugality, and virtue, and by frequent recurrence to fundamental principles.

16. That religion, or the duty which we owe to our CREATOR, and the manner of discharging it, can be directed only by reason and conviction, not by force or violence; and therefore all men are equally entitled to the free exercise of religion, according to the dictates of conscience; and that it is the mutual duty of all to practice Christian forbearance, love, and charity, towards each other.

FOUR

Amendments Proposed by the Virginia Convention June 27, 1788

That there be a Declaration or Bill of Rights asserting and securing from encroachment the essential and unalienable Rights of the People in some such manner as the following;

First, That there are certain natural rights of which men, when they form a social compact cannot deprive or divest their posterity, among which are the enjoyment of life and liberty, with the means of acquiring, possessing and protecting property, and pursuing and obtaining happiness and safety.

Second. That all power is naturally vested in and consequently derived from the people; that Magistrates, therefore, are their trustees and agents and at all times amenable to them.

Third, That Government ought to be instituted for the common benefit, protection and security of the People; and that the doctrine of non-resistance against arbitrary power and oppression is absurd slavish, and destructive of the good and happiness of mankind.

Fourth, That no man or set of Men are entitled to exclusive or seperate [sic] public emoluments or privileges from the community, but in Consideration of public services; which not being descendible, neither ought the offices of Magistrate, Legislator or Judge, or any other public office to be hereditary.

Fifth, That the legislative, executive, and judiciary powers of Government should be seperate [sic] and distinct, and that the members of the two first may be restrained from oppression by feeling and participating the public burthens, they should, at fixt periods be reduced to a private station, return into the mass of the people; and the vacancies be supplied by certain and regular elections; in which all or any part of the former members to be eligible or ineligible, as the rules of the Constitution of Government, and the laws shall direct.

Sixth, That elections of representatives in the legislature ought to be free and frequent, and all men having sufficient evidence of permanent common interest with and attachment to the Community ought to have the right of suffrage: and no aid, charge, tax or fee can be set, rated, or levied upon the people without their own consent, or that of their representatives so elected, nor can they be bound by any law to which they have not in like manner assented for the public good.

Seventh, That all power of suspending laws or the execution of laws by any authority, without the consent of the representatives of the people in the legislature is injurious to their rights, and ought not to be exercised.

Eighth, That in all capital and criminal prosecutions, a man hath a right to demand the cause and nature of his accusation, to be confronted with the accusers and witnesses, to call for evidence and be allowed counsel in his favor, and to a fair and speedy trial by an impartial Jury of his vicinage, without whose unanimous consent he cannot be found guilty, (except in the government of the land and naval forces) nor can he be compelled to give evidence against himself.

Ninth. That no freeman ought to be taken, imprisoned, or disseised of his freehold, liberties, privileges or franchises, or outlawed or exiled, or in any manner destroyed or deprived of his life, liberty or property but by the law of the land.

Tenth. That every freeman restrained of his liberty is entitled to a remedy to enquire into the lawfulness thereof, and to remove the same, if unlawful, and that such remedy ought not to be denied nor delayed.

Eleventh. That in controversies respecting property, and in suits between man and man, the ancient trial by Jury is one of the greatest Securities to the rights of the people, and ought to remain sacred and inviolable.

Twelfth. That every freeman ought to find a certain remedy by recourse to the laws for all injuries and wrongs he may receive in his person, property or character. He ought to obtain right and justice freely without sale, compleatly [sic] and without denial, promptly and without delay, and that all establishments or regulations contravening these rights, are oppressive and unjust.

Thirteenth, That excessive Bail ought not to be required, nor excessive fines imposed, nor cruel and unusual punishments inflicted.

Fourteenth, That every freeman has a right to be secure from all unreasonable searches and siezures [sic] of his person, his papers and his property; all warrants, therefore, to search suspected places, or sieze [sic] any freeman, his papers or property, without information upon Oath (or affirmation of a person religiously scrupulous of taking an oath) of legal and sufficient cause, are grievous and oppressive; and all general Warrants to search suspected places, or to apprehend any suspected person, without specially naming or describing the place or person, are dangerous and ought not to be granted.

Fifteenth, That the people have a right peaceably to assemble together to consult for the common good, or to instruct their Representatives; and that every freeman has a right to petition or apply to the legislature for redress of grievances.

Sixteenth, That the people have a right to freedom of speech, and of writing and publishing their Sentiments; but the freedom of the press is one of the greatest bulwarks of liberty and ought not to be violated.

Seventeenth, That the people have a right to keep and bear arms; that a well regulated Militia composed of the body of the people trained to arms is the proper, natural and safe defence of a free State. That standing armies in time of peace are dangerous to liberty, and therefore ought to be avoided, as far as the circumstances and protection of the Community will admit; and that in all cases the military should be under strict subordination to and governed by the Civil power.

Eighteenth, That no Soldier in time of peace ought to be quartered in any house without the consent of the owner, and in time of war in such manner only as the laws direct.

Nineteenth, That any person religiously scrupulous of bearing arms ought to be exempted upon payment of an equivalent to employ another to bear arms in his stead.

Twentieth, That religion or the duty which we owe to our Creator, and the manner of discharging it can be directed only by reason and conviction, not by force or violence, and therefore all men have an equal, natural and unalienable right to the free exercise of religion according to the dictates of conscience, and that no particular religious sect or society ought to be favored or established by Law in preference to others.

AMENDMENTS TO THE BODY OF THE CONSTITUTION

First, That each State in the Union shall respectively retain every power, jurisdiction and right which is not by this Constitution delegated to the Congress of the United States or to the departments of the Foederal [sic] Government.

Second, That there shall be one representative for every thirty thousand, according to the Enumeration or Census mentioned in the Constitution, until the whole number of representatives amounts to two hundred; after which that number shall be continued or encreased [sic] as the Congress shall direct, upon the principles fixed by the Constitution by apportioning the Representatives of each State to some greater number of people from time to time as population encreases [sic].

Third, When Congress shall lay direct taxes or excises, they shall immediately inform the Executive power of each State of the quota of such state according to the Census herein directed, which is proposed to be thereby raised; And if the Legislature of any State shall pass a law which shall be effectual for raising such quota at the time required by Congress, the taxes and excises laid by Congress shall not be collected, in such State.

Fourth, That the members of the Senate and House of Representatives shall be ineligible to, and incapable of holding, any civil office under the authority of the United States, during the time for which they shall respectively be elected.

Fifth, That the Journals of the proceedings of the Senate and House of Representatives shall be published at least once in every year, except such parts thereof relating to treaties, alliances or military operations, as in their judgment require secrecy.

Sixth, That a regular statement and account of the receipts and expenditures of all public money shall be published at least once in every year.

Seventh, That no commercial treaty shall be ratified without the concurrence of two thirds of the whole number of the members of the Senate; and no Treaty ceding, contracting, restraining or suspending the territorial rights or claims of the United States, or any of them or their, or any of their rights or claims to fishing in the American seas, or navigating the American rivers shall be [made] but in cases of the most urgent and extreme necessity, nor shall any such treaty be ratified without the concurrence of three fourths of the whole number of the members of both houses respectively.

Eighth, That no navigation law, or law regulating Commerce shall be passed without the consent of two thirds of the Members present in both houses.

Ninth, That no standing army or regular troops shall be raised or kept up in time of peace, without the consent of two thirds of the members present in both houses.

Tenth, That no soldier shall be inlisted [sic] for any longer term than four years, except in time of war, and then for no longer term than the continuance of the war.

Eleventh, That each State respectively shall have the power to provide for organizing, arming and disciplining it's own Militia, whensoever Congress shall omit or neglect to provide for the same. That the Militia shall not be subject to Martial law, except when in actual service in time of war, invasion, or rebellion; and when not in the actual service of the United States, shall be subject only to such fines, penalties and punishments as shall be directed or inflicted by the laws of its own State.

Twelfth That the exclusive power of legislation given to Congress over the Foederal [sic] Town and its adjacent District and other places purchased or to be purchased by Congress of any of the States shall extend only to such regulations as respect the police and good government thereof.

Thirteenth, That no person shall be capable of being President of the United States for more than eight years in any term of sixteen years.

Fourteenth That the judicial power of the United States shall be vested in one supreme Court, and in such courts of Admiralty as Congress may from time to time ordain and establish in any of the different States: The Judicial power shall extend to all cases in Law and Equity arising under treaties made, or which shall be made under the authority of the United States; to all cases affecting ambassadors other foreign ministers and consuls; to all cases of Admiralty and maritime jurisdiction; to controversies to which the United States shall be a party; to controversies between two or [more] States, and between parties claiming lands under the grants of different States. In all cases affecting ambassadors, other foreign ministers and Consuls, and those in which a State shall be a party, the supreme court shall have original jurisdiction; in all other cases before mentioned the supreme Court shall have appellate jurisdiction as to matters of law only: except in cases of equity, and of admiralty and maritime juris-diction, in which the Supreme Court shall have appellate jurisdiction both as to law and fact, with such exceptions and under such regulations as the Congress shall make. But the judicial power of the United States shall extend to no case where the cause of action shall have originated before the ratification of this Constitution; except in disputes between States about their Territory, disputes between persons claiming lands under the grants of different States, and suits for debts due to the United States.

Fifteenth, That in criminal prosecutions no man shall be restrained in the exercise of the usual and accustomed right of challenging or excepting to the Jury.

Sixteenth, That Congress shall not alter, modify or interfere in the times, places, or manner of holding elections for Senators and Representatives or either of them, except when the legislature of any State shall neglect, refuse or be disabled by invasion or rebellion to prescribe the same.

Seventeenth, That those clauses which declare that Congress shall not exercise certain powers be not interpreted in any manner whatsoever to extend the powers of Congress. But that they may be construed either as making exceptions to the specified powers where this shall be the case, or otherwise as inserted merely for greater caution.

Eighteenth, That the laws ascertaining the compensation to Senators and Representatives for their services be postponed in their operation, until after the election of Representatives immediately succeeding the passing thereof; that excepted, which shall first be passed on the Subject.

Nineteenth, That some Tribunal other than the Senate be provided for trying impeachments of Senators.

Twentieth, That the Salary of a Judge shall not be encreased [sic] or diminished during his continuance in Office, otherwise than by general regulations of Salary which may take place on a revision of the subject at stated periods of not less than seven years to commence from the time such Salaries shall be first ascertained by Congress.

FIVE

Amendments Offered in Congress by James Madison June 8, 1789

First. That there be prefixed to the Constitution a declaration, that all power is originally vested in, and consequently derived from, the people.

That Government is instituted and ought to be exercised for the benefit of the people; which consists in the enjoyment of life and liberty, with the right of acquiring and using property, and generally of pursuing and obtaining happiness and safety.

That the people have an indubitable, unalienable, and indefeasible right to reform or change their Government, whenever it be found adverse or inadequate to the purposes of its institution.

Secondly. That in article 1st, section 2, clause 3, these words be struck out, to wit: "The number of Representatives shall not exceed one for every thirty thousand, but each State shall have at least one Representative, and until such enumeration shall be made;" and that in place thereof be inserted these words, to wit: "After the first actual enumeration, there shall be one Representative for every thirty thousand, until the number amounts to ——, after which the proportion shall be so regulated by Congress, that the number shall never be less than ——, nor more than ——, but each State shall, after the first enumeration, have at least two Representatives; and prior thereto."

Thirdly. That in article 1st, section 6, clause 1, there be added to the end of the first sentence, these words, to wit: "But no law varying the compensation last ascertained shall operate before the next ensuing election of Representatives."

Fourthly. That in article 1st, section 9, between clauses 3 and 4, be inserted these clauses, to wit: The civil rights of none shall be abridged on account of religious belief or worship, nor shall any national religion be established, nor shall the full and equal rights of conscience be in any manner, or on any pretext, infringed.

The people shall not be deprived or abridged of their right to speak, to write, or to publish their sentiments; and the freedom of the press, as one of the great bulwarks of liberty, shall be inviolable.

The people shall not be restrained from peaceably assembling and consulting for their common good; nor from applying to the Legislature by petitions, or remonstrances, for redress of their grievances.

The right of the people to keep and bear arms shall not be infringed; a well armed and well regulated militia being the best security of a free country: but no person religiously scrupulous of bearing arms shall be compelled to render military service in person.

No soldiers shall in time of peace be quartered in any house without the consent of the owner; nor at any time, but in a manner warranted by law.

No person shall be subject, except in cases of impeachment, to more than one punishment or one trial for the same offence; nor shall be compelled to be a witness against himself; nor be deprived of life, liberty, or property, without due process of law; nor be obliged to relinquish his property, where it may be necessary for public use, without a just compensation.

Excessive bail shall not be required, nor excessive fines imposed, nor cruel and unusual punishments inflicted.

The rights of the people to be secured in their persons, their houses, their papers, and their other property, from all unreasonable searches and seizures, shall not be violated by warrants issued without probable cause, supported by oath or affirmation, or not particularly describing the places to be searched, or the persons or things to be seized.

In all criminal prosecutions, the accused shall enjoy the right to a speedy and public trial, to be informed of the cause and nature of the accusation, to be confronted with his accusers, and the witnesses against him; to have a compulsory process for obtaining witnesses in his favor; and to have the assistance of counsel for his defence.

The exceptions here or elsewhere in the Constitution, made in favor of particular rights, shall not be so construed as to diminish the just importance of other rights retained by the people, or as to enlarge the powers delegated by the Constitution; but either as actual limitations of such powers, or as inserted merely for greater caution.

Fifthly. That in article 1st, section 10, between clauses 1 and 2, be inserted this clause, to wit:

No State shall violate the equal rights of conscience, or the freedom of the press, or the trial by jury in criminal cases.

Sixthly. That, in article 3d, section 2, be annexed to the end of clause 2d, these words, to wit:

But no appeal to such court shall be allowed where the value in controversy shall not amount to —— dollars: nor shall any fact triable by jury, according to the course of common law, be otherwise re-examinable than may consist with the principles of common law.

Seventhly. That in article 3d, section 2, the third clause be struck out, and in its place be inserted the clauses following, to wit:

The trial of all crimes (except in cases of impeachments, and cases arising in the land or naval forces, or the militia when on actual service, in time of war or public danger) shall be by an impartial jury of freeholders of the vicinage, with the requisite of unanimity for conviction, of the right of challenge, and other accustomed requisites; and in all crimes punishable with loss of life or member, presentment or indictment by a grand jury shall be an essential preliminary, provided that in cases of crimes committed within any county which may be in possession of an enemy, or in which a general insurrection may prevail, the trial may by law be authorized in some other county of the same State, as near as may be to the seat of the offence.

In cases of crimes committed not within any county, the trial may by law be in such county as the laws shall have prescribed. In suits at common law, between man and man, the trial by jury, as one of the best securities to the rights of the people, ought to remain inviolate.

Eighthly. That immediately after article 6th, be inserted, as article 7th, the clauses following, to wit:

The powers delegated by this Constitution are appropriated to the departments to which they are respectively distributed: so that the Legislative Department shall never exercise the powers vested in the Executive or Judicial, nor the Executive exercise the powers vested in the Legislative or Judicial, nor the Judicial exercise the powers vested in the Legislative or Executive Departments.

The powers not delegated by this Constitution, nor prohibited by it to the States, are reserved to the States respectively.

Ninthly. That article 7th be numbered as article 8th.

SIX

Amendments Reported
by the Select Committee
July 28, 1789

In the introductory paragraph before the words, "*We the people,*" add, "Government being intended for the benefit of the people, and the rightful establishment thereof being derived from their authority alone."

ART. 1, SEC. 2, PAR. 3—Strike out all between the words, "*direct*" and "*and until such,*" and instead thereof insert, "After the first enumeration there shall be one representative for every thirty thousand until the number shall amount to one hundred; after which the proportion shall be so regulated by Congress that the number of Representatives shall never be less than one hundred, nor more than one hundred and seventy-five, but each State shall always have at least one Representative."

ART. 1, SEC. 6—Between the words "*United States,*" and "*shall in all cases,*" strike out "*they,*" and insert, "But no law varying the compensation shall take effect until an election of Representatives shall have intervened. The members."

ART. 1, SEC. 9—Between PAR. 2 and 3 insert, "No religion shall be established by law, nor shall the equal rights of conscience be infringed."

"The freedom of speech, and of the press, and the right of the people peaceably to assemble and consult for their common good, and to apply to the government for redress of grievances, shall not be infringed."

"A well regulated militia, composed of the body of the people, being the best security of a free State, the right of the people to keep and bear arms shall not be infringed, but no person religiously scrupulous shall be compelled to bear arms."

"No soldier shall in time of peace be quartered in any house without the consent of the owner, nor in time of war but in a manner to be prescribed by law."

"No person shall be subject, except in case of impeachment, to more than one trial or one punishment for the same offence, nor shall be compelled to be a witness against himself, nor be deprived of life, liberty, or property without due process of law; nor shall private property be taken for public use without just compensation."

"Excessive bail shall not be required, nor excessive fines imposed, nor cruel and unusual punishments inflicted."

"The right of the people to be secure in their person, houses, papers and effects, shall not be violated by warrants issuing, without probable cause supported by oath or affirmation, and not particularly describing the places to be searched, and the persons or things to be seized."

"The enumeration in this Constitution of certain rights shall not be construed to deny or disparage others retained by the people."

ART. 1, SEC. 10, between the 1st and 2d PAR. inset, "No State shall infringe the equal rights of conscience, nor the freedom of speech, or of the press, nor of the right of trial by jury in criminal cases."

ART. 3, SEC. 2, add to the 2d PAR. "But no appeal to such court shall be allowed, where the value in controversy shall not amount to one thousand dollars; nor shall any fact, triable by a Jury according to the course of the common law, be otherwise re-examinable than according to the rules of common law."

ART. 3, SEC. 2—Strike out the whole of the 3rd paragraph, and insert—"In all criminal prosecutions the accused shall enjoy the right to a speedy and public trial, to be informed of the nature and cause of the accusation, to be confronted with the witnesses against him, to have compulsory process for obtaining witnesses in his favor, and to have the assistance of counsel for his defence."

"The trial of all crimes (except in cases of impeachment, and in cases arising in the land or naval forces, or in the militia, when in actual service in time of war or public danger) shall be by an impartial jury of freeholders of the vicinage, with the requisite of unanimity for conviction, the right of challenge and other accustomed requisites;

and no person shall be held to answer for a capital, or otherwise infamous crime, unless on a presentment or indictment by a Grand Jury; but if a crime be committed in a place in the possession of an enemy, or in which an insurrection may prevail, the indictment and trial may by law be authorized in some other place within the same State; and if it be committed in a place not within a State, the indictment and trial may be at such place or places as the law may have directed."

"In suits at common law the right of trial by jury shall be preserved."

"Immediately after Art. 6, the following to be inserted as Art. 7."

"The powers delegated by this Constitution to the government of the United States, shall be exercised as therein appropriated, so that the Legislative shall never exercise the powers vested in the Executive or the Judicial; nor the Executive the powers vested in the Legislative or Judicial; nor the Judicial the powers vested in the Legislative or Executive."

"The powers not delegated by this Constitution, nor prohibited by it to the States, are reserved to the States respectively."

Art. 7 to be made Art. 8.

SEVEN

Amendments Passed by the House of Representatives August 24, 1789

ARTICLE THE FIRST.

After the first enumeration, required by the first Article of the Constitution, there shall be one Representative for every thirty thousand, until the number shall amount to one hundred, after which the proportion shall be so regulated by Congress, that there shall be not less than one hundred Representatives, nor less than one Representative for every forty thousand persons, until the number of Representatives shall amount to two hundred, after which the proportion shall be so regulated by Congress, that there shall not be less than two hundred Representatives, nor less than one Representative for every fifty thousand persons.

ARTICLE THE SECOND.

No law varying the compensation to the members of Congress, shall take effect, until an election of Representatives shall have intervened.

ARTICLE THE THIRD.

Congress shall make no law establishing religion or prohibiting the free exercise thereof, nor shall the rights of Conscience be infringed.

*This word in the Archives copy is spelled "offense."

ARTICLE THE FOURTH.

The Freedom of Speech, and of the Press, and the right of the People peaceably to assemble, and consult for their common good, and to apply to the Government for a redress of grievances, shall not be infringed.

ARTICLE THE FIFTH.

A well regulated militia, composed of the body of the People, being the best security of a free State, the right of the People to keep and bear arms, shall not be infringed, but no one religiously scrupulous of bearing arms, shall be compelled to render military service in person.

ARTICLE THE SIXTH.

No soldier shall, in time of peace, be quartered in any house without the consent of the owner, nor in time of war, but in a manner to be prescribed by law.

ARTICLE THE SEVENTH.

The right of the People to be secure in their persons, houses, papers and effects, against unreasonable searches and seizures, shall not be violated, and no warrants shall issue, but upon probable cause supported by oath or affirmation, and particularly describing the place to be searched, and the persons or things to be seized.

ARTICLE THE EIGHTH.

No person shall be subject, except in case of impeachment, to more than one trial, or one punishment for the same offence,* nor shall be compelled in any criminal case, to be a witness against himself, nor be deprived of life, liberty or property, without due process of law; nor shall private property be taken for public use without just compensation.

ARTICLE THE NINTH.

In all criminal prosecutions, the accused shall enjoy the right to a speedy and public trial, to be informed of the nature and cause of the accusation, to be confronted with the witnesses against him, to have compulsory process for obtaining witnesses in his favor, and to have the assistance of counsel for his defence.

ARTICLE THE TENTH.

The trial of all crimes (except in cases of impeachment, and in cases arising in the land or naval forces, or in the militia when in actual service in time of War or public danger) shall be by an Impartial Jury of the Vicinage, with the requisite of unanimity for conviction, the right of challenge, and other accostomed [sic] requisites; and no person shall be held to answer for a capital, or otherways [sic] infamous crime, unless on a presentment or indictment by a Grand Jury; but if a crime be committed in a place in the possession of an enemy, or in which an insurrection may prevail, the indictment and trial may by law be authorised in some other place within the same State.

ARTICLE THE ELEVENTH.

No appeal to the Supreme Court of the United States, shall be allowed, where the value in controversy shall not amount to one thousand dollars, nor shall any fact, triable by a Jury according to the course of the common law, be otherwise re-examinable, than according to the rules of common law.

ARTICLE THE TWELFTH.

In suits at common law, the right of trial by Jury shall be preserved.

ARTICLE THE THIRTEENTH.

Excessive bail shall not be required, nor excessive fines imposed, nor cruel and unusual punishments inflicted.

ARTICLE THE FOURTEENTH.

No State shall infringe the right of trial by Jury in criminal cases, nor the rights of conscience, nor the freedom of speech, or of the press.

ARTICLE THE FIFTEENTH.

The enumeration in the Constitution of certain rights, shall not be construed to deny or disparage others retained by the people.

ARTICLE THE SIXTEENTH.

The powers delegated by the Constitution to the government of the United States, shall be exercised as therein appropriated, so that the Legislative shall never exercise the powers vested in the Executive or Judicial; nor the Executive the powers vested in the Legislative or Judicial; nor the Judicial the powers vested in the Legislative or Executive.

ARTICLE THE SEVENTEENTH.

The powers not delegated by the Constitution, nor prohibited by it, to the States, are reserved to the States respectively.

EIGHT

Amendments Passed
by the Senate
September 9, 1789

ARTICLE THE FIRST.

After the first enumeration, required by the first article of the Constitution, there shall be one Representative for every thirty thousand, until the number shall amount to one hundred; to which number one Representative shall be added for every subsequent increase of forty thousand, until the Representatives shall amount to two hundred, to which number one Representative shall be added for every subsequent increase of sixty thousand persons.

ARTICLE THE SECOND.

No law, varying the compensation for the services of the Senators and Representatives, shall take effect, until an election of Representatives shall have intervened.

ARTICLE THE THIRD.

Congress shall make no law establishing articles of faith, or a mode of worship, or prohibiting the free exercise of religion, or abridging the freedom of speech, or of the press, or the right of the people peaceably to assemble, and to petition to the government for a redress of grievances.

ARTICLE THE FOURTH.

A well regulated militia, being necessary to the security of a free State, the right of the people to keep and bear arms, shall not be infringed.

ARTICLE THE FIFTH.

No soldier shall, in time of peace, be quartered in any house, without the consent of the owner, nor in time of war, but in a manner to be prescribed by law.

ARTICLE THE SIXTH.

The right of the people to be secure in their persons, houses, papers, and effects, against unreasonable searches and seizures, shall not be violated, and no warrants shall issue, but upon probable cause, supported by oath or affirmation, and particularly describing the place to be searched, and the persons or things to be seized.

ARTICLE THE SEVENTH.

No person shall be held to answer for a capital, or otherwise infamous crime, unless on a presentment or indictment of a Grand Jury, except in cases arising in the land or naval forces, or in the militia, when in actual service in time of war or public danger; nor shall any person be subject for the same offence to be twice put in jeopardy of life or limb; nor shall be compelled in any criminal case, to be a witnesses against himself, nor be deprived of life, liberty or property, without due process of law; nor shall private property be taken for public use without just compensation.

ARTICLE THE EIGHTH.

In all criminal prosecutions, the accused shall enjoy the right to a speedy and public trial, to be informed of the nature and cause of the accusation, to be confronted with the witnesses against him, to have compulsory process for obtaining witnesses in his favour, and to have the assistance of counsel for his defence.

ARTICLE THE NINTH.

In suits at common law, where the value in controversy shall exceed twenty dollars, the right of trial by Jury shall be preserved, and no fact, tried by a Jury, shall be otherwise re-examined in any court of the United States, than according to the rules of the common law.

ARTICLE THE TENTH.

Excessive bail shall not be required, nor excessive fines imposed, nor cruel and unusual punishments inflicted.

ARTICLE THE ELEVENTH.

The enumeration in the Constitution, of certain rights, shall not be construed to deny or disparage others retained by the people.

ARTICLE* THE TWELFTH.

The powers not delegated to the United States by the Constitution, nor prohibited by it to the States, are reserved to the States respectively, or to the people.

*This word in the printed document reads ACTICLE.

NINE

Amendments Agreed to After Conference and Proposed by Congress to the States September 25, 1789

Article the first . . . After the first enumeration required by the first Article of the Constitution, there shall be one Representative for every thirty thousand, until the number shall amount to one hundred, after which, the proportion shall be so regulated by Congress, that there shall be not less than one hundred Representatives, nor less than one Representative for every forty thousand persons, until the number of Representatives shall amount to two hundred, after which the proportion shall be so regulated by Congress, that there shall not be less than two hundred Representatives, nor more than one Representative for every fifty thousand persons.

Article the second . . . No law, varying the compensation for the services of the Senators and Representatives, shall take effect, until an election of Representatives shall have intervened.

Article the third . . . Congress shall make no law respecting an establishment of religion, or prohibiting the free exercise thereof; or abridging the freedom of speech, or of the press, or the right of the people peaceably to assemble, and to petition the Government for a redress of grievances.

Article the fourth . . . A well regulated Militia, being necessary to the security of a free State, the right of the people to keep and bear Arms, shall not be infringed.

Article the fifth . . . No Soldier shall, in time of peace be quartered in any house, without the consent of the Owner, nor in time of war, but in a manner to be prescribed by law.

Article the sixth . . . The right of the people to be secure in their persons, houses, papers, and effects, against unreasonable searches and seizures, shall not be violated, and no Warrants shall issue, but upon probable cause, supported by Oath or affirmation, and particularly describing the place to be searched, and the persons or things to be seized.

Article the seventh . . . No person shall be held to answer for a capital, or otherwise infamous crime, unless on a presentment or indictment of a Grand Jury, except in cases arising in the land or naval forces, or in the Militia, when in actual service in time of War or public danger; nor shall any person be subject for the same offence to be twice put in jeopardy of life or limb, nor shall be compelled in any criminal case to be a witness against himself, nor be deprived of life, liberty, or property, without due process of law; nor shall private property be taken for public use without just compensation.

Article the eighth . . . In all criminal prosecutions, the accused shall enjoy the right to a speedy and public trial, by an impartial jury of the State and district wherein the crime shall have been committed, which district shall have been previously ascertained by law, and to be informed of the nature and cause of the accusation; to be confronted with the witnesses against him; to have compulsory process for obtaining witnesses in his favor, and to have the Assistance of Counsel for his defence.

Article the ninth . . . In suits at common law, where the value in controversy shall exceed twenty dollars, the right of trial by jury shall be preserved, and no fact tried by a jury shall be otherwise reexamined in any Court of the United States, than according to the rules of the common law.

Article the tenth . . . Excessive bail shall not be required, nor excessive fines imposed, nor cruel and unusual punishments inflicted.

Article the eleventh . . . The enumeration in the Constitution, of certain rights, shall not be construed to deny or disparage others retained by the people.

Article the twelfth . . . The powers not delegated to the United States by the Constitution, nor prohibited by it to the States, are reserved to the States respectively, or to the people.

Bibliography

Chafee, Zechariah, Jr. *Free Speech in the United States.* Cambridge: Harvard University Press, 1948.

Chafee, Zechariah, Jr. *How Human Rights Got into the Constitution.* Boston: Boston University Press, 1952.

Duker, William F. *A Constitutional History of Habeas Corpus.* Westport, Conn.: Greenwood, 1980.

Dumbauld, Edward. *The Bill of Rights and What It Means Today.* Norman: University of Oklahoma Press, 1957.

Goldwin, Robert A., and William A. Schambra, eds. *How Does the Constitution Secure Rights?* Washington, D.C.: American Enterprise Institute, 1985.

Hickock, Eugene W., Jr. *The Bill of Rights: Original Meaning and Current Understanding.* Charlottesville: University Press of Virginia, 1991.

Pound, Roscoe. *The Development of Constitutional Guarantees of Liberty.* New Haven: Yale University Press, 1957.

Rutland, Robert A. *Birth of the Bill of Rights, 1776–1791.* Chapel Hill: University of North Carolina Press, 1955.

Schwartz, Bernard. *The Great Rights of Mankind: A History of the Bill of Rights.* New York: Oxford University Press, 1977.

Sigler, Jay A. *Double Jeopardy: The Development of a Legal and Social Policy.* Ithaca: Cornell University Press, 1969.

Smith, James Morton. *Freedom's Fetters: The Alien and Sedition Acts and American Civil Liberties.* Ithaca: Cornell University Press, 1956.

Younger, Richard D. *The People's Panel: The Grand Jury in the United States, 1634–1941.* Providence: Brown University Press, 1963.

Index